Terim Richards *Nursing student*

"I immediately went to my nurse manager after I failed the NCLEX® and she referred me to ATI. I was able to discover the areas I was weak in, and focused on those areas in the review modules and online assessments. I was much more prepared the second time around!"

Molly Obetz *Nursing student*

"The ATI review books were very helpful in preparing me for the NCLEX®. I really utilized the review summaries and the critical thinking exercises at the end of each chapter. It was nice to review the key points in the areas I was weak in and not have to read the entire book."

Lindsey Koeble *Nursing student*

"I attribute my success totally to ATI. That is the one thing I used between my first and second attempt at the NCLEX®....with ATI I passed!"

Danielle Platt *Nurse Manager • Children's Mercy Hospital • Kansas City, MO*

"The year our hospital did not use the ATI program, we experienced a 15% decrease in the NCLEX® pass rates. We reinstated the ATI program the following year and had a 90% success rate."

"As a manager, I have witnessed graduate nurses fail the NCLEX® and the devastating effects it has on their morale. Once the nurses started using ATI, it was amazing to see the confidence they had in themselves and their ability to go forward and take the NCLEX® exam."

Mary Moss *Associate Dean of Nursing and Health Programs • Mid-State Technical College • Rapids, WI*

"I like that ATI lets students know what to expect from the NCLEX®, helps them plan their study time and tells them what to do in the days and weeks before the exam. It is different from most of the NCLEX® review books on the market."

Practical Nurse Mental Health Nursing Care
Review Module Edition 6.0

Contributors

Lucindra Campbell, APRN, PhD, BC
Associate Professor
Houston Baptist University
Houston, Texas

Anita W. Finkelman, RN, MSN
Adjunct Associate Professor, Clinical Nursing
College of Nursing, University of Cincinnati
Cincinnati, Ohio
President, Resources for Excellence
Textbook Author

Sue Kilgore, RN, MSN
Park University
Parkville, Missouri
Shawnee Mission Medical Center
Shawnee Mission, Kansas

Patricia Nutz, RN, MSN, MEd
Professional Nurse Educator
Jameson Memorial Hospital School of Nursing
New Castle, Pennsylvania

Netha O'Meara, RN, MSN
Professor of Nursing
Wharton County College
Wharton, Texas

Barbara Schoen Johnson, RN, PhD, CS, PMHNP
Psychiatric Mental Health Nurse Practitioner
Cook Children's Behavioral Health Services
Fort Worth, Texas
Textbook Author

Jeana Wilcox, RN, MSN, MHNP
Associate Professor of Nursing
University of Missouri-Kansas City
Kansas City, Missouri

Editor-in-Chief

Leslie Schaaf Treas, RN, PhD(c), MSN, CNNP

Director of Research and Development
Assessment Technologies Institute™, LLC
Overland Park, Kansas

Managing Editor

Jim Hauschildt, RN, EdD, MA

Director of Product Development
Assessment Technologies Institute™, LLC
Overland Park, Kansas

Sixth Edition Copyright© 2005 by Assessment Technologies Institute™, LLC. Previous editions copyrighted 1999-2004.

Copyright Notice

Important Notice to the Reader of this Publication

Assessment Technologies Institute™, LLC is the publisher of this publication. The publisher reserves the right to modify, change, or update the content of this publication at any time. The content of this publication, such as text, graphics, images, information obtained from the publisher's licensors, and other material contained in this publication are for informational purposes only. The content is not providing medical advice, and is not intended to be a substitute for professional medical advice, diagnosis, or treatment. Always seek the advice of your primary care provider or other qualified health provider with any questions you may have regarding a medical condition. Never disregard professional medical advice or delay in seeking it because of something you have read in this publication. If you think you may have a medical emergency, call your primary care provider or 911 immediately.

The publisher does not recommend or endorse any specific tests, primary care providers, products, procedures, processes, opinions, or other information that may be mentioned in this publication. Reliance on any information provided by the publisher, the publisher's employees, or others contributing to the content at the invitation of the publisher, is solely at your own risk. Health care professionals need to use their own clinical judgment in interpreting the content of this publication, and details such as medications, dosages or laboratory tests and results should always be confirmed with other resources.†

This publication may contain health or medical-related materials that are sexually explicit. If you find these materials offensive, you may not want to use this publication.

The publishers, editors, advisors, and reviewers make no representations or warranties of any kind or nature, including but not limited to the accuracy, reliability, completeness, currentness, timeliness, or the warranties of fitness for a particular purpose or merchantability, nor are any such representations implied with respect to the content herein (with such content to include text and graphics), and the publishers, editors, advisors, and reviewers take no responsibility with respect to such content. The publishers, editors, advisors, and reviewers shall not be liable for any actual, incidental, special, consequential, punitive or exemplary damages (or any other type of damages) resulting, in whole or in part, from the reader's use of, or reliance upon, such content.

Introduction to Assessment–Driven Review

To prepare candidates for the licensure exam, many different methods have been used. Assessment Technologies Institute™, LLC, (ATI) offers Assessment–Driven Review™ (ADR), a newer approach for customized board review based on candidate performance on a series of content-based assessments.

The ADR method is a four-part process that serves as a type of competency assessment for preparation for the NCLEX®. The goal is to increase preparedness and subsequent pass rate on the licensure exam. Used as a comprehensive program, the ADR is designed to help learners focus their review and remediation efforts, thereby increasing their confidence and familiarity with the NCLEX® content. This type of program identifies learners at risk for failure in the early stages of nursing education and provides a path for prescriptive learning prior to the licensure examination.

The ADR approach may be preferable to a traditional "crash course" style of review for a variety of reasons. Time restriction is a fundamental barrier to comprehensive review. Because of the difficulty in keeping up with the expansiveness of information available today, a more efficient and directed approach is needed. Individualized review that starts with the areas of deficit helps the learner narrow the focus and begin customized remediation instead of a blanket A-to-Z approach. Additionally, review that occurs sequentially over time may be preferable to after-the-fact efforts after completion of a program when faculty are no longer available to assist with remediation.

Early identification of content weaknesses may prove advantageous to progressive program success. "Smaller bites" for content achievement and a shortened lapse of time between the introduction of course content and remediation efforts is likely to be more effective in catching the struggling learner before it is too late. Regular feedback keeps learners "on track" and reduces attrition rate by identifying the learner who is "slipping."

This approach provides the opportunity to tutor or implement intensified instruction before the learner reaches a point of no return and drops out of the program.

Step I: Proctored Assessment

The ADR program is a method using a prescriptive learning strategy that begins with a proctored, diagnostic assessment of the learner's mastery of nursing content. The topics covered within the ADR program are based on the current NCLEX® Test Plan. Proctored assessments are administered in paper-pencil and online formats. Scores are reported instantly with Internet testing or within 24 hours for paper-pencil testing. Individual performance profiles list areas of deficiencies and guide the learner's review and remediation of the missed topics. This road map serves as a starting point for self-directed study for NCLEX® success. Learners receive a cumulative Report Card showing scores from all assessments taken throughout the program—beginning to end. Like reading a transcript, the learner and educator can monitor the sequential progress, step-by-step, an assessment at a time.

Step II: Modular Reviews

A good test is one that supports teaching and learning. The score report identifies areas of content mastery as well as providing a means for correction and improvement of weak content areas. Eight review modules contain concise summaries of topics with a clinical overview, therapeutic nursing management, and client teaching. Key concepts are provided to streamline the study process. The ATI modules are not intended to serve as a primary teaching source. Instead, they are designed to summarize the material relevant to the licensure exam and entry-level practice.

Learners are taught to integrate holistic care with a critical thinking approach into the review material to promote clinical application of course content. The learner constructs responses to open-ended questions to stimulate higher-order thinking. The learner may provide rationales for actions in various clinical scenarios and generate explanations of why the solution may be effective in similar clinical situations. These exercises serve as the venue to shift from traditional didactic memorization of facts toward the use of analytical and evaluative reasoning in a client-related situation. The clinical application scenarios involve the learner actively in the problem-solving process and stimulate an attitude of inquiry.

These exercises are designed to provoke creative problem-solving for the individual learner as well as stimulate collaborative dialogue for groups of learners in the classroom. Through group discussion, learners discover the technique of elaboration. Learners use group dialogue to increase their understanding of nursing content. In study groups, they may pose questions to their peers or explain various topics in their own words, adding personal experiences with clients and examples from previously acquired knowledge of the topic. Together they learn to reframe problems and assemble evidence to support conclusions. Through the integration of multiple perspectives and the synergy involved in the exchange of ideas, this approach may also facilitate the development of effective working relationships and patterns for lifelong learning. Critical thinking exercises for each topic area situate instruction into a problem-solving environment that can capture learners' attention, increase motivation to learn, and frame the content into an application context. Additionally, the group involvement can model the process for effective team interaction.

Step III: Non-Proctored Assessments

The third step is the use of online assessments that allow users to test from any site with an Internet connection. This online battery identifies specific areas of content weakness for further directed study. The interactive style provides the learner with immediate feedback on all response options. Rationales provide additional information about the correctness of an answer to supplement learners' understanding of the concept. Detailed explanations are provided for each incorrect response to clarify topics that learners often confuse, misunderstand, or fail to remember. Readiness to learn is often peaked when errors are uncovered; thus, immediate feedback is provided when learners are most motivated to find the answer. A Performance Profile summarizes learners' mastery of content. Question descriptors for each missed item are used to stimulate inquiry and further exploration of the topic. The online assessment is intended to extend the learners' preparation for NCLEX® in a way that is personally suited to their deficiencies.

Step IV: ATI-PLAN™ DVD Series

This 12-disk set contains more than 28 hours of nursing review material. The DVD content is designed to complement ATI's Content Mastery Series™ review modules and online assessments. Using the ATI-PLAN™ navigational points, learners can easily find the content areas they want to review.

Recognizing that individuals process information in a variety of ways, ATI developed the ATI- PLAN™ DVD series to offer nursing review in a way that simulates the classroom. However, individuals viewing the ATI-PLAN™ DVDs can navigate through more than 28 hours of material to their topics of choice. Nursing review is available at the convenience of the learner and can be replayed as often as necessary to ensure mastery of content.

The regulation of personal learning goals and the ability to plan and pursue academic intentions are the keys to successful learning. The expert teacher is the one who can determine individual learning needs and appropriate strategies to master learning. The ADR program is an efficient method of helping students prepare for the nursing licensure exam using frequent and systematic content review directed by the identified areas of content weakness. The interactive approach for mastery of nursing content focused in the areas of greatest need is likely to increase student success on the licensure exam.

ATI's ADR method parallels the nursing process in concept and in design. Both provide a framework for solving actual and potential problems purposefully and methodically. Assessment ADR-style is accomplished with ATI's battery of proctored assessments. Diagnosis is facilitated by the individual and group score reports the proctored assessments generate. Planning for improving performance in identified areas of weakness incorporates ATI's modular review system. Implementation begins with modular review and culminates in use of ATI's online assessments to validate improvement. Evaluation is reflected in the score reports, and performance can then be strengthened or further improved with the ATI-PLAN™ DVD series. Just like the nursing process, ATI's ADR prescriptive learning method often leads to specific, measurable results and highly desirable outcomes.

Table of Contents

Psychiatric Mental Health Assessment

> ### Key Points
>
> - Accuracy in assessment determines whether the following steps of the nursing process will produce accurate nursing diagnoses, planning, and intervention.
> - Clients expect that interviewers will exhibit:
>   - Confidentiality
>   - Expertise
>   - Professional confidence
>   - Warmth and genuineness
>   - Nonjudgmental attitude
>   - Recognition of clients' knowledge about themselves
> - **Key Terms/Concepts**: Assessment, subjective data, objective data, client expectations

Overview

Assessment is the first step of the nursing process. Psychiatric-mental health assessment is the gathering, organizing, and documenting of data about the psychiatric and mental health needs of the client and family.

Health care providers must be encouraged to consider the strengths and resources, needs and goals of clients as family members, in the context of family life, rather than as individuals living in isolation to enhance family and family member functioning as well as quality of life.

Interview

The degree to which the interview is therapeutic, or helpful, to the client may determine the extent and honesty of the information shared by the client. Clients expect the interviewer to be an expert who is confident in the professional role, maintains confidentiality, demonstrates warmth and genuineness, is nonjudgmental toward them and their past or current behavior, and recognizes that clients are experts on themselves and their behavior.

During the interview, the nurse uses verbal and nonverbal therapeutic communication techniques to collect subjective and objective data about the client. These data include the client's current mental health problem; past medical, social, family, academic/vocational, psychiatric, and substance abuse histories; medications and allergies; health habits; interests; strengths and weaknesses; behavior; cultural beliefs and practices; and mental status. Psychiatric-mental health assessments are conducted in all care settings. Quality care necessitates that the assessment be thorough and objective. The use of assessment tools provides additional objective information from other sources, as well as from standardized psychological testing.

Assessment Data

- Subjective
  - Client's current problem and reason for seeking help
  - Past mental illnesses and treatment
  - Family history of mental illness
  - Medical history
  - Allergies to medications, foods, and other substances
  - Past and present medications and their effects
  - Social history including relationships with family, friends, coworkers, neighbors, authority figures
  - Past and present abuse
  - Substance abuse history
  - Educational and/or vocational history
  - Health habits
  - Safety issues
  - Cultural beliefs and practices
- Objective
  - Behavior
  - Communication
  - Physical assessment
  - Laboratory/testing data
  - Mental status exam
  - Examination of the mental state is essential in evaluating clients.
    - **Appearance**: Hygiene, grooming, appropriateness of clothing, posture, gestures
    - **Behavior**: Eye contact, motor behavior, body language, behavioral responses to others and environment, volume and speed of speech, tone of voice, flow of words
    - **Affect and mood**: Happy, sad, anxious, sullen, hostile, inappropriate for situation, silly, range of emotions
    - **Orientation**: To person, place, time, situation, relationship with others
    - **Memory**: Immediate recall; recent and remote memory
    - **Sensorium/attention**: Ability to concentrate on a task or conversation; perception of stimuli
    - **Intellectual functioning**: General fund of knowledge about the world, cognitive abilities such as simple arithmetic; ability to think abstractly or symbolically
    - **Judgment**: Decision-making ability, especially regarding delay of gratification
    - **Insight**: Awareness of one's responsibility for and analysis of current problem; understanding of how client arrived in current situation
    - **Thought content**: Recurrent topics of conversation; themes

- **Thought process**: Processing of events in the situation, awareness of one's thoughts, logic of thought
- **Perception**: Awareness of reality vs. fantasy, hallucinations, delusions, illusions, suicidal or homicidal ideation/plans
- Formalized assessment instruments provide fuller information from psychological testing (responses to ambiguous stimuli, ability to focus on a task, performance, and verbal IQs)
- Reports from other sources (family, friends, teachers)
- The "Mini" Mental Status Exam (MMS) is a quick way to evaluate cognitive function. It is often used to screen for dementia or monitor its progression.

The MMS exam includes eleven questions, requires only 5 - 10 minutes to administer, and is practical to use. It concentrates only on the cognitive aspects of mental functions, and excludes questions concerning mood, abnormal mental experiences and the form of thinking.

Mini Mental Status Examination

Folstein Mini Mental Status Examination

Task	Instructions	Scoring	
Date Orientation	"Tell me the date." Ask for omitted items.	One point each for year, season, date, day of week, and month	5
Place Orientation	"Where are you?" Ask for omitted items.	One point each for state, county, town, building, and floor or room	5
Register 3 Objects	Name three objects slowly and clearly. Ask the client to repeat them.	One point for each item correctly repeated	3
Serial Sevens	Ask the client to count backwards from 100 by 7. Stop after five answers. (Or ask them to spell "world" backwards.)	One point for each correct answer (or letter)	5
Recall 3 Objects	Ask the client to recall the objects mentioned above.	One point for each item correctly remembered	3
Naming	Point to your watch and ask the client "what is this?" Repeat with a pencil.	One point for each correct answer	2
Repeating a Phrase	Ask the patient to say "no ifs ands, or buts."	One point if successful on first try	1
Verbal Commands	Give the client a plain piece of paper and say "Take this paper in your right hand, fold it in half, and put it on the floor."	One point for each correct action	3

Task	Instructions	Scoring	
Written Commands	Show the client a piece of paper with "CLOSE YOUR EYES" printed on it.	One point if the client's eyes close	1
Writing	Ask the client to write a sentence.	One point if sentence has a subject, a verb, and makes sense	1
Drawing	Ask the client to copy a pair of intersecting pentagons onto a piece of paper.	One point if the figure has ten corners and two intersecting lines	1
Scoring	A score of 24 or above is considered normal.		30
Adapted from Folstein et al, Mini Mental State, (1975)			

Critical Thinking Exercise: Psychiatric Mental Health Assessment

Situation: In an outpatient treatment setting, you meet a young man who is about to undergo an initial psychiatric-mental health nursing assessment. He asks you, a student nurse, what will happen in the assessment interview.

1. How would you respond to his question?

2. After the interview, he asks you why it was necessary to know all those things about him, his family, and his job.

Legal Issues and Liability

Key Points

- A legal right is the entitlement of an individual to have, to do, or to receive.
- Examples of legal issues important in mental health include:
    - Privacy
    - Informed consent
    - Commitment
    - Client rights
- Liability refers to legal responsibilities that are important for all nurses.
- Important liability issues include:
    - Malpractice
    - Negligence
    - Invasion of privacy
    - Defamation of character
    - False imprisonment
- **Key Terms/Concepts**: Privacy, informed consent, commitment, client rights, malpractice, negligence, invasion of privacy, defamation of character, false imprisonment

Legal Considerations

Privacy: Being apart from others for observation.

Informed consent: The health care provider, usually the primary care provider, has a responsibility to communicate pertinent information in a manner that the client is able to understand. The purpose of informed consent is to allow clients to exercise their decision-making skills in relation to health care.

Commitment: The legal process by which clients who have psychiatric problems are brought to and confined in a secure area because their behaviors are so extreme and severe that they pose a harm to themselves or others. Mental health personnel are frequently involved; however, the commitment process varies from state to state.

Client rights: Clients retain all of the basic rights that every citizen has, i.e., the right to vote or buy property. Important rights during hospitalization are to receive mail, telephone calls, visits from clergy and/or attorney, confidentiality, and privacy. Clients also expect that treatment will be individualized and collaborative with no verbal or physical abuse. If rights are taken away, they must be done for clinical reasons and with a primary care provider's order. These orders must be reviewed every 24 hours. Hospitals should have policies related to these matters. In non-hospital treatment, client rights include privacy, confidentiality, and expectation that treatment will be appropriate to needs with client participation.

Humane research: Entails voluntary participation, informed consent, and freedom to withdraw from the study at any time for any reason, without penalty. The study needs to show a clear benefit with no undue risks to clients. Institutional review boards regulate research protocols and subject participation. Restraints and seclusions may be considered punitive, rather than therapeutic in nature; therefore, these methods are rarely used in clinical practice today.

Liability

Malpractice: Incorrect or negligent treatment by a professional that causes injury or harm to a client. The injury may result from a lack of professional knowledge, experience, or skills that should be expected of those in the profession.

Negligence: The commitment of an act that a reasonable and prudent person would not have done, or the omission of a duty that a prudent person would have completed, resulting in harm to a client. In particular, such as in a malpractice suit, a professional person is negligent if harm to a client results from an act or failure to act, but it must be proven that other prudent persons of the same profession would ordinarily have acted differently under the same circumstances.

Invasion of privacy: The violation of another person's right to be left alone and free from unwarranted contact, intrusion, and publicity.

Defamation of character: Any untrue communication, written (libel) or spoken (slander) that injures the good name or reputation of another, or in any way brings that person into disrepute.

False imprisonment: The intentional, unjustified, nonconsensual detention or confinement of a client for any length of time. This also includes the interference with a voluntarily committed client to leave against medical advice (AMA). If the primary care provider thinks the client should stay but is not committable, the primary care provider will ask the client to sign an AMA form.

Respondeat superior: The employer is ultimately responsible for the acts of its employees, and is thus liable for damage to the third parties.

Critical Thinking Exercise: Legal Issues and Liability

Situation: Staff members working on the psychiatric unit are reviewing their policies and procedures, an annual event. Usually they are not too happy about having to do this; however, there is one particular topic of interest due to some recent incidents on the unit. Client rights have been questioned. A client was recently told that he could not receive mail. He called an attorney. When the attorney reviewed the client's medical record he noted that there was no primary care provider's order to deny the client the right of receiving mail.

1. The first task of the staff is to identify the important client rights that need to be addressed. What are these?

2. Why was it important to have a primary care provider's order to withhold mail?

Confidentiality

Key Points

- Confidentiality is a critical element of trust between the client and the nurse. There are important legal issues associated with confidentiality, such as what information may be shared and with whom. For most situations, the client must consent to divulging information about his/her health care.
- Breach of confidentiality may be required in the following situations:
  - Child or adult abuse allegations
  - Sexual misconduct between therapist and client
  - Threats of self-injury or harm to others, including provider
- **Key Terms/Concepts**: Confidentiality, trust, privileged communication

Overview

It is the professional and ethical duty of the nurse to gather and express information about the client solely for the enhancement of care. Confidentiality is the foundation for establishing trust. Mental health clients often have difficulty establishing trust, so the basis of confidentiality becomes a key issue in therapy. Legal issues are of concern with confidentiality, as revealing private information without the client's approval can lead to lawsuits. In general, the psychiatric nurse has the legal privilege of not being required to release client-nurse dialogue unless the client's consent is obtained or a subpoena is filed. Many problems can be avoided if the confidentiality of the relationship is clearly defined during the initial meeting. Usually signatures are obtained to verify that the information was discussed. Client records must be protected from unauthorized personnel. No information is given to telephone callers or visitors. The nurse never agrees to keep secrets with the client that relate to client safety or the safety of others.

Breach of Confidentiality

It is the nurse's duty to report:

- Any threat or harm to person(s) in the community
- Suspected child or adult abuse
- Allegations of sexual misconduct with any member of the health care team

Critical Thinking Exercise: Confidentiality

Situation: You are working on an inpatient psychiatric unit. The telephone at the desk keeps ringing and no one is around to answer it, so you pick it up. After you identify yourself and the unit, the person asks to speak with P.B., a client admitted to the unit. You tell the person that P.B. is available but that he must be reached on the client payphone, and you give the caller the telephone number.

1. Why does the nurse manager become upset when she finds out that you have provided this information over the telephone?

2. As the nurse manager speaks with you, what does she tell you is the purpose of confidentiality?

Situation: The following day you are assigned a client who requires one-to-one supervision following a suicide attempt. She tells you that she has something special to tell only you, and asks if you can keep a secret.

3. How do you respond?

Client Protection in the Mental Health Setting

Key Points

- Physical restraint is only appropriate after all other types of interventions are used to assist the client to control his/her behavior and remain safe.
- Documentation of all interventions and the results are critical. This documentation should include:
  - Description of a clear process from less restrictive interventions
  - Criteria for removal of restraints
  - Care and observation during the use of restraints
  - Regular assessment of the client and potential complications of restraints
  - Reasons for removal of restraints
  - Follow-up interventions, including processing event leading to restraint
- Types of restraints include:
  - Physical
  - Chemical
  - Seclusion/observation room
  - One-to-one supervision
- **Key Terms/Concepts:** Physical restraints, chemical restraints, seclusion/observation room

Overview

Before any physical restraint or intervention that confines the client is applied, every effort must be made to assist the client with other types of intervention. These efforts must be documented in the client's medical records, along with the results of alternate attempts to de-escalate clients. Persons reviewing the record should be able to see a clear process from less restrictive interventions, ineffective results from these interventions, reasons for using more restrictive interventions, criteria for their removal, care and observation during their use, regular assessment of client, potential complications of restraints, reasons for removal, and follow-up interventions. A staff member must help the client process the event leading to restraint. This documentation is absolutely critical for legal protection and quality assurance purposes.

Restraints

Physical: Any manual method, physical or mechanical device, material or equipment that is attached or adjacent to the client's body and cannot be easily removed, restricting freedom of movement or normal access to one's body. Physical restraints are not a standard treatment for any medical or psychiatric condition. The most common restraint devices are roll belts, vests, wrist/hand mitts, or the Vail bed®. They are used to prevent wandering and falls, facilitate treatment, and control self-harm and disruptive or violent behavior. Criteria for removal are clearly articulated at the time of use and used to determine removal.

Chemical: Medication therapy may be used to sedate, calm, and de-escalate client behavior. Medications are used to prevent wandering, facilitate treatment, and alter disruptive or aggressive behavior.

Seclusion/Observation Room: Isolation of a client in a special room is used to decrease stimuli that might exacerbate the client's emotional stress. This intervention is used to decrease stimuli and protect the client and/or others, as well as to avoid property damage. This approach is intended for therapeutic purposes only, and not to serve as a punitive function. Criteria for removal are clearly articulated at the time of use and used to determine removal.

One-to-One Supervision

One-to-one supervision is implemented for protection of the client, (e.g., self harm through suicidal acts or self-mutilation, vomiting following mealtime). Policies and procedures must be followed as determined by the health care facility. At no time should the client be left alone if the policy requires it. Frequently the client may attempt to convince staff to leave him/her alone for just a few minutes. The nurse is required to reinforce to the client that this is not an option under any circumstances.

The staff must ensure that the client receives appropriate nutrition and fluids, sleep, hygiene, exercise, communication with staff, support from staff, and regular assessment that is clearly defined. Client status is assessed carefully for physical and mental complications. Documentation of the adherence to the policy and procedure established by the facility is a necessary role of the nurse providing mental health care. If the client is cooperative, a no-harm contract may be drawn up to give him/her and the staff a mutual agreement. Always document this in the client's record.

Critical Thinking Exercise: Client Protection in the Mental Health Setting

Situation: O.W. is admitted to the inpatient psychiatric unit. She is diagnosed with major depression. Shortly after admission, she attempts self-injury. The client requires one-to-one supervision. You have been asked to explain the supervision to a new staff member.

1. How would you describe one-to-one supervision to the new staff member?

Situation: You read O.W.'s medical record. It states, "10 a.m.: Client participated in group meeting. 11:30 a.m.: Client put on one-to-one supervision."

2. How would you critique this documentation? What would need to be documented after instituting the supervision?

Culture

Key Points

- Cultural competence allows individuals to understand and appreciate cultural differences.
- Culturally-competent mental health care includes:
  - Accessible services
  - Culturally similar providers
  - Understanding of the client's interpretation of illness
  - Rapport
  - Acknowledging the importance of religious beliefs and cultural health practices
  - Awareness of the nurse's own feelings and attitudes about people who are different from self
- **Key Terms/Concepts**: Culture, culturally-competent

Overview

Culture is the composite of human behavior, including customs, beliefs, values, institutions, languages, rituals, and practices of an ethnic, racial, social, or religious group. Cultural competence refers to the skills that allow individuals to understand and appreciate cultural differences. The cultural diversity of America is expanding. During the last decade, twelve million new immigrants came to the United States.

Culturally-competent mental health care involves respect for the individual, regardless of cultural differences. Typically, psychiatric-mental health care has not met the needs of minority clients and gaps in care exist. Ethnic and racial minorities are admitted to psychiatric hospitals at higher rates, drop out of services at a higher rate, and enter mental health treatment at a later stage in the illness.

Culturally Competent Care

Nurses must be knowledgeable of their own cultural background and recognize and acknowledge the influence of their experiences with people who are different from themselves. Providing culturally competent care is an essential aspect of psychiatric mental health nursing that includes:

- Understanding how the client interprets his or her illness
- Focusing on establishing rapport
- Recognizing and supporting the importance of religious beliefs

- Being familiar with health practices and healers of particular cultures
- Assessing whether behavior is usual within the culture
- Determining the client's expectations and misconceptions regarding treatment
- Incorporating cultural health practices and healers into plan of care
- Supporting the spiritual beliefs about the illness and treatment

Cultural barriers to treatment

- Language differences
- Inaccessibility of services
- Insensitivity of staff to clients' cultural beliefs
- Misunderstanding of procedures

Critical Thinking Exercise: Culture

Situation: As a student nurse, you are assigned to care for G.R., a 60-year-old man of a different cultural background, who is being treated for depression. He tells you that he does not think anyone truly understands why he has suffered with his problem.

1. How should you respond to him?

2. G.R. says that he is being punished for the "awful things" he did when he was young. He asks you to pray for him. What should you say to him?

Spirituality

Key Points

- Spirituality is important to a client's health-related quality of life.
- The goals of collaborative management include:
  - Promoting spiritual well-being
  - Incorporating a therapeutic presence, listening, and dialogue
  - Promoting a positive sense of meaning
  - Facilitating religious rituals and practices
  - Protecting clients' religious beliefs
- **Key Terms/Concepts**: Spirituality, religious practices

Overview

Spirituality is the life principle that pervades a client's entire being, integrating and transcending one's biological and psychosocial nature. It is considered a core dimension and critical determinant of health-related quality of life. Spiritual well-being typically affirms the unity of the person with the environment and is important for social connection. Spiritual distress is demonstrated by concern about the meaning of life, inner conflict, questions about one's existence, and the inability to practice one's religion.

Defining Characteristics of Spiritual Distress

- Expresses concern with the meaning of life
- Shows anger toward a higher power
- Verbalizes inner conflict about beliefs
- Questions the meaning of his/her own existence
- Is unable to participate in his/her usual religious practices
- Is concerned about moral/ethical implications of therapeutic regimen

Therapeutic Nursing Management

- Promote spiritual well-being by informing a clergy member (with permission of the client) and arranging a visit.
- Provide spiritual art work, music, or reading material.
- Be therapeutically present with active listening and dialogue.
- Promote a positive sense of meaning by facilitating experiences that are known to create a sense of purpose.
- Facilitate religious rituals and practices.

Critical Thinking Exercise: Spirituality

Situation: During an interdisciplinary team meeting on a medical unit, a staff member mentions that spirituality has no place in the discussion of a client's care. Several other staff members agree; however, you do not. Feeling somewhat uncomfortable, you do not say anything. Two weeks later, the team discusses a client who was admitted with multiple sclerosis. You admitted the client and indicated in the record that one nursing diagnosis for the client was spiritual distress. The team is discussing this diagnosis, and again some disagree with its use. You must defend your decision by educating the staff members about spirituality and relevant nursing care.

1. You begin by giving them a definition of spirituality, which is:

2. What data might you identify in the client's behavior to support the nursing diagnosis of spiritual distress?

3. You anticipate that one of the client's concerns likely to be verbalized is: "What can we possibly do about this problem?" How will you answer this question?

Grief and Loss

Key Points

- Several authorities have described the process of dying by identifying stages or phases. When applying these stages or phases it is important to remember that each client is an individual who may not neatly fit into a stage or phase and may also move back and forth between stages.
- Kubler-Ross' stages include:
  - Denial
  - Anger
  - Bargaining
  - Depression
  - Acceptance
- Glaser and Strauss' stages include:
  - Closed awareness
  - Suspicion awareness
  - Mutual pretense awareness
  - Open awareness
- Colin Murray Parkes' phases of grief include:
  - Shock and disbelief
  - Expressions of the emotions of grief
  - Disorganization
  - Recovery
- **Key Terms/Concepts**: Dying process, grieving, dysfunctional grieving, denial, depression, anger

Emotional Response to Dying According to Kubler-Ross

First Stage: Denial: Clients deny their diagnosis, feeling that there must be a mistake, and often shop for different doctors. Denial is a mechanism used by most clients, and it is usually a temporary defense. Denial may return as the client continues through different stages (e.g., "No, not me! It cannot be true.")

Second Stage: Anger: Clients become angry at the world, including loved ones who are closest to them. Loved ones often have a difficult time with these intense emotions and also need support through this period (e.g., "Why me?")

Third Stage: Bargaining: Most bargaining is made with their God, requesting more time. Once their request has been fulfilled, then another request may be stated (e.g., "Let me live just until....").

Fourth Stage: Depression: This is when the client can no longer deny his/her illness and physical symptoms begin to appear. Depression is a preparatory period in order to prepare the client for the separation from loved ones (e.g., "What is the use?")

Fifth Stage: Acceptance: If the client has had enough time and help in working through the previous stages, the client will reach a period when he/she is neither angry nor sad about dying (e.g., "I am ready to die." "I am at peace.")

Glaser and Strauss' Stages in the Process of Dying

Closed awareness: The client is unaware that he/she is dying, but family and staff may be aware.

Suspicion awareness: The client has a feeling that death may occur without sufficient information to verify it.

Mutual pretense awareness: All people involved are aware of the dying process, but maintain a ritual of pretense.

Open awareness: All people involved are aware of the dying process and demonstrate the awareness in actions, communication, and taking care of unfinished business.

Colin Murray Parkes' Phases of the Grief Process

Shock and disbelief: Denial, which protects from overwhelming pain

Expressions of the emotions of grief: Intense yearning or loneliness for the deceased; anger, or guilt

Disorganization: Apathy, depression, and emptiness

Recovery: Readjustment to life

Dysfunctional Grieving

- Dysfunctional grieving may manifest in several possible ways. There may be an absence of a grief response.
- A delayed reaction to loss may be related to chronic depression or other pathological states.
- Prolonged grief is evident when the bereaved remains intensely preoccupied with the memories of the deceased for a year or more after the death.
- Suicide is more common in persons experiencing dysfunctional grieving. Substance abuse (drugs and alcohol), self-neglect, and susceptibility to disease may also be evident.

Nursing Interventions

- Encourage client's verbalization of feelings of grief, loss, and anticipatory fear.
- Explore the meaning the loss holds for the client.
- Allow progression through the normal states of grief, including adaptive denial.
- Encourage the client to examine patterns of coping (what has worked in the past).
- Encourage client to review personal strengths and areas in which he/she maintains control.

Critical Thinking Exercise: Grief and Loss

Situation: You are working for a hospice home care agency. You have been assigned a client, P.S., who has breast carcinoma. She is 42, married, and has three children, ages 14, 10, and 8. You make your first visit to her home, and her husband answers the door. He tells you that he is so glad you are there. He is very concerned about his wife. You ask him what specifically concerns him today. "My wife has always been upbeat but has had tough times too. Three weeks ago I could not get her to talk about her feelings, and she seemed to not care about anything. Before that, she would break into rages about her illness, and sometimes would say, 'I'd do anything just to live to see my children as adults.'" You ask him how his wife is responding now. He says, "That is the strange part. She seems at peace now. I don't like this and am not sure what it all means."

1. How would you explain P.S.'s emotions and reactions to her husband? (Apply Kubler-Ross' responses to dying.)

2. According to Colin Murray Parkes' phases of dying, which phase is P.S. experiencing?

Diagnosis of Mental Illness

Key Points

- The Diagnostic and Statistical Manual of Mental Illness (DSM-IV) is used to diagnose mental illness. It provides diagnostic criteria for each mental disorder and a system of five axes to give a comprehensive view of the client's mental illness and functioning.
- The five axes of the DSM are:
  - Axis I: The clinical disorder that is the focus of treatment
  - Axis II: Personality disorders and mental retardation
  - Axis III: Medical conditions
  - Axis IV: Psychosocial and environmental problems
  - Axis V: Global assessment of functioning (GAF)
- Nursing diagnosis is a statement of the client's response to a health disruption. The nursing diagnosis is a method to describe the condition and its effect on the individual/family. It also serves to direct the nursing management.
- **Key Terms/Concepts**: Diagnoses, DSM-IV, axes, nursing diagnosis, NANDA, defining characteristic

Overview

Mental health professionals use the Diagnostic and Statistical Manual of Mental Illness (DSM-IV) to diagnose mental illness. The DSM's classification system includes a list of diagnostic criteria for each mental disorder. The DSM uses a multiaxial system of five axes to give a comprehensive view of the client's mental illness and functioning level. Each axis represents another aspect of the client's illness or condition and levels of functioning. The five axes of the DSM are:

- Axis I: The clinical disorder that is the focus of treatment
- Axis II: Personality disorders and mental retardation
- Axis III: Medical conditions
- Axis IV: Psychosocial and environmental problems
- Axis V: Global assessment of functioning (GAF), written as numbers 0-100 that represent current level of functioning/highest level of functioning in the past year, such as a GAF of 45/70.

For example, major depression, obsessive-compulsive disorder, and autism are clinical conditions that are the foci of psychiatric treatment and the diagnosis is Axis I. Borderline personality disorder is an Axis II diagnosis. Asthma is a medical condition; therefore, the diagnosis is Axis III. Psychosocial and environmental problems such as problems of primary support, occupational problems, educational problems, and financial problems are placed on Axis IV. A current GAF between 50 and 60 indicates moderate severity of symptoms or moderate level of functioning. The higher numbers in the GAF indicate higher levels of functioning.

Nursing diagnoses are formulated by analyzing client data. The North American Nursing Diagnosis Association (NANDA) endorses the taxonomy for nursing diagnoses. The format for a nursing diagnosis includes three parts: (1) diagnostic label from the NANDA list; (2) etiology and causative factors ("related to"); and (3) defining characteristics (signs and symptoms). Nursing diagnoses should be descriptive enough to label the condition accurately and to direct nursing interventions. In the nursing diagnosis, "Ineffective Individual Coping, related to impulsivity and lack of responsibility for own behavior, as evidenced by angry outbursts, destruction of property, and threats to harm others," the etiology/causative factors (2nd part of diagnosis) guide nursing interventions. A nursing diagnosis can also be a potential diagnosis, such as "Risk for Self-Directed Violence, related to feelings of hopelessness, helplessness, unresolved grief, and statements like, 'I can't live like this anymore.'"

Critical Thinking Exercise: Diagnosis of Mental Illness

Situation: A newly admitted client has the following diagnoses written in the chart:
Axis I: Alcohol dependence
Axis II: Mild mental retardation
Axis III: Bronchitis
Axis IV: Problems related to primary support and occupational problems
Avis V: 40/55

1. Which of these axes and diagnoses is the reason why this client is receiving treatment?

2. The numbers, "40/55" refer to:

3. What is identified in Axis IV in the DSM's multiaxial system?

Situation: The nurse working with an anxious client formulates the nursing diagnosis, "Sleep Pattern Disturbance, related to anxiety and exaggerated fears, as evidenced by subjective complaints of fitful sleep and fatigue, observed pacing at 4 a.m., lack of daytime alertness, and repeated requests for a 'stronger' sleep medication."

4. Which part of the nursing diagnosis will guide nursing interventions?

5. What data could you, as a student, gather to support the nursing diagnosis of Sleep Pattern Disturbance?

Therapeutic Relationships

Key Points

- Therapeutic relationships are focused on the needs and problems of the client.
- Through therapeutic relationships, nurses strive to help clients understand their behavior, explore problems, and develop healthier coping skills.
- Therapeutic relationships are marked by mutually-determined goals that are aimed toward meeting the clients' needs and increasing their repertoire of coping skills.
- The nurse's approach must be accepting and nonjudgmental of clients and their life circumstances.
- Phases of the therapeutic relationship:
  - Preinteraction (Preorientation)—Planning, information-gathering
  - Phase I—Orientation, introduction, establishing rapport (follow the rhythm of the client)
  - Phase II—Working, learning, developing skills
  - Phase III—Termination, evaluation, discussion of accomplishments
- **Key Terms/Concepts**: Therapeutic relationship, characteristics, phases

Overview

Nurse-client relationships are the core of nursing. Through predetermined goals, therapeutic relationships help clients work toward achieving their goals and regaining their health or optimal functioning. Nurse and client work together collaboratively in a therapeutic relationship to meet the client's needs. The therapeutic relationship requires purposeful interactions that are designed to help the client learn new coping skills. Maladaptive behaviors of the client that were learned in former relationships can be changed within the new therapeutic relationship to become adaptive, effective behaviors.

Therapeutic relationships differ from social and intimate relationships. Social relationships occur commonly among persons, such as friends, coworkers, and neighbors, whose aim is to meet their own needs through the relationship. Intimate relationships occur between two people, such as a married couple, who are committed to care for and about each other.

Phases of Therapeutic Relationships

Preinteraction (Preorientation Phase): Includes the thoughts, ideas, and exchange of information that occurs prior to the first contact with the client. Information may be obtained from the client's chart, significant others, or health team members.

Phase I (Introductory Phase): Nurse and client discuss expectations and goals; rapport and trust are established; data are gathered, nursing diagnoses are made; goals and client outcomes are formed.

Phase II (Working Phase): The "work" of the relationship, such as exploring problems, overcoming resistance, learning and practicing new coping skills and ways of thinking, is done during this phase.

Phase III (Termination Stage): Together, the nurse and client review the progress made by the client, reassess goals, and explore feelings about termination.

Types of Relationships

- Social
- Intimate
- Therapeutic

Characteristics of Therapeutic Relationships

- Mutually-determined goals
- Goal-directed toward meeting client's needs
- Provision of environment to maximize client's potential for growth
- Client learning new coping skills
- Predictable phases of relationship

Relationship Issues

Transference: Client's unconscious displacement upon the nurse of feelings or attitudes experienced in another relationship.

Countertransference: Nurse's conscious or unconscious displacement upon the client of feelings or attitudes experienced in the past.

Anger: The nurse may feel angry with the client's behavior (past or present). Healthy expression of the anger (talking with coworkers) is necessary to facilitate a therapeutic relationship with the client.

Critical Thinking Exercise: Therapeutic Relationships

Situation: As a student nurse, you observe the RN interacting with a severely depressed female client who sits with shoulders slumped and eyes downcast. You note that the client answers the nurse's occasional questions with one or two-word answers. The nurse sits quietly by the client's side.

1. Why is the nurse just sitting next to the client? How does that behavior promote a therapeutic relationship?

Situation: After weeks of meeting with two clients to discuss their problems and establish a therapeutic relationship, you meet with your nursing instructor and report the following, "M.A. and I seem to be making progress. He wants to discuss the difficulty he has with meeting new people. I taught him some social skills and he practiced them with me. M.J. and I have also met together. We talk about what she wants to accomplish in our time together."

2. The instructor asks you to identify which phase of the therapeutic relationship you are engaging in with each of your clients.

Therapeutic Communication

Key Points

- The goal of therapeutic communication is to help the client replace dysfunctional behaviors with more functional, effective behaviors.
- Essential conditions for therapeutic communication are:
    - Rapport
    - Trust
    - Respect
    - Empathy/positive regard
- Variables that influence communication include:
    - Perception
    - Values/beliefs
    - Culture
    - Gender
    - Age and developmental level
    - Environmental factors
- Types of communication include:
    - Nonverbal
    - Verbal
    - Active listening
    - Genuineness
- Therapeutic communication techniques are:
    - Listening alone is quite useful when clients are disclosing painful memories or experiences. Though it may be difficult to remain silent, it is most useful for the client.
    - Broad opening
    - Clarification
    - Reflection
    - Confrontation
    - Giving information
    - Seeking validation
    - Self-disclosure
    - Silence
    - Summarizing

- Barriers or factors affecting therapeutic communication include:
  - Culture
  - Beliefs/values
  - Religion
  - Social status
  - Gender
  - Age/developmental level
  - Environment
- The nurse should be advised to stay away from using these nontherapeutic communication mistakes:
  - Changing the subject
  - Interrupting
  - Approving
  - Moralizing
  - Social response
  - Belittling
  - Giving advice
- **Key Terms/Concepts**: Barriers, therapeutic communication, nontherapeutic communication, rapport, confidentiality

Overview

Communication is a personal, interactive system between a sender and a recipient. Verbal and nonverbal cues and feedback are important to successful communication. The nurse and client's personal variables affect communication. The three essential components of the communication process are the encoding of information, the meaning of the transmission, and the behavioral effect of information. There are two levels to every message: content and process (or tone) of the message.

Therapeutic communication is a way of interacting in a purposeful manner to promote the client's ability to express his thoughts and feelings openly. In therapeutic communication, the nurse uses verbal and nonverbal therapeutic communication techniques to attend to and listen to the client, express empathy for the client's condition, obtain information, and intervene appropriately. The goals of therapeutic communication include the following: establishing a therapeutic nurse/client relationship, identifying issues of significant concern to the client, evaluating what the client's "true" issues are, recognizing underlying needs not verbalized, and guiding the client to determine a socially acceptable, healthy resolution of issues. The nurse's interactions with the client are designed to discourage dysfunctional behaviors and to introduce and encourage more functional, effective behaviors. Some interaction behaviors are therapeutic (they promote continued and open communication) and some are barriers to therapeutic communication.

Variables that Influence Communication

Perception: The experience of sensing, interpreting, and comprehending the world in which one lives. This is a highly personal and internal act. Perception influences behavior.

Values/Beliefs: Past experiences prepare us to view things, people and events in a particular way. Some past experiences may encourage the client to view a situation in an inaccurate way.

Culture: Each culture provides its members with ideas of how the world is structured and what it means. These views are learned at an early age and often affect communication and interaction with others. Stereotyping may have a profound effect on relationships with others. For example: Latino and Native American youth avoid direct eye contact with elders and authority figures as a sign of respect. Some may view these downcast eyes as guilt or dishonesty.

Gender: Differences in personality and temperament are found between the sexes. Cultural values vary depending upon gender. Chemical properties within the body are different.

Age and Developmental Level: Communication skills are influenced by age and developmental level of the client.

Environmental Factors: External influences, which have an impact on communication patterns and client response, may include: lighting, room/outside temperature, smells, noise, level of privacy, interruption, and expectations of others. Nurses enter any communication with clients, families, and other staff with their own variables that affect communication. Likewise, the client's communication is influenced by many factors, both internal and external.

Types of Communication

Nonverbal: Actions or behaviors that communicate a message without speaking. Examples may include facial expressions, body language, posture, hand gestures, or dress. The use of space and territory is a form of nonverbal communication. The proximity a person maintains to another person or group is an expression of interpersonal communication.

Verbal: The transmission of a message using the spoken language.

Therapeutic: Communication that pertains to treatment and healing. Important elements contributing to the establishment of the therapeutic relationship are empathy, attending, observing, and listening. Therapeutic communication is intended to help clients see themselves and their situations more objectively. This often helps the client to practice new ways of feeling and acting, gradually leading to the development of both courage and the ability to take responsibility for his/her actions in socially acceptable ways. Therapeutic communication techniques may include silence, acknowledgment, positive regard, and restating ideas for clarity; these methods encourage open communication.

Nontherapeutic: Communication that is a barrier to free expression of feelings. Nontherapeutic communication may provide a disruption of the treatment process. Examples include giving false reassurance, using closed-ended questions, rejecting a behavior or feeling, giving advice, belittling, stereotyping, and judging.

Active Listening: Attentiveness to the client in a physical and psychological manner.

Essential Components of Therapeutic Communication

- Rapport
- Trust
- Respect
- Empathy/Positive regard
- Genuineness

Essential Conditions for Therapeutic Communication

Rapport: Interpersonal relationship characterized by a spirit of cooperation, confidence, and harmony

Trust: A risk-taking process whereby a person's situation and feeling of well-being depends on the actions of another

Respect: A relationship in which one considers the other in high esteem or regard.

Empathy/positive regard: The ability to try and understand what another person is feeling; NOT actually feeling what the other person is feeling. Restating what someone states they are feeling is often most helpful and conveys the impression you, as the nurse, are trying to understand their feelings.

Genuineness: Being as one appears, sincere, honest

Therapeutic Communication Techniques

Listening: The nurse focuses on or attends to all the client's behaviors; this is communicated nonverbally to the client by means of facing and leaning toward him/her, using eye contact and open, relaxed body posture. Listening alone is quite useful when clients are disclosing painful memories or experiences. Though it may be difficult to remain silent, it is most useful for the client.

- Nonverbal behaviors that signal active listening:
  - Position facing the client
  - Open posture
  - Leaning forward toward the client
  - Establishment of eye contact
  - Relaxed body language

Broad opening: The nurse uses open-ended comments that help the client express himself/herself (e.g., "Go on. Tell me what happened. How are you today?").

Clarification: The nurse communicates an understanding of the thought or feeling tone of the client's message back to him/her to offer another perspective on the situation (e.g., "You did not see any other way to cope with the problem. You feel your family is ashamed of you.").

Reflection: The nurse reflects back to the client the feeling or thought message that the client expressed to help him/her identify the emotions and events that are troubling him (e.g., "You think your mother loved your brother more than you. You feel trapped in your current job.").

Confrontation: The nurse describes contradictions in the client's behavior or feelings that are sending mixed messages to others (e.g., "You complain about your wife's lack of concern for you, but you refuse to respond to her gestures for reconciliation.").

Giving information: The nurse provides facts or information that the client requests (e.g., "Your doctor is ill today, so your appointment will be held tomorrow instead.").

Seeking validation: The nurse asks the client to give feedback about the accuracy of the nurse's perceptions (e.g., "Is this what you're experiencing? Do I understand you to say...?").

Self-disclosure: The nurse occasionally and cautiously reveals something from her own experience to make a connection with the client and his/her experience.

Silence: The nurse uses silence to communicate presence and acceptance of the client.

Summarizing: The nurse summarizes the work of the session, progress made, or client's goals at the end of the interview (e.g., "We have been discussing how you perceive your sister's comments to you and ways to handle your anger differently than you have in the past.").

Nontherapeutic Communication

Changing the subject: The nurse communicates an unwillingness to continue with the client's topic, usually due to personal discomfort with the subject matter.

Interrupting: The nurse shows disrespect for the client by breaking into and interfering with his/her communication.

Approving: The nurse uses approval and disapproval to control the client and his/her behavior.

Moralizing: The nurse passes judgment on the client by telling him/her what is right and wrong, good and bad, instead of letting the client decide.

Social response: The nurse uses superficial, social conversation that is not client-centered.

Belittling: The nurse discounts the client's feelings and experiences as not being valuable or worthwhile.

Giving advice: The nurse gives advice to the client, indicating that he/she is incapable of solving his/her own problems.

Factors Affecting or Barriers to Communication

Culture: Cultural norms/ideas/customs provide the basis or our way of thinking. Cultural values are learned and differ from society to society.

Religion: Religion can influence communication. Example: Priest/Minister wearing clerical collar publicly.

Social Status: Nonverbal indicators of social status. Example: High status persons communicate their status through gestures. Example: Decreased eye contract, louder pitch voice, dress, distance when talking to individuals considered to be lower status.

Gender: Traditionally roles have been identified as male or female. Masculinity: husband, father, breadwinner, doctor, engineer. Femininity: wife, mother, homemaker, nurse, teacher, or secretary. Gender signals which are recognized as masculine/feminine. Example: Women tend to sit more upright in the chair with their legs together

Age/developmental level: May be related to physiologic alterations. Example: Hearing loss - cannot hear vocal tone; Blindness - unable to see nonverbal communication.

Background knowledge/experience: During adolescence, teens struggle to establish their own identity and generate their own communication.

Environment/Territoriality: Individuals lay claim to areas around them as their own.

Critical Thinking Exercise: Therapeutic Communication

Situation: A 40-year-old male client is discussing his family situation with a nurse. State whether the nurse's responses are therapeutic or nontherapeutic.

1. **Client**: "I don't know what to do any more. My wife has left me and she took the children." **Nurse**: "Go on."

2. **Client**: "Our 15-year-old son has been smoking dope and he says it's because I don't spend enough time with him." **Nurse**: "Smoking marijuana leads to the use of other drugs. That is terrible for a 15-year-old. Why don't you put him into sports?"

3. **Client**: "What will I do without her?" **Nurse**: (Sits silently with him.)

4. **Client**: "I feel so lonely without her and the kids. The house is empty and there's nothing left of me." **Nurse**: "You feel sad and empty without your wife and children."

Defense Mechanisms

> **Key Points**
>
> - Types of defense mechanisms include:
>   - Denial
>   - Repression
>   - Rationalization
>   - Projection
>   - Reaction formation
>   - Displacement
>   - Isolation
>   - Intellectualization
>   - Identification
>   - Undoing
>   - Regression
>   - Dependency
>   - Suppression
>   - Sublimation
>   - Fantasy
>   - Compensation
>   - Introjection
> - **Key Terms/Concepts:** Each of the types of defense mechanisms listed above

Overview

A defense mechanism is a type of coping technique that protects one's ego against anxiety, unpleasant feelings, or impulses. All people use defense mechanisms; however, some are maladaptive or are overused. Persons with mental illness inappropriately or excessively use these mechanisms, which affects their behavior, communication, and ability to cope with stress and crises. Defense mechanisms are unconscious and distort reality. The purpose of defense mechanisms is to decrease stress and anxiety. A common coping mechanism is evident when a person denies the existence of some external reality such as an illness.

Types of Defense Mechanisms

Denial: Protecting the self from an unpleasant reality by the refusal to perceive or face it

Repression: Preventing painful or dangerous thoughts from entering the consciousness

Rationalization: Using contrived explanations to conceal, disguise, or justify unworthy motives for one's behavior; one of the most common defense mechanisms

Projection: Placing responsibility for one's unacceptable motives, characteristics, or behaviors on another person

Reaction formation: Preventing the awareness or expression of unacceptable desires or feelings by an exaggerated adoption of seemingly opposite behavior

Displacement: Discharging pent-up feelings, often of hostility, on people or objects less dangerous than those arousing the feelings

Isolation: Reducing ego involvement by protective withdrawal or passivity

Intellectualization: Cutting off affective charge from harmful situations or separating incompatible attitudes; reasoning and analyzing in order to avoid emotional issues

Undoing: Atoning for or trying to magically dispel unacceptable desires or acts

Regression: Retreating to an earlier developmental level involving less mature behavior or responsibilities

Dependency: Constantly seeking approval or assistance from others

Sublimation: Channeling unacceptable impulses into acceptable behavior

Fantasy: The non-rational mental escape from everyday life. This break in the boundaries of reality allows for pleasurable experience to aid in coping with stress

Identification adopting: Unconsciously assuming the personality characteristics, values, attitudes, and behaviors of another. When this process becomes conscious, it is called imitation

Suppression: Excluding certain anxiety-producing thoughts from the conscious mind. This is when a person puts something out of his/her mind

Compensation: Overachievement in one area to compensate for a perceived deficiency in another area; covering up a weakness by emphasizing a more desirable characteristic of self

Introjection: The adoption of someone else's beliefs as though they were one's own.

Critical Thinking Exercise: Defense Mechanisms

Identify the defense mechanism in each statement and indicate why the client's reasoning is not accurate.

1. P.J. is a 47-year-old smoker. She smokes three packs of cigarettes per day and claims that many people who smoke do not get lung cancer. In fact, she says, smokers can be some of the healthiest people you meet.

   Defense mechanism:

   Explanation:

2. A little league baseball coach becomes excessively demanding with his young players. When asked why he acted this way, he responded that he had a football coach who was extremely tough and the football team won the conference. He added that the football team was the "talk of the town."

   Defense mechanism:

   Explanation:

3. A man who is troubled by his attraction to gambling begins a campaign to force a casino out of town.

   Defense mechanism:

   Explanation:

4. A boy does not make the soccer team so he puts all of his energy into academics.

    Defense mechanism:

    Explanation:

5. L.K. is an unmarried 47-year-old who continues to rely on his 77-year-old mother to meet his basic needs.

    Defense mechanism:

    Explanation:

6. A woman who is harassed by her boss at work initiates an argument with her husband.

    Defense mechanism:

    Explanation:

7. An emotionally distraught mother of three teenage boys cannot recognize individual qualities of her children. Instead, she views them all as either all good or all bad.

    Defense mechanism:

    Explanation:

Hospitalization and Milieu Therapy/Outpatient Treatment

Key Points

- Hospitalization may be voluntary or involuntary.
- The client's safety, as well as the safety of others, is a critical factor in hospitalization.
- Therapeutic milieu is used during hospitalization to provide support and opportunities for the client to learn new coping strategies, problem-solving, and communication skills.
- Outpatient therapy allows for treatment in a least restrictive and a more cost effective environment.
- Approximately 70% of all mental health costs are for inpatient treatment.
- Psychiatric hospitalization occurs for less than one percent of the general population, but accounts for half or more of the total cost of treatment.
- Much of inpatient treatment can be as effectively delivered in outpatient settings.
- The goals of collaborative management include:
  - Providing a safe environment
  - Using the environment to provide positive growth opportunities
  - Ensuring that all basic needs are met
- **Key Terms/Concepts**: Milieu, commitment (voluntary, involuntary), outpatient treatment

Overview

The involuntary commitment to a mental health facility is allowed only for clients with psychological problems or behaviors so severe that they pose a threat to themselves or others. The anticipated harm must be imminent, represent clear and present danger, or have been demonstrated by an overt act of violence within the previous thirty days. The steps in the protective confinement process may vary from state to state. Mental illness alone is not sufficient ground for restricting an individual to a facility against his or her will. Clients may also be admitted voluntarily.

Conditions for Hospitalization

- Dangerous to oneself or others
- Incapable of providing for one's basic physical needs
- Unable to make reasonable decisions regarding hospitalization
- In need of care or treatment in the hospital

Hospitalization

Voluntary commitment (admission): In most cases, the client enters a mental health facility without a court order. The client can leave without notice, but this varies from state to state.

Involuntary commitment (admission): The client is not agreeable to the hospitalization; however, if the client is found to be dangerous or unable to provide basic self-care, then the client loses the right to sign out against medical advice (AMA).

Insurance coverage is a major factor today in determining if a client will be admitted (if not committed), and the type, extent, and the duration of treatment that will be provided.

Milieu Therapy

A therapeutic milieu is an environment designed to promote healing experiences and to provide a corrective setting for the enhancement of the client's coping abilities. A comfortable, secure physical environment coupled with a qualified mental health care team is essential to the therapeutic milieu.

Outpatient

Partial hospitalization programs are focused on providing specific treatments such as medication and individual, group and family therapy in a highly organized, structured program. This is an effective treatment modality approach for a variety of client diagnoses and are more cost effective than inpatient care.

Therapeutic Objectives

- Correcting the client's perceptions of stressors
- Changing the client's coping mechanisms from maladaptive to adaptive
- Improving interpersonal relationship skills
- Learning effective stress management strategies. Milieu therapy may occur in a partial hospitalization, inpatient, intensive outpatient, or classroom setting.

Principles of Therapy

- Promote respect for client, other clients, and staff.
- Use the opportunities for communication between client and staff for maximum therapeutic benefit.
- Encourage clients to act at a level equal to their ability to enhance their self-esteem.
- Promote socialization.
- Provide opportunities for the client to be part of the management of therapy.

Critical Issues

Boundaries serve to define functions in the therapeutic relationship and consequently imply responsibility. The nurse must clarify boundaries to make the client more at ease in the new relationship and environment. Boundaries provide structure for individual work by defining the work, its goals, and the time frame. Limit-setting and boundaries are mandatory to keep the interpersonal relationship between the client and nurse at a professional level.

Safety is provided by knowing what the client's responsibilities are in a given relationship. This makes the client feel more comfortable within the environment. The client is assured of being kept safe in the milieu.

Trust requires consistency between words and actions. The nurse acts in a consistent manner to achieve defined purposes.

Critical Thinking Exercise: Hospitalization and Milieu Therapy/Outpatient Treatment

Situation: The staff team on a new psychiatric inpatient unit is meeting to discuss the purposes of therapeutic milieus. The criteria for admission to the unit must also be identified. The unit is a 25-bed unit in an acute care hospital. It is a locked unit. Most staff members have little psychiatric experience. You are one of the more experienced nurses; therefore, the staff seeks your advice and help.

A staff member comes to you and asks, "I am not sure what a therapeutic milieu really is. We certainly did not have anything like that on the medical unit I just came from. Is it something I am supposed to do or does it just happen? Why have it anyway?"

1. How do you respond?

Situation: Two staff members have met with the medical director to draft the admission criteria.

2. What would you expect those criteria to include?

General Nursing Interventions

Key Points

- General nursing interventions in a therapeutic environment focus on:
  - One-to-one relationship
  - Constructive feedback
  - Trust
  - Assessment
  - Safety
  - Environment
  - Physical needs
  - Collaborative treatment planning
  - Medications
  - Education
  - Discharge planning
  - Coping
- **Key Terms/Concepts**: One-to-one relationship, constructive feedback, consistency, ADL, coping mechanisms (relaxation techniques, guided imagery, cognitive therapy, thought stopping)

General Nursing Interventions

- Forming a **one-to-one relationship** with the client will help the client to enhance communication, problem-solving, and social skills. Coping skills and trust in relationships may be learned or enhanced. The nurse who establishes this relationship needs to be clear about its purpose and provide positive interactions with the client. Establishment of a specific meeting time, expectations for interaction, and the duration of therapy are important boundaries to establish.

- **Constructive feedback** is given to the client so that the client's self-esteem will not be compromised. When the confrontation technique is used, the nurse needs to discuss the discrepancies between the client's verbalized intentions and nonverbal behavior carefully, without appearing to be attacking the client.

- **Trust** is essential to establish a therapeutic relationship. Consistency is the key. If the nurse cannot meet with client at an appointed time, the client must be informed at the earliest possible time. A new meeting time is scheduled. Direct communication is essential for the building of a therapeutic relationship. Other factors that facilitate trust within the nurse/client relationship include:
  - Recognizing the client's feelings

- Honesty
- Respect for the client
- Non-judgmental attitude

- **Emphasize positive results** and progress in learning new coping skills. Do not argue with the client. Recognize that the client is experiencing pain, but do not dwell on that pain.

- **Assessment** of client behavior is critical at the time of admission or initial treatment. Reassessment is indicated at appropriate intervals. The client must also learn how to self-monitor his/her symptoms.

- **Safety** is a primary concern. The client may require protection interventions; if so, these must be provided in a safe manner with respect for the client. The milieu may need to be evaluated for safety (e.g., the number of clients with escalating behaviors and adequacy of staff for client acuity and census).

- The **environment** should provide privacy and time with decreased stimuli. It should be a calm environment in which the client feels safe from psychological and physical threats.

- **Physical needs** are intricately related to psychological function. Ensure that the client's nutritional, fluid, sleep, hygiene, ADL, and exercise needs are met.

- The client should be encouraged to participate in **treatment planning**, and the client's feedback needs to be considered.

- Administer **medications** as ordered and assess results. Approach the confused or combative client in a calm, firm manner when administering medication. Restraints or the assistance of another care provider may be necessary for injections. Ensure that the client takes medication and is not hoarding pills. Client will need to learn about his/her medications and how to maintain this treatment without direct staff supervision. Be aware of side effects of medications.

- **Client and family education** is important throughout treatment.

- **Discharge planning** begins when the client is admitted, whether it is the hospital, home care, or any other treatment program. The client, and when appropriate, the family, must be involved in this process for it to be successful. It should include all relevant aspects of the client's life.

- Some methods, including **relaxation techniques**, **thought stopping**, and **guided imagery** (be careful with clients who are hallucinating or delusional), may be taught to clients to help with coping.

Critical Thinking Exercise: General Nursing Interventions

Situation: L.Z. has been on the inpatient psychiatric unit for two days. He is diagnosed with bipolar disorder and has a history of violence. You are his primary nurse. In spite of the prescribed medication therapy, L.Z. remains very active on the unit, often pacing, fidgeting, and restless. He displays aggressive behavior toward others around him. You perceive that he does not trust others. His insurance will only cover 10 days of treatment.

1. Prioritize his problems and describe the most important nursing interventions for L.Z.

Behavior Therapy

> ## Key Points
>
> - Behavior includes feelings, thoughts, words, actions, and physiological responses. Behaviors, or overt responses, are measurable and can be changed through therapy.
> - Types of behavior therapy include:
>   - Classical conditioning
>   - Operant conditioning
>   - Modeling and observational learning
>   - Cognitive therapy
> - **Key Terms/Concepts**: Behavior therapy, target behaviors, behavior modification, cognition, imagery, behavioral rehearsal, assertiveness, thought stopping

Overview

Behavior is the internal and external response (feelings, thoughts, words, actions, and physiological responses) a person makes to environmental stimuli. Behaviors (overt responses) are measurable and able to be altered through behavior therapy. Behavior and cognitive therapy is based on the concept that mental disorders represent learned behavior. Learning principles are applied to modifying these behaviors. Behavior therapy uses behavior modification techniques and cognitive interventions to change maladaptive behavior and focuses on specific target behaviors. Behavioral techniques include the use of token economies, time out (from positive reinforcement), and rewards or reinforcements for desired behaviors.

Types of Behavior Therapy

Classical conditioning: If an **unconditioned stimulus** (food) elicits an unconditioned response (salivation in a hungry dog), then a **conditioned stimulus** (a bell) paired with food, over time will condition the dog to salivate, a **conditioned response**, upon hearing a bell. This conditioning can be used to explain and treat learned anxiety, helplessness, phobias, obsessive-compulsive disorder, somatoform disorders, and sexual disorders.

Operant conditioning: **Operant behavior** (eating or dieting/exercise) is activity that is strengthened or weakened by its consequences (weight gain or loss). Operant behavior is influenced by a reinforcement (something that increases the probability of the response). The reinforcement meets a need and is goal directed. **Positive reinforcement** (reward) strengthens a behavior; as well as removal of a **negative reinforcement**. **Punishment** suppresses, but does not eliminate a behavior. These behavioral principles can be applied in many clinical situations.

Modeling and observational learning: A person can imitate or learn through another's performance. Observing the behavior of another can influence a person to behave similarly, especially when the model is rewarded for his/her behavior.

Cognitive therapy (or cognitive processing): This form of therapy corrects distorted thinking and its underlying faulty assumptions, beliefs, and attitudes.

Other Techniques

Imagery: Mental pictures are initiated by the client to correct faulty thinking.

Behavioral rehearsal: Role-playing, usually along with modeling, is used to rehearse new responses to problems.

Assertiveness training: This technique promotes positive interpersonal relations and strengthens effective coping.

Progressive muscle relaxation: Contracting and relaxing muscles in a systematic way reduces psychosomatic distress and stress-related problems.

Problem-solving: Involves learning and using the steps of the problem-solving process.

Thought stopping: A technique used to stop irrational, brooding, self-deprecating, anxious, and other negative thoughts and self-perceptions.

Behavioral contracts: A collaborative process during which client and provider identify behaviors to be changed and plan rewards/reinforcements to be received when the desired behaviors are achieved.

Critical Thinking Exercise: Behavior Therapy

Situation: A mother says to the pediatric nurse, "I can't understand why my 3-year-old son throws such a fit whenever we're in the grocery store. He screams and cries for candy at the checkout counter and I always say no. But then he carries on so loudly until everyone nearby is looking at us and I have to give in and buy him candy. I don't understand why he is not learning that he cannot have candy every time he's in the grocery store."

1. What is the target behavior that the mother is trying to change?

2. What has the mother's behavior taught her young son?

Individual Therapy

> ## Key Points
>
> - Individual therapy focuses on the needs and problems of the client.
> - Individual therapy can be supportive, re-educative, or reconstructive.
> - Stages of individual therapy are:
>   - Introductory
>   - Working
>   - Working-through
> - Issues in therapy include:
>   - Free association
>   - Transference
>   - Countertransference
>   - Resistance
>   - Treatment alliance
> - **Key Terms/Concepts**: Therapy, stages of therapy, re-educative, reconstructive, free association, transference, countertransference, resistance, treatment alliance

Overview

Individual therapy focuses on the needs and problems of the client. The work of therapy is dependent on the therapeutic relationship of the client and therapist. Most individual therapy (except play therapy) is accomplished through verbal communication. The therapist strives to become significant in the life of the client and to help guide him or her through the process of personal growth.

Purposes of Individual Therapy

- Treat mental illness
- Gain insight and self-knowledge
- Help people without mental illness learn more effective ways to solve problems
- Decrease stress and anxiety
- Deal with traumatic situations

Levels of Individual Therapy

Supportive: The client is provided a caring, safe relationship in which to explore problems and make decisions. The therapist reinforces client's existing coping skills and does not attempt to teach him/her new coping methods.

> **Re-educative**: The client explores new ways to perceive and behave through a systematic approach. The client and therapist sign a contract that identifies goals and desired changes in behavior and feelings. An effective approach is reality-based, focused on solutions, and directly deals with concrete issues. Examples of re-educative techniques include cognitive restructuring and behavior modification.

> **Reconstructive**: The client may spend two to five years exploring all aspects of his/her life through analysis or deep psychotherapy. Outcomes include self-understanding and understanding of others, greater emotional freedom, maximizing one's potential, and a greater capacity for love and work.

Types of Individual Therapy

> **Psychoanalysis**: Focuses on client's unconscious repressed thoughts and memories as the root of the mental illness. This often involves long-term, in-depth therapy (rarely covered by current insurance policies).

> **Brief psychotherapy**: Addresses a certain issue in a specified amount of time. Other issues that are outside the central issue are not discussed. The exploration is open and solution focused.

> **Play therapy**: A way for a child to express fears, feelings, conflicts, and aggression through play, and to learn to work through, manage, or discard these feelings and conflicts.

> **Behavior therapy**: Based on the concept that mental disorders represent learned behavior. Learning principles are applied to modify these behaviors. Reward and punishment are used to encourage the client to repeat certain behaviors and extinguish others.

> **Cognitive therapy**: Assists with problem solving and stopping negative self-perceptions by teaching the client to think a different way.

Issues in Therapy

> **Free association**: The free expression of thoughts and feelings as they come to mind; a technique that lowers the client's defenses.

> **Transference**: Client transfers feelings and attitudes held toward significant others onto the therapist; a tool that can be used to increase self-understanding when the therapist responds differently than significant others responded.

> **Countertransference**: Therapist transfers feelings and attitudes held toward significant others onto the client, which must be detected and changed for the therapist to become therapeutic.

> **Resistance** (or blocking): Resisting offering or receiving information or recalling feelings, which a client may use to avoid remembering painful knowledge or experiences.

> **Treatment alliance**: Ability of client and therapist to work together and be invested emotionally in the therapy.

Stages in Therapy

> **Introductory stage**: Client and therapist meet and start to work together, history is gathered, medical problems are identified, and client expresses his/her perceptions about problems and desired outcomes of therapy. Logistics of therapy (meeting dates,

length, location, and fees) are discussed. The beginning of a treatment alliance is formed. Purpose of introductory stage is to establish trust so client can move to the second or working stage of therapy.

Working stage: The client becomes more trusting, disclosing and exploring his or her thoughts, feelings, and behaviors that lead to the problem. Increased trust leads to increased recall, insight, and expression of previously repressed feelings and thoughts. The client's greater understanding results in more effective functioning.

Working-through stage: In this final stage of therapy, the client uses his/her improved understanding of self and others to try out new ways of thinking, perceiving, feeling, acting, and coping. Clients need considerable support during this stage of altering their internal behaviors and interactions with others. Termination of therapy is viewed as a loss or separation and the client may respond with grief.

Principles of Individual Therapy

- Desired outcomes of individual therapy are greater self-understanding, symptom reduction, improved judgment and insight, and a change toward healthier behavior.

- An effective therapist pays attention to the process of therapy, does not control the client, allows the client to move at his/her own pace, and uses therapeutic communication skills in a genuine, caring way.

Critical Thinking Exercise: Individual Therapy

Situation: During P.J.'s monthly visit at the Outpatient Clinic, she tells the nurse, "I have started therapy like the doctor recommended and have been going to therapy weekly for about two months. Lately, when I leave the therapist's office, I don't feel good. In fact, I feel kind of upset and stressed about our talking about all the bad things that have happened in my life. I thought therapy was going to help me feel better."

1. What stage of therapy is P.J. currently engaged in?

2. What occurs in that stage of therapy?

Family Therapy

> ## Key Points
>
> - Optimal, or high-functioning, families produce competent people.
> - Optimal families are marked by:
>   - Openness to others
>   - Permeable boundaries
>   - Clear communication and generational lines
>   - Power shared between the parents
>   - Autonomous thinking and behavior
>   - Warm and caring emotions
>   - Negotiated tasks decided by parents
>   - Values and beliefs that strengthen its members
> - Many troubled or dysfunctional families communicate with each other in negative ways through:
>   - Discounting
>   - Scapegoating
>   - Training
>   - Passive aggression
> - Family therapy addresses the needs and problems of the entire family
> - Family therapy is based on the belief that the behavior of one family member affects the other members
> - **Key Terms/Concepts**: Families, family therapy, family functioning, parental coalition, triangling, scapegoating, discounting, dysfunctional, genogram

Overview

All families do not function or deal with their problems at similar levels of functioning. Family functioning ranges from limited, troubled, or dysfunctional in some families to high functioning or optimal in others. Optimal families produce competent people.

Characteristics of Optimal Families

Open system: The family and its members are encouraged to interact with the environment outside of the family.

Permeable boundaries: The family uses input from other people to strengthen its members' lives. There are boundaries between parents and children, males and females, but it does not exclude members.

Contextual clarity: The family uses clear verbal and nonverbal communication with each other. Developmental issues are resolved appropriately. Family has a strong parental coalition: parents present a "united front" to their children.

Power: Power in the family is shared and comes from the parents. Roles of parents are complementary. A member's gender does not dictate his/her roles or power. Children do not try to take on parents' roles or responsibilities.

Autonomy: Parents are aware that, and act as though, they are preparing their children to leave their home and become responsible, capable adults. They encourage their children to act and think more independently as appropriate for their ages. The family respects each member's views.

Affective (emotional) tone: The family members are warm and caring to each other. Members pay attention to their own and others' feelings. The family confronts and resolves conflicts in a way that strengthens the relationships amongst the members.

Negotiation and task performance: Family tasks or chores are shared, after all members give input. Parents lead the discussions and make the decisions.

Transcendent values: The family's values and beliefs support and strengthen it in difficult times.

Benefits to society/humanity: The family's actions are guided by what is good for society and humankind.

Characteristics of Dysfunctional Families

Families who experience emotional difficulties usually have communication problems. They may discount or ignore each other's communication. They may "scapegoat" one of their members by viewing and treating that member as though he or she is the cause of all the family's problems. They may create "triangles," in which two family members form an alliance and exclude the third person. Passive-aggressive behavior is common.

Family-Centered Approach

Family therapy is therapy for the entire family. It is based on the beliefs that the behavior of one person in the family affects everyone else in the family, and that the presence of symptoms such as depression or anger in one family member is a sign of disorder, pain, or problems in the whole family system. The behavior of an individual cannot be understood without understanding the behavior of other family members. Interventions are directed at the family as a whole and their behaviors, not at an identified client. Family therapy promotes family cohesion.

Goals of Family Therapy

- Identify and express each family member's thoughts and feelings.
- Define family roles and rules.
- Explore and try new, more effective ways of relating to each other.
- Return the power to and strengthen the parental coalition (the parents as united leaders of the family).

Techniques for Family Therapy

- **Genogram**: A three-generational map of family structure and relationships, which may be used to diagram and understand the family's history, problems, roles, and values.
- Communication techniques include:
  - Discussing painful events or family problems openly
  - Clarifying members' thoughts, feelings, and messages
  - Dealing with anger openly and nonjudgmentally
  - Connecting feelings and facts
  - Never blaming
  - Expressing empathy with family members
  - Experiential and homework activities, such as planning a family vacation, doing a fun activity together, or eating meals together

Critical Thinking Exercise: Family Therapy

Situation: A family, consisting of mother, father, 14-year-old daughter, and 11-year-old son, attends its first family therapy session. The daughter has been withdrawn recently and spends a great deal of time in her room. She is not interested in her friends and prefers to be alone. The son, who has ADHD, continues to struggle in his schoolwork. Last year, he barely passed 5th grade.

1. What is unique about family therapy? How does that apply to this family?

The session reveals that the parents disagree and argue about whether or not their son should take medicine for his ADHD. The father says his son "is what's wrong with this family" and should "just buckle down and work harder," but mother says he needs his medication to focus on his work.

2. The father's comments about the son are an example of what communication problem that occurs in troubled families?

Group Therapy

Key Points

- Critical characteristics of therapeutic groups include:
  - Cohesiveness
  - Goal direction
  - Interpersonal communication
  - Group atmosphere
  - Leader behavior
- Types of groups include:
  - Content-oriented
  - Process-oriented
  - Mid-range groups
  - Educational groups
- **Key Terms/Concepts**: Cohesiveness, goal direction, interpersonal communication, group atmosphere, democratic styles of leadership, types of groups

Overview

The goal of group therapy is to help individuals develop more functional and satisfying relationships. An individual's behavior in group therapy is thought to imitate his/her behavior in other group settings. When an individual's dysfunctional pattern is demonstrated in the group, the task of the group is to assist members to understand the patterns of interacting within the group and to help clients generalize this information to their lives outside the group.

Goals of Individuals in the Group

The group will give input regarding the manner in which the individual:

- Represents him/herself to others
- Presents beliefs and evaluates them as to whether they are fixed and realistic
- Discovers previously unknown characteristics of himself/herself (strengths, skills, abilities, desires)
- Tries new behaviors within the safety of the group
- Accepts ultimate responsibility for behavior

Characteristics of Therapeutic Group

Cohesiveness: The degree to which group members work together. Cohesion is associated with positive group outcomes.

Goal-directed: Clear goals are set based on similar values and interests.

Interpersonal communication: Decentralized communication so that all members have increased member interaction. Interpersonal communication increases morale and satisfaction among members.

Group atmosphere: Individuals respond in an environment in which they feel valued and accepted.

Leader behavior: Democratic styles of leadership promote a more cohesive environment. Leaders continually monitor group interactions. The leader as a facilitator of interpersonal communication is neither passive nor overly aggressive, but will be both observer and reflector of what is going on in the group. The leader also models helpful group behavior to the members by providing respectful attention, giving full weight to what is being disclosed and allowing the opportunity to communicate and listen in a non-judgmental, non-directive, and non-manipulative way.

Therapeutic Factors of Group Therapy

Instillation of hope: Client believes he/she will get better through group therapy.

Universality: Client learns that other group members have similar problems and feelings.

Imparting of information: Client learns didactic information, which occurs in a group setting.

Altruism: Clients help each other in the group, resulting in increased self-esteem.

Corrective recapitulation of the primary family group: Client's family background influences client behavior, and client can relive and correct early conflicts.

Development of socializing techniques: Clients develop social skills in the group.

Imitative behavior: Client identifies with and imitates healthier behavior of group members.

Interpersonal learning: Client's interpersonal distortions are corrected.

Group cohesiveness: Client experiences bonding with the group, group norms are protected, and positive client outcomes result.

Catharsis: Group members express feelings, even deep and powerful emotions, and then learn new ways to handle their problems.

Existential factors: Responsibility, existence, awareness, and mortality are explored.

Types of Groups

Content-oriented: Discussion of goals and tasks. Task groups focus on defining tasks and what needs to be accomplished.

Process-oriented: Focus on relationships among members and their communication styles or patterns. Inpatient therapy and encounter groups fall into this category.

Mid-range groups: Combines both tasks and processes. Support groups are included in this category.

Educational groups: Focus on medication and health teaching.

Critical Thinking Exercise: Group Therapy

Situation: As an observer to a group therapy meeting, you observe the following: The group is talking about reactions that members have to one another. At times, the group interaction is very emotional. Members seem to feel comfortable with this emotional sharing and confrontation. The group seems close and productive.

1. How would you describe the characteristics of this group? State three characteristics that are evident from these data.

2. What type of group is this? Provide your rationale.

Psychopharmacotherapy

Key Points

- Principles of psychopharmacotherapy:
  - Psychopharmacologic agents/psychotropic medications do not "cure" mental illness.
  - Clients require physical and psychiatric assessments before psychiatric medication is prescribed for them.
  - Clients hold various views about the use of psychotropic medications; some of these views may bring about nonadherence to medication treatment.
  - Clients must give informed consent prior to administration of psychopharmacologic agents, including an explanation of risks versus benefits.
  - Psychotropic medications have different onsets of actions. Most medications (Lithium, antidepressants) require daily administration for one to several weeks before their intended effects are evident; some medications (benzodiazepines, antipsychotics) act more immediately.
- Categories of psychopharmacotherapy are:
  - Anxiolytics (antianxiety drugs): to decrease anxiety and treat anxiety disorders
  - Antipsychotics (neuroleptics): to decrease psychotic symptoms and reduce aggression
  - Antimuscarinics, antihistaminics, dopamine agonists: to decrease side effects of antipsychotic medications
  - Antidepressants: to decrease symptoms of depression, improve mood, and reduce vegetative signs of depression
  - Mood stabilizers: to decrease manic symptoms and provide maintenance therapy for bipolar disorder
  - Psychostimulants: to improve attention and to decrease hyperactivity, distractibility, and impulsivity
  - Sedative-hypnotics: to sedate in low doses and to induce sleep in larger doses
- Medication administration must include:
  - Assessment data when medications are selected and during reassessment
  - Awareness of possible non-adherence
  - Awareness that these medications can have negative effects on the elderly due to the aging process
- **Key Terms/Concepts**: Psychopharmacotherapy, psychotropic, adherence, compliance, anxiolytic, refractory, toxicity, tolerance, dependency

Overview

Psychopharmacologic agents (also called psychotropic or psychotherapeutic medications) are able to relieve symptoms, but not "cure" mental illness. Some clients may view medications as the solution to all their problems, while others adamantly oppose medication for a variety of reasons (e.g., unfounded beliefs that the medications are addicting, harmful to the personality or development, or a sign of weakness, etc.). Nonadherence must be managed; client may not remember to take psychotropic medications or may refuse to take them at all or as prescribed. Clients taking psychotropic medications and families of clients need education regarding the medication's action, purpose, intended effects, side effects, toxic or dangerous effects, treatment for side effects, and what to do about adverse or toxic effects. Clinical observation of clients taking psychotropic medications includes affective and behavioral responses to medication, complaints about medication, and beliefs about medication (e.g., its purpose, benefit, effects). Medications may need to be changed and/or dosages adjusted in accordance with drug effectiveness and client response. Clients must give informed consent prior to administration of psychopharmacologic agents, including an explanation of risks versus benefits. Nurses must observe and document the clients' responses to and beliefs about medications.

Purposes of Psychotropic Medications

- Relieve or reduce symptoms of dysfunctional thoughts, moods, or actions, mental illness or disorder
- Improve client's functioning
- Increase client's adherence (or compliance) and amenability to other therapies

Most psychotropic medications act by modulating neurotransmitters (brain chemicals), specifically serotonin, norepinephrine (noradrenaline), dopamine, acetylcholine, and glutamate.

Reasons for Nonadherence to Psychotropic Medication Regimen

- Medications may be expensive and the client cannot afford them.
- Clients may refuse to take medications because of their unpleasant or distressing side effects.
- Clients may stop taking their medications because they begin to feel better and believe that they no longer need the medications.
- Clients may not believe they have any illness requiring medication or fear the stigma associated with having a mental illness and taking medication.
- Mental illness itself, such as paranoia, contributes to the client's denial or fears about medication usage.

Services that Encourage Adherence to Medication Regimen

- Follow-up interactions with the client will help the nurse verify that the client understands the purpose, proper administration, intended effects, side and toxic effects of, and how to treat serious problems associated with psychotropic medication.
- Support persons can encourage and assist the client's adherence to his or her psychotropic medication regimen.

- Appropriate laboratory tests must be conducted to prevent serious complications and assure safe and therapeutic levels of psychotropic medication.
- Medication groups often provide not only education, but also peer support to those taking psychotropic medication. Often clients and their families have misconceptions that are preventing the client from taking his or her medication.
- Depot injections of antipsychotic medication can provide two to four weeks' dosage of the medication to clients who have difficulty adhering to their medication schedule.

Client and Family Teaching

- Nurses must ensure and document that any client taking a psychotropic medication is informed about:
  - The purpose of the medication and how it will benefit him or her, specifically side effects that may occur and how to treat them
  - What symptoms indicate a toxic or adverse effect, how to treat effect(s), and whom to notify
  - Specific instructions about drug administration or monitoring

Effects on Special Populations

Psychotropic medications should be administered with great caution to children and the elderly. Many of the medications used to treat mental illness in children have not received approval from the FDA to be given to children; such testing was not required until recently. Initiating treatment with small dosages and increasing the dosages slowly diminishes the likelihood of side effects.

The elderly client may be more susceptible to side effects of psychotropic medications, especially cardiac effects, and may metabolize or excrete the drugs more slowly, requiring lower doses of medications. Also, the elderly client is likely to be taking other medication; therefore, the client is at increased risk for drug-drug interactions.

Elderly clients may have decreased liver and renal function, therefore, their BUN (blood urea nitrogen), creatinine, and liver enzymes should be monitored routinely. Regular use of sedating medications for sleep should be discouraged because of the elderly person's usual return to normal sleeping patterns after only a few nights of medication use and because sedating medications may cause excessive sedation, confusion, or disorientation in the elderly person, (resulting in falls and other injuries).

- Psychotropic medications are often not approved for children by FDA.
- Elderly clients are more susceptible to side effects, especially cardiac effects.
- Lower doses are needed for the elderly client because of decreased liver and renal function.
- Elderly clients are likely to be taking other drugs; therefore, they have an increased risk for drug-drug interactions.

Psychopharmacotherapy: Antianxiety (Anxiolytic) Medications

Overview

Antianxiety medications or minor tranquilizers, are medications prescribed on a short-term basis to decrease anxiety and treat sleep disorders. Anxiolytic agents are used to reduce the manifestations of anxiety: trembling, sweating, chest pain, dizziness, fear of losing control or dying, and feelings of panic. The two basic categories are benzodiazepines and nonbenzodiazepines. The benzodiazepines are commonly prescribed because of their effectiveness and wide margin of safety. This class of anxiolytics has nearly replaced barbiturates for the treatment of anxiety disorders.

Benzodiazepine Anxiolytics

Action

- Potentiate effects of gamma-aminobutyric acid (GABA), an inhibitory neurotransmitter

Commonly used drugs

- Chlordiazepoxide hydrochloride (Librium, Lipoxide)
- Diazepam (Valium, Diastat)
- Alprazolam (Xanax)
- Oxazepam (Serax)
- Clorazepate (Tranxene)
- Clonazepam (Klonopin)

Intended effects

- Decreased anxiety
- Treatment of panic disorder, alcohol detoxification and withdrawal, skeletal muscle spasms, and status epilepticus
- Single doses induce sedation
- Long-term administration reduces symptoms of generalized anxiety disorder; however, long-term use leads to dependence on the drug
- Clonazepam also has anticonvulsant properties

Side or adverse effects

- Drowsiness, confusion, and lethargy
- Tolerance to the medication resulting in physical and psychological dependence
- Potentiation of other central nervous system (CNS) depressants
- Aggravation of depression
- Orthostatic hypotension
- Dizziness and ataxia
- Paradoxical excitement where the client experiences a period of unexpected excitability or rage

- Dry mouth
- Nausea and vomiting
- Blood dyscrasias

Toxic efects

- Respiratory depression in conjunction with CNS depressants, such as alcohol

Contraindications

- Combination with other CNS depressants
- Renal or hepatic dysfunction
- History of drug abuse or addiction
- Depression and suicidal tendencies

Unique teaching needs

- Should be taken only on a short-term basis or results in drug dependence
- Avoid alcohol and other CNS depressants
- Sedation impairs ability to drive or use machinery
- Not to be taken by anyone with prior or current drug dependence
- Discontinuation of the benzodiazepines causes withdrawal symptoms

Nonbenzodiazepine Anxiolytic

Action

- Agonist or partial agonist on serotonin type 1A receptors

Commonly used drugs

- Buspirone hydrochloride (BuSpar)

Intended effects

- Decreased anxiety
- Treatment of anxiety disorders, specifically generalized anxiety disorder
- Augmented antidepressant therapy

Side or adverse effects

- Dizziness
- Nausea
- Headache
- Nervousness
- Lightheadedness
- Dry mouth
- Diarrhea
- Excitement

Toxic effects

- Lethal dose is 160-550 times the daily recommended dose.

Contraindications

- Used with caution in pregnant women
- Nursing mothers
- Clients with hepatic or renal disease
- Anyone taking MAOs

Unique teaching needs

- BuSpar is not associated with sedation, cognitive impairment, or withdrawal symptoms.
- Therapeutic effect is not experienced for two to four weeks.
- Some clients feel slight restlessness, which could be incompletely treated anxiety.

Psychopharmacotherapy: Antipsychotic Medications

Overview

Antipsychotic medications (neuroleptics) are effective in the treatment of psychoses. Clients with schizophrenia, schizophreniform disorders, schizoaffective disorder, manic phase of bipolar disorders, and delusional disorder may benefit from antipsychotic medications. Exacerbations may be prevented with medication use. Antipsychotic medication is used to lessen symptoms, including hallucinations, dementia, delusions, illusions, aggressive behavior, disorganized speech, and inappropriate affect and behavior. Currently, the most commonly used category of antipsychotics are the atypical antipsychotics (serotonin-dopamine antagonists).

Atypical Antipsychotics (serotonin–dopamine agonists)

Action

- Block postsynaptic dopamine receptors in the basal ganglia, hypothalamus, limbic system, brainstem, and medulla. The newer medications also affect serotonin levels.

Commonly used drugs

- Clozapine (Clozaril)
- Risperidone (Risperdal)
- Olanzapine (Zyprexa)
- Quetiapine (Seroquel)
- Ziprasidone (Geodon)

Intended effects

- Treatment of psychotic symptoms (e.g., hallucinations and delusions), also called **positive symptoms**, that may be seen in schizophrenia, bipolar disorder, major depression, and delusional disorders
- Treatment of **negative symptoms** of schizophrenia (e.g., flat affect, apathy, lack of motivation, social withdrawal)
- Reduction in aggressive behavior

Side or adverse effects

- Sedation
- Weight gain
- Insomnia
- Agitation
- Minimal anticholinergic effects
- Clozaril has greater sedation, anticholinergic effects, and orthostatic hypotension than the other two

Toxic effects

- Clozaril can cause bone marrow toxicity
- Respiratory depression is possible with concomitant ingestion of alcohol

Contraindications

- Known hypersensitivity
- Central nervous system (CNS) depression
- Blood dyscrasias in clients with Parkinson's disease
- Liver, renal, or cardiac insufficiency
- Use with caution in diabetics, elderly, or debilitated.
- Central nervous system (CNS) depressants, including alcohol, in conjunction with antipsychotics induces addictive central nervous system (CNS) depression.
- Tegretol (carbamazepine) in conjunction with antipsychotics causes up to 50% reduction in antipsychotic concentrations.
- Cigarette smoking causes reduced plasma concentrations of antipsychotics.
- Luvox (fluvoxamine) in conjunction with antipsychotics causes increased concentrations of Haldol (haloperidol) and Clozaril.
- Beta-blockers in conjunction with antipsychotics cause severe hypotension.
- Antidepressants in conjunction with antipsychotics may cause increased antidepressant concentration.
- SSRIs in conjunction with antipsychotics may cause sudden onset of extrapyramidal side effects (EPS).

Unique teaching needs

- Regular administration of antipsychotic medications provides maintenance treatment and can prevent exacerbations of psychosis.
- Those taking Clozaril must have their blood counts monitored frequently because of the drug's potential for bone marrow toxicity.

Traditional/Conventional Antipsychotics (Neuroleptics)

Action

- Blocks postsynaptic dopamine-2 receptors in the basal ganglia, hypothalamus, limbic system, brainstem, and medulla.

Commonly used drugs

- Haloperidol (Haldol)
- Trifluoperazine (Stelazine)
- Thiothixene (Navane)
- Fluphenazine (Prolixin)
- Chlorpromazine (Thorazine)
- Loxapine (Loxitane)
- Molindone (Moban)

Intended effects

- Treatment of psychotic symptoms (e.g., hallucinations and delusions), also called positive symptoms, that may be seen in schizophrenia, bipolar disorder, major depression, and delusional disorders

- Treatment of tics and vomiting, as well as intractable hiccoughs
- Reduction in aggressive behavior

Side or adverse effects

- Extrapyramidal side effects (EPS), including acute dystonia, akathisia, pseudoparkinsonism, and tardive dyskinesia
- Sedation
- Anticholinergic effects (dry mouth, constipation, urinary retention, blurred vision)
- Skin rash
- Weight gain
- Photosensitivity
- Reduction of seizure threshold
- Orthostatic hypotension
- Galactorrhea/amenorrhea
- Sexual dysfunction

Toxic effects

- Respiratory depression is possible with concomitant ingestion of alcohol

Contraindications

- Blood dyscrasias
- Liver, renal, or cardiac insufficiency
- Cautious use in the elderly, debilitated, and diabetic clients
- CNS depressants, including alcohol, in conjunction with antipsychotics induces additive CNS depression.
- Tegretol in conjunction with antipsychotics causes up to 50% reduction in antipsychotic concentrations.
- Cigarette smoking causes reduced plasma concentrations of antipsychotics.
- Luvox in conjunction with antipsychotics causes increased concentrations of Haldol and Clozaril.
- Beta-blockers in conjunction with antipsychotics cause severe hypotension.
- Antidepressants in conjunction with antipsychotics may cause increased antidepressant concentration.
- SSRIs in conjunction with antipsychotics may cause sudden onset of EPS.

Unique teaching needs

- Regular administration of antipsychotic medications provides maintenance treatment and can prevent exacerbations of psychosis; therefore, failure to take antipsychotic medication as prescribed can lead to relapses and repeated hospitalizations.
- Antipsychotic dosages in the elderly should be lowered. Haldol and Prolixin are available in decanoate form for depot injections that are helpful for clients who refuse or forget to take their medications.

Psychopharmacotherapy: Antidepressant Medications

Overview

Antidepressants are used in the treatment of depressive mood disorders, including bipolar disease and depression. There are four categories of antidepressants: tricyclics, monoamine oxidase inhibitors (MAOI), selective serotonin reuptake inhibitors (SSRI), and non-tricyclics. Research has indicated the use of antidepressants in a wide variety of disorders other than depression, such as enuresis, eating disorders, and anxiety disorders. Medication is used primarily to treat the related symptoms of dysphoria, anhedonia, reduced energy level, change in appetite and sleep, hopeless feelings, and suicidal ideations.

Selective Serotonin Reuptake Inhibitors (SSRIs)

Action

- Block the reuptake of serotonin into the neuron, thus increasing the amount of serotonin in the synapse

Commonly used drugs

- Paroxetine (Paxil)
- Citalopram (Celexa)
- Fluoxetine (Prozac)
- Sertraline (Zoloft)
- Fluvoxamine (Luvox)
- Nefazodone (Serzone)

Intended effects

- Treatment of depressive disorders
- Decreased symptoms of depression
- Improvement of mood, reduction in anxiety, and treatment of depression associated with organic illness and addiction
- Treatment of anxiety disorders, including obsessive compulsive disorder (OCD), social anxiety disorder, post-traumatic stress disorder (PTSD), and panic disorder
- Treatment of eating disorders
- Dysphoria of PMS
- Treatment of enuresis

Side or adverse effects

- Sexual dysfunction (lack of desire, orgasm, or ejaculation)
- Insomnia
- Agitation
- Akathisia
- Anxiety
- Panic attacks

- Nausea
- Gastrointestinal distress
- Diarrhea
- Headache
- Withdrawal effects
- Efficacy wears off after long term use

Toxic effects

- SSRIs have improved safety and tolerability and are not lethal in overdose.
- SSRIs in conjunction with MAOIs may cause Serotonin Syndrome. Serotonin Syndrome consists of autonomic instability, fever, tremor, rigidity, delirium, seizures, coma, and even death.
- SSRIs in conjunction with tricyclic antidepressants (TCA) may cause TCA toxicity.

Contraindications

- Cardiac dysrhythmias

Unique teaching needs

- The effects of SSRIs are generally not seen for 10 to 21 days, and it will take weeks longer to reach full clinical benefit.
- Client must be taught that relief will not be immediate but will be experienced, and warned not to discontinue medications prematurely.
- Most SSRIs cause sexual side effects and some SSRIs cause weight gain. Antidepressant, trazodone (Desyrel), is commonly used as a hypnotic to induce drowsiness and sleep.

Serotonin Norepinephrine Reuptake Inhibitor (SNRI)

Action

- Blocks the reuptake of serotonin, norepinephrine, and possibly dopamine at high doses in the neurons of the brain

Commonly used drugs

- Venlafaxine (Effexor)

Intended effects

- Decreased symptoms of depression, especially in clients with concurrent anxiety or refractory to SSRIs

Side or adverse effects

- At low doses: sexual dysfunction, insomnia, agitation, and nausea
- At medium to high doses: hypertension, severe insomnia, severe agitation, severe nausea, and headache
- Withdrawal effects: dizziness, gastrointestinal distress, and sweating

Toxic effects

- SNRIs have improved safety and tolerability.
- Effexor in conjunction with Haldol may cause increased Haldol levels.
- Effexor in conjunction with MAOI may cause Serotonin Syndrome.
- Effexor in conjunction with SSRIs may cause increased venlafaxine levels.

Contraindications

- Borderline or labile hypertension
- Insomnia
- Agitation

Unique teaching needs

- Skipping a dose of venlafaxine may cause withdrawal symptoms.
- Low-to-medium dose Effexor may cause sexual side effects.

Norepinephrine Dopamine Reuptake Inhibitor (NDRI)

Action

- Blocks the reuptake of norepinephrine and dopamine in the neurons of the brain

Commonly used drugs

- Bupropion (Wellbutrin)

Intended effects

- Decreased symptoms of depression
- Treatment of attention-deficit disorder
- Reversed SSRI sexual dysfunction
- Treatment of retarded depression with hypersomnia, and/or pseudodementia (cognitive slowing)
- Those who fail to respond to SSRIs
- Treatment of nicotine dependence
- May be used in treatment of stimulant withdrawal and craving

Side or adverse effects

- Agitation
- Stimulation
- Nausea
- Weight loss
- Insomnia
- Seizures (4/1,000) by reducing the seizure threshold

Toxic effects

- There is an increased risk of seizures, particularly in individuals who have a history of seizures.

Contraindications

- Seizure disorders
- Seizure-prone clients (head injury)
- Nonadherence to twice-daily dosing, agitation or insomnia

Unique teaching needs

- Verify that client has not had seizures

Tricyclic Antidepressants (TCAs)

Action

- Block the reuptake of norepinephrine and serotonin by the neurons, thus increasing their concentrations. TCAs have five separate actions: serotonin reuptake inhibitor, norepinephrine reuptake inhibitor, anticholinergic-antimuscarinic drug, alpha 1 adrenergic antagonist, and antihistamine. These actions account for TCA side effects.

Commonly used drugs

- Amitriptyline (Elavil)
- Imipramine (Tofranil)
- Clomipramine (Anafranil)
- Nortriptyline (Aventyl)
- Amoxapine (Asendin)

Intended effects

- Decreased symptoms of depression
- Treatment of chronic pain, fibromyalgia, migraine, and severe depression
- Used as sedative/hypnotic
- Treatment of depression associated with organic illness and addiction
- Amoxapine has neuroleptic properties.
- Clomipramine is effective in treating obsessive-compulsive disorder.

Side or adverse effects

- Anticholinergic effects (dry mouth, constipation, blurred vision, urinary retention)
- Sedation
- Orthostatic hypotension
- Dizziness
- Weight gain
- Confusion, especially in elderly
- Arrhythmias

Toxic effects

- TCAs have possibility of cardiac toxicity and are toxic in overdose

Contraindications

- Alcohol intake
- Dementia
- Suicidal clients (toxic in overdose)
- Cardiac disease
- Multiple concomitant medications (TCA-drug interactions)
- Those who cannot tolerate daytime sedation, urinary retention, or constipation

Unique teaching needs

- Dosage for elderly is usually $1/2$ of adult dosage.
- Alcohol intake in conjunction with TCA will cause sedation and ataxia.
- Suicidal client cannot take TCA because of the fatal cardiac toxicity in overdose.
- TCAs and MAOIs (classic antidepressants) are effective in treating depression, but are not as safe or well tolerated as the newer antidepressants (SSRIs, SNRI, NDRI).

MAO Inhibitors

Action

- Inhibits monoamine oxidase (MAO), thus interfering with the enzymatic breakdown of norepinephrine, dopamine, and serotonin

Commonly used drugs

- Classical MAOIs (irreversible and nonselective)
  - Phenelzine (Nardil)
  - Tranylcypromine (Parnate)
  - Isocarboxazid (Marplan)
- Reversible inhibitors of MAO A (RIMAs)
  - Moclobemide (Manerix)
- Selective inhibitors of MAO B
  - Deprenyl (Selegiline)

Intended effects

- Reduces atypical depression (with weight gain and hypersomnia) or refractory depression in compliant clients

Side or adverse effects

- Orthostatic hypotension
- Insomnia
- Sexual dysfunction
- Drug and dietary interactions/restrictions
- Palpitations
- Headaches

Toxic effects

- Hypertensive crisis
- MAOI in conjunction with sympathomimetic amine medications and dietary tyramine (found in aged cheese, chocolate, beer, wine, etc.) may cause a hypertensive crisis.
- MAOI in conjunction with barbiturates may cause increased sedation.
- MAOI in conjunction with meperidine, SSRI, or TCA may cause serotonin syndrome.

Contraindications

- Noncompliant (or nonadherent) or poorly-motivated clients, agitation and insomnia.

Drug interactions

- Acetaminophen/opiate combinations (Tylenol 3)
- Antihistamines
- Antihypertensives
- Caffeine
- Beta-2 agonists (albuterol)
- Decongestants
- Pseudoephedrine

Unique teaching needs

- Client and family require extensive instruction about foods and medications to avoid, including: cheese, liver, avocados, figs, anchovies, yeast extract, deli meats, herring, bananas, sardines, Brewer's yeast, beer, red wine, ale, liqueurs, chocolate, protein extracts and stimulants, diet pills, cold and decongestant medications, and nasal sprays.
- If client develops severe headache, excess perspiration, lightheadedness, vomiting, or increased heart rate, an MAO hypertensive crisis is likely. Hold the medication, contact the prescribing practitioner, and go to nearest emergency department immediately.
- MAOIs can never be combined with SSRIs.

Psychopharmacotherapy: Mood Stabilizing Medications

Overview

A manic disorder is characterized by an expansive emotional state, extreme excitement, and elation, flight of ideas, increased psychomotor activity, and sometimes violent and self-destructive behavior.

Lithium has traditionally been the most common drug of choice for mood disorders because of its effectiveness for treatment of bipolar disorder in both the acute mania phase and in long-term maintenance therapy. Lithium is also commonly used in the treatment of schizoaffective disorders and as an adjunct therapy in clients with depression, impulse control disorders, conduct disorders, pervasive development disorders, and mental retardation. It takes two to three weeks for lithium to be effective, so many clients are placed on antipsychotics until lithium becomes effective. Cautious use is indicated due to the narrow therapeutic range.

Other newer agents are now used to treat bipolar disorders, including carbamazepine and valproic acid. These medications are effective in controlling seizures and other impulse-control disorders. However, the adverse side effects are serious and can cause liver failure.

Lithium

Action

- Lithium is a salt that may modify second messenger systems; it may alter G-proteins or enzymes that interact with the second messenger system.

Commonly used drugs

- Lithium carbonate:
  - Lithobid
  - Lithonate
  - Eskalith
  - Lithotabs

Intended effects

- Treatment of mania (marked by mood swings, excitement, elation, flight of ideas, and sometimes violent/self-destructive behavior)
- Long-term (or maintenance) treatment of bipolar disorder
- Augmented antidepressant treatment, reduction in frequency and intensity of mood swings, reduction in aggressive behavior, augmented antidepressants, and treatment of bipolar disorder or disorders with expansive emotional states
- Also may be used to treat schizoaffective disorders, impulse control disorders, conduct disorders, and pervasive developmental disorders

Side or adverse effects

- Nausea
- Polyuria

- Polydipsia
- Fine hand tremor
- Weight gain
- Dry mouth
- Maintenance therapy can cause hypothyroidism, leukocytosis (reversible when lithium is discontinued), acne, psoriasis, and kidney damage

Toxic effects

- Vomiting, diarrhea, ataxia, sedation, or confusion, severe tremor, drowsiness, muscular weakness, loss of coordination, and seizures
- Lithium serum concentrations are increased by fluoxetine, ACE inhibitors, diuretics, and NSAIDs
- Lithium serum concentrations are decreased by theophylline, osmotic diuretics, and urinary alkalinizers

Contraindications

- Renal disease
- Cardiac disease
- Severe dehydration
- Sodium depletion
- Brain damage
- Pregnancy or lactation
- Use with caution in the elderly or clients with diabetes, thyroid disorders, urinary retention, and seizures.

Unique teaching needs

- Blood levels of Lithium, Depakote, and Tegretol must be monitored regularly to prevent toxicity. (Not all mood stabilizers require blood monitoring. Maintenance blood levels of lithium are usually 0.5-1.2 mEq and toxic levels are those equal to or greater than 1.5 mEq.)
- If any toxic symptoms occur, discontinue the drug and notify health care provider.
- Client must take in adequate fluid (about two to three liters/day) and eat a balanced diet with normal sodium intake.
- It takes 2-3 weeks for lithium to become effective; clients who are psychotic may be placed on antipsychotic medication while lithium is taking effect.
- Lithium should be taken with food.

Anticonvulsants

Action

- Cause a decrease in the catabolism of GABA, resulting in increased concentration of GABA in the central nervous system

Commonly used drugs

- Carbamazepine (Tegretol)

- Valproic acid (Depakote, Depakene, Valproate)
- Clonazepam (Klonopin)

Intended effects

- Treatment of bipolar disorder, acute mania, and aggressive behavior
- Reduction in mood swings
- Maintenance treatment of bipolar disorder (and seizure disorders)
- May be used for schizoaffective disorders, impulse control disorders, and aggression
- Depakote and Tegretol are useful for rapid-cycling bipolar disorder.

Side or adverse effects

- Depakote:
  - Gastrointestinal distress
  - Nausea
  - Diarrhea
  - Headache
  - Dizziness
  - Anxiety
  - Confusion
  - Sedation
  - Diplopia
  - Edema
  - Tremor
  - Weight gain
  - Alopecia
  - Jaundice
- Tegretol:
  - Dizziness
  - Drowsiness
  - Nausea
  - Vomiting
  - Ataxia
  - Confusion
  - Disturbed vision
  - Memory impairment
  - Skin rash, and weight gain

Toxic effects

- Tegretol can cause agranulocytosis and aplastic anemia.
- Depakote can cause liver dysfunction, hepatic failure, and blood dyscrasias including thrombocytopenia.
- Depakote interacts with drugs that are hepatically metabolized.

Contraindications

- Hepatic or renal disease
- Pregnancy
- Lactation
- Presence of blood dyscrasias

Unique teaching needs

- Blood levels of mood stabilizers must be monitored regularly to prevent toxicity. The normal ranges for Tegretol and Depakote are: Tegretol (4-12), Depakote (50-110).
- Liver and renal function tests and complete blood counts with differential are monitored regularly to prevent serious complications involving the liver, kidneys, and blood cell elements.
- Depakote must be swallowed whole, not cut, chewed, or crushed to prevent irritation to the mouth, throat, and stomach.
- Client should not take any other medication without permission of his/her doctor, should take the medication with food, report bruising, and not use heavy equipment if drowsy.
- Client should understand the importance and reasons for regular blood monitoring.

Psychopharmacotherapy: Psychostimulant (Sympathomimetic) Medications

Action

- Causes catecholamines, particularly dopamine, to be released from presynaptic neurons and inhibits the reuptake of released catecholamines back into the presynaptic neurons. As a result, several brain regions are stimulated, especially the ascending reticular activating system (RAS).

Commonly used drugs

- Methylphenidate (Ritalin, Concerta)
- Combination of amphetamine salts (Adderall)
- Dextroamphetamine (Dexedrine)

Intended effects

- Increased attention and concentration
- Decreased distractibility, hyperactivity, and impulsivity
- Treatment of attention-deficit hyperactivity disorder
- Treatment of narcolepsy

Side or adverse effects

- Anorexia
- Weight loss (and possibly growth delay)
- Insomnia
- Headache

- Tachycardia
- Precipitation or exacerbation of tic disorder

Toxic effects

- Potential for abuse or overdose (delirium, psychosis, palpitations, arrhythmias, hypertension, hyperpyrexia, seizures, coma)

Contraindications

- History of drug abuse or dependence, severe anxiety, anorexia nervosa, MAOIs

Unique teaching needs

- Eat meals before taking medication.
- Do not take medication after 4 p.m.
- As with all medication for children, parents should safeguard and dispense psychostimulants.
- Children and adults taking psychostimulants should be regularly monitored and assessed regarding whether the medication is still needed.

Psychopharmacotherapy: Sedative-Hypnotic Medications

Overview

Sedatives and hypnotics are drugs that are used to reduce anxiety and insomnia. These agents act as depressants to slow the action of the central nervous system (CNS). Shortly after taking the medication, the client experiences a feeling of relaxation as tensions disappear. This experience is followed by a physical and mental lassitude and tendency toward sleep. Excessive use may lead to increased tolerance as well as psychological and physiological dependency. Sedative-hypnotics are usually prescribed in small doses for short periods of time. This classification of medication is also indicated for use in the preoperative and postoperative periods.

Benzodiazepines

Action

- Acts mainly at subcortical levels of central nervous system (CNS), potentiates the effects of GABA, an inhibitory neurotransmitter, producing central nervous system (CNS) depression.

Commonly used erugs

- **Non-barbiturates**
  - Flurazepam (Dalmane)
  - Temazepam (Restoril)
- **Barbiturates**
  - Secobarbital (Seconal)
  - Pentobarbital (Nembutal)

Intended effects

- Sedation in low doses
- Induced sleep in higher doses
- Treatment of acute anxiety and panic attacks
- May be used for preoperative and postoperative sedation

Side or adverse effects

- Drowsiness
- Ataxia
- Hangover effect (sluggish and slow speech, impaired comprehension)
- Confusion
- Sudden mood swings
- Loss of weight, fatigue
- Lightheadedness
- Dizziness

Toxic effects

- Respiratory depression in conjunction with other CNS depressants leading to death
- Symptoms of abrupt withdrawal (depression, paranoia, delirium, seizures)

Contraindications

- Alcohol use
- Addiction
- Central nervous system (CNS) depressants
- Hepatic or renal impairment
- Cardiac disease
- Pregnancy
- Lactation

Unique teaching needs

- Use for short periods of time (1-2 weeks) usually does not lead to tolerance, dependence, or withdrawal. Longer use causes tolerance and physical and psychological dependence to develop and often, withdrawal syndrome.
- Benzodiazepines must be carefully tapered on discontinuation and never stopped abruptly.
- Do not take benzodiazepines with other medications without consulting your health care provider.
- Do not drive or use heavy machinery if sedated.

Nonbenzodiazepines

Action

- Modulate GABA receptors to cause suppression of neurons, leading to sedation, anticonvulsant, and relaxant properties

Commonly used erugs

- Zolpidem (Ambien)
- Zaleplon (Sonata)

Intended effects

- Induced drowsiness and sleep
- Sonata has very short duration of effect, so it can be repeated in the night and given up to four hours before arising.

Side or adverse effects

- Drowsiness
- Dizziness
- Blurred vision
- Gastrointestinal upset
- Hangover effect

- Confusion
- Depression
- Paradoxical excitement

Toxic effects

- Seizures
- Ataxia
- Hallucinations

Contraindications

- Hepatic and renal disease
- Addiction
- Pregnancy
- Lactation

Unique teaching needs

- Long-term use is not recommended.
- Do not drive or use heavy machinery if sedated.
- Can repeat Sonata up to four hours before arising.

Psychopharmacotherapy: Medications Used to Treat Extrapyramidal Side Effects (EPS)

Overview

The dopamine blockade of antipsychotic medications can cause a variety of movement-related side effects in which normal motor activity is disrupted. These side effects are collectively known as extrapyramidal side effects (EPS). They are troubling to clients and a major reason for nonadherence to medication treatment.

Antipsychotic Medications

Extrapyramidal side effects

Acute dystonia: Painful and frightening spasms of tongue, throat, face, jaw, eyes, neck, or back muscles; occurs in up to 10% of clients. Symptoms may present as eye closing, severe upward deviation of the eyeballs, neck muscle contraction that pulls the neck to one side, severe dorsal arching of the neck and back, and difficulty swallowing. Fortunately, anticholinergic drugs (in oral or IM forms) are rapidly effective in relieving acute dystonia.

Akathisia: Occurs in 25% of persons taking antipsychotics. Clients verbalize an inner restlessness described as irritability or tension. Outward signs are motor restlessness, pacing, foot tapping, rocking, and inability to remain still.

Pseudoparkinsonism: Bradykinesia or akinesia, rigidity, resting tremor, rabbit syndrome, sialorrhea (hypersalivation with drooling), flat affect, cogwheel rigidity, postural instability, hunched and shuffling gait, and mask-like faces. Symptoms are due to cholinergic predominance resulting from dopamine blockade because dopamine and acetylcholine usually exist in balance in the brain.

Tardive dyskinesia (TD): An abnormal condition characterized by involuntary, repetitious movements of the muscles of the face, limbs, and trunk. Facial movements may include tongue thrusting and writhing, lip pursing or smacking, facial grimaces, and chewing movements. Rapid, jerking and slow, writhing movements may, at the outset, occur anywhere in the body; these movements are usually first noticed by family members. TD occurs in 4% of clients. Symptoms of TD may decrease or disappear for a while, but typically TD is permanent. Newer, atypical antipsychotics tend to carry lower risk of causing TD.

Medications to Treat EPS

Action

- Antihistamines block the effects of histamine and have anticholinergic effects.
- Antiparkinsonian medications increase dopamine release in the nigrostriatal pathway.
- Anticholinergics normalize the imbalance of cholinergic/dopaminergic neurotransmission in the basal ganglia of the brain.

Commonly used drugs

- Antimuscarinics
    - Benztropine (Cogentin)
    - Trihexyphenidyl (Artane)
    - Biperiden (Akineton)
    - Procyclidine (Kemadrin)
- Antihistaminic
    - Diphenhydramine hydrochloride (Benadryl)
- Dopamine agonists
    - Amantadine (Symmetrel)
    - Ropinirole (Requip)

Intended effects

- Decreased EPS
- Reversed acute dystonia by reducing severity of rigidity
- Suppression of drooling and other signs of parkinsonism

Side or adverse effects

- Dry mouth
- Constipation
- Blurred vision
- Dizziness
- Drowsiness, nausea
- Orthostatic hypotension
- Tachycardia
- Palpitations
- Confusion
- Memory loss
- Urinary retention
- Some psychiatric symptoms (e.g., depression, hallucinations)

Toxic effects

- Potentially fatal cardiac arrhythmia if taken with erythromycin

Contraindications

- Benadryl cannot be taken with erythromycin because the combination could cause a potentially fatal cardiac arrhythmia.
- Benadryl should not to be taken in pregnancy and lactation, during asthmatic attacks, with obstructions of bladder neck or pylorus-duodenum or prostatic hypertrophy.
- Symmetrel should not be taken with history of seizures, liver disease, eczema-like rash, congestive heart failure (CHF), renal disease, or lactation.
- Cogentin cannot be taken if client has glaucoma, myasthenia gravis, obstructions of pylorus-duodenum or bladder neck, or prostatic hypertrophy.

Unique teaching needs

- These medications should be taken simultaneously with antipsychotic medication to prevent EPS.
- Acute dystonia can be treated with Benadryl.
- Use caution, especially around machinery, if medication causes drowsiness, dizziness, or lightheadedness.
- Report swelling, difficulty urinating, shortness of breath, difficulty walking, tremors, or slurred speech immediately to health care provider.

Critical Thinking Exercise: Psychopharmacotherapy

Situation: You are the medication nurse for one week on a psychiatric unit. You have a busy week. The following are short client descriptions regarding problems and questions about psychopharmacology that you encountered this week. Respond to the questions for each example given.

1. Your client has been prescribed fluphenazine (Prolixin). The client has never taken this medication. What type of medication is this? Identify four side effects that the client might experience.

2. M.H. is taking procyclidine (Kemadrin). Why would this medication be prescribed?

3. A.P. has been prescribed lithium soon after her admission. She is very angry and aggressive. What is wrong with the statement, "The lithium will soon stop that behavior?"

4. A.P. begins to experience hand tremors, polyuria, confusion, and ataxia. What is happening to A.P.? What do you need to do initially?

5. A.P. will need to be taught about her diet. What will you teach her?

6. B.F. has been taking secobarbital (Seconal) for sleep. He has found that he needs a higher dose to obtain sleep. What has happened to B.F.?

7. A.K. is taking alprazolam (Xanax). She says, "I have a fear of addiction, but I don't mind taking this medication because I know I can't get addicted to it." How would you respond to this statement?

8. You are assessing a new client who has schizophrenia. You note that the client has facial grimaces, tongue thrusting, and makes a smacking sound. What is the client's problem? What is a cause of this problem?

9. Elderly clients will need higher doses of medications in order to obtain positive results from psychotropic medications. Why is this a false statement?

10. A client on the unit has been prescribed isocarboxazid (Marplan). What intervention is critical for this client?

Electroconvulsive Therapy

Key Points

- Electroconvulsive therapy (ECT) is used:
  - For severe depression when antidepressant medications are ineffective
  - For manic episodes when lithium and other medications are ineffective
  - With some clients who have acute schizophrenia
- Risks associated with ECT include:
  - Death
  - Temporary or permanent memory loss
  - Brain damage
- **Key Terms/Concepts:** Depression, manic episode, acute schizophrenia, general anesthesia

Overview

Electroconvulsive therapy (ECT) is the procedure for the induction of a grand mal seizure through the application of an electric current to the brain while the client is under general anesthesia. The current is applied through electrodes placed bilaterally on the frontal temporal region or unilaterally on the same side as the dominant hand. The amount of electricity is determined by the client's condition. Most clients require six to 10 treatments; however, some clients do not reach a maximum response until 20 to 25 treatments. Maintenance ECT is also used after the initial therapy every six weeks to six months.

Indications for Use

- Treatment of intractable depression, that is, severe depressions in which antidepressant medications have been ineffective or not tolerated well
- Treatment of manic episodes of bipolar disorders where therapy with lithium or other medications are ineffective or not tolerated well
- Shown to induce remission with clients who present with acute schizophrenia, but is of little value to treat chronic schizophrenia

Types

- **Modified:** Treatment approach whereby pretreatment medications are utilized to initiate treatment.
- **Unmodified:** Treatment without the aid of medication. A concern with this approach is the high morbidity associated with treatment, thus this method's no longer used.

Risks Associated with ECT

- **Mortality**: Death is rare and usually is related to cardiovascular complications. Thus, ECT is contraindicated for clients with cerebrovascular disease, myocardial infarction, hypertension, increased intracranial pressure, or congestive heart failure. EKG is assessed before the procedure. ECT is also contraindicated for pregnant women.

- **Temporary or permanent memory loss**: Studies have shown that a small subgroup may suffer from short-term confusion, disorientation, and memory loss. Memory loss may be permanent, but usually is not.

- **Brain damage**: Critics believe that there is always some degree of immediate brain damage. However, there have been no substantial data that prove ECT produces any brain changes in structure or function.
  - ICP
  - HTN, COPD
  - Cardiac arrhythmias
  - Cervical injury or problem
  - Head injuries

Medications Used in ECT

- **Glycopyrrolate (Robinul)**
  - Used to dry secretions
  - If given IM, must be given 20 minutes prior to procedure
  - Dosing: 0.1 mg to 0.2 mg
- **Methohexital (Brevital Sodium)**
  - Anesthetic
  - PT feels a burning sensation when administered
  - Works immediately
  - Common side effect: hiccups
  - Dosing: 1 mg/kg
- **Succinylcholine (Anectine)**
  - Muscle relaxant
  - Lasts 2 - 3 minutes
  - Diaphragm is last muscle to relax
  - Dosing: 1 mg/kg

Issues Related to the Procedure

- The client should take nothing by mouth (NPO) after midnight to prevent aspiration during anesthesia.
- The anesthesia that is usually used is methohexital sodium (Brevital).
- ECT may be given on an inpatient or outpatient basis. If it is administered to an outpatient, the client will need transportation home after the procedure and help with care at home. There will be some memory loss, which is usually temporary.

- Recovery requires the typical postanesthesia nursing care. The client recovers quickly from the brief procedure. Vital signs and observation are important. When the client has recovered, provide fluids and food and assist client in walking until stable.
- **Course** (six to 12 treatments): QOD (average of 15 treatments; maximum of 24 per year)
    - Seizures should last between 20-180 seconds at 40-110 Joules
        - 15-20 = abortive seizure
        - 0-20 - absent seizure
- **Maintenance**: One ECT every two to four weeks, seizures get progressively shorter
- Lead Placement:
    - **Bitemporal**: easier to obtain a seizure. However, more cognitive problems
    - **Right unilateral**: most favorable, more energy, less cognitive problems
    - **Bifrontal**: Anterior forehead lead placement above each eye orbit; equally effective as bitemporal placement with fewer memory and cognitive side effects
- Memory Issues:
    - **Retrograde amnesia**: Loss of memory up to time of treatment. Memory will return slowly.
    - **Anterograde amnesia**: Loss of memory from treatment forward. Unable to remember the treatment nor events beyond.
- **History**: (Should be completed within the last 30 days)
- **Consultation**: Assure the diagnosis is correct.
    - Full history and physical assessment
    - SMAC, CBC PT, PTT LIVER, RPR, thyroid function
    - EKG
    - Chest x-ray
- **Important related information**:
    - CT of brain
    - EEG
    - Cervical lumbar x-rays

Critical Thinking Exercise: Electroconvulsive Therapy

Situation: Unit A provides electroconvulsive therapy (ECT) for clients who need this treatment. V.R. is 60 years old and has been admitted for major depression. She has lost weight, is very withdrawn, and is unable to leave home. V.R. is not able to carry on a conversation for more than a few minutes. She has threatened to kill herself. Her primary care provider has tried her on several antidepressants, but they do not relieve the symptoms. She has been admitted to begin an ECT series. You are assigned to her care.

1. To decrease her risk during the treatment, what interventions are needed? What is the reason for these?

2. After the treatment, you are assigned to care for V.R. What should you expect to do?

3. Will V.R. experience memory loss? If so, will it be permanent?

Stress Management

Key Points

- Stress is the body's nonspecific response to any demand made on it, according to Selye.
- Stressors are physical or psychological factors that produce stress. Any stressor produces the same biological response in the body.
- Distress is a damaging stressor such as anxiety or anger.
- The General Adaptation Syndrome (GAS) is the body's response to an increased demand, its "flight or flight" mechanism.
- Stages of the GAS include:
  - Alarm reaction
  - Stage of resistance
  - Stage of exhaustion
- Stress management is a person's ability to experience appropriate emotions and cope with stress. The person who manages stress in a healthy manner is flexible and uses a variety of coping mechanisms.
- Many factors increase a person's resilience or ability to resist the effects of stress, including:
  - Physical health
  - Strong sense of self
  - Religious foundation
  - Optimism
  - Hobbies and outlets
  - Satisfying interpersonal relationships
  - Humor
- Cultural differences exist among a person's perception, experience, and management of stress.
- **Key Terms/Concepts**: Stress, stressor, General Adaptation Syndrome, distress, stress management, eustress

Overview

Stress is the body's nonspecific response to any demand made on it, according to the biologist, Hans Selye. Stressors are factors that produce stress; stressors may be physical or psychological, but any stressor produces the same biologic response. Stress is not the same as distress, which is a damaging stressor (such as anxiety, hopelessness, fatigue, or anger). Eustress is the positive, motivating influence that results in action, success, or fulfillment. All of life involves stress; the absence of stress is death.

Types of Stressors

The perception of the significance of an event or situation is an important determinant of the degree of stress that it is likely to produce. Developed in 1967 by Holmes and Rahe, the classic stress rating scale identifies the degree of social and personal stressors.

- Physical: Extreme heat or cold, malnutrition, disease, infection, or pain
- Psychological: Fear, failure, move, success, holiday, or vacation are among the many stressors identified

The General Adaptation Syndrome (GAS)

The GAS is a term used by Selye to describe the body's biochemical changes and manner of responding to any increased demand. These responses are the body's "fight or flight" mechanism. The GAS occurs in three stages:

Alarm reaction: The body starts to adjust and respond to the stressor by releasing hormones that initiate physical responses, but resistance is being decreased; death may occur if the stressor is strong enough.

Stage of resistance: The body continues to resist the stressor and compensate physiologically, so the level of resistance is stronger than usual.

Stage of exhaustion: Due to the sustained biochemical response, the body's ability to resist the stressor becomes depleted; illness or death could result.

Physical Findings

- Increased heart rate
- Pupillary dilation
- Increased blood pressure
- Increased oxygen consumption
- Sweat gland stimulation
- Elevated blood glucose, cholesterol, and free fatty acid levels
- Polyuria
- Peripheral vasoconstriction
- Nausea

Behavioral Cues

- Insomnia
- Scattered thoughts
- Disorganized speech
- Restlessness
- Irritability
- Impaired concentration

Therapeutic Nursing Management

- Listen

- Assess for:
  - Level of stress
  - Support systems/other coping mechanisms
  - Thought patterns
  - Behavioral patterns
  - Energy/activity level
- Teach:
  - Prioritizing
  - Relaxation techniques
  - Coping strategies:
    - Positive self-talk
    - Reframing
    - Altruism
    - Sublimation
    - Suppression
    - Music
    - Pets
    - Humor
    - Biofeedback
    - Deep breathing
    - Progressive muscle relaxation
    - Imagery
    - Yoga
    - Meditation
    - Physical exercise
    - Hobbies
    - Support systems
- Stress management is a person's ability to experience appropriate emotions and cope with stress. The person who manages stress in a healthy manner is flexible and uses a variety of coping mechanisms. The mechanisms to resist and cope with stress are:
  - A strong sense of self
  - Satisfying interpersonal relationships/social network (church, work, school)
  - Problem-solving skills (prioritizing actions, budgeting)
  - Humor
  - Hobbies and outlets for feelings (sublimating energies into positive forms)
  - Optimism
  - Physical health and good health habits
  - Interpersonal skills, such as listening and setting personal boundaries
  - Techniques such as reframing, deep breathing, imagery, meditation, yoga, progressive muscle relaxation, and positive self-talk
- Refer to a specialist (doctor, counselor, psychiatrist, support group).

Critical Thinking Exercise: Stress Management

Situation: T.C., a 17-year-old girl, comes into the nurse's office at her high school. T.C. says she has been upset, is having trouble sleeping, and has lost her appetite. On further exploration, she reveals that her parents have been arguing quite a bit related to financial difficulties, her college applications are due and she has not started on them, and her grades are suffering. She asks the nurse to help.

1. What symptoms indicate that T.C. is having problem with stress?

2. T.C. says she feels worried all the time. What three techniques could help T.C. relax and decrease her stress?

Crisis and Crisis Intervention

Key Points

- Crisis is a state of emotional pain, distress, instability, or disordered function that is usually triggered by a situational event or radical change in a person's life.
- Caplan's four phases of crisis development:
  - Exposure to conflict or problem
  - Failure of usual defense responses
  - Trial-and-error attempts fail
  - Overwhelming anxiety and resulting maladaptive behavior
- The goals for collaborative management include:
  - Protecting the client from harm
  - Providing crisis intervention that considers the crisis situation and responses
  - Providing a safe environment: hospital and home
  - Adhering to medication treatment
  - Teaching coping and self-monitoring skills
- **Key Terms/Concepts**: Crisis, disequilibrium, anxiety, coping, self-monitoring, crisis intervention

Overview

A crisis is the state of psychological disequilibrium resulting from an overwhelmingly stressful situation in which there is no escape or resolution through the usual problem-solving resources. All people experience stress, and most learn how to cope effectively. However, individuals with a mental illness have an impaired capacity to cope with stress and crisis.

Phases in the Development of a Crisis

- Client is exposed to a precipitating stressor or an overwhelming event.
- Anxiety increases when the usual problem-solving techniques do not relieve the stressor.
- All possible resources, both internal and external, are called upon to resolve the problem and relieve the discomfort.
- If resolution still does not occur, the tension may increase to an intolerable point. Significant disorganization and deterioration may occur and the stress reaches crisis level.

Types of Crisis

Situational: Arises from external, rather than internal, source

Maturational: The stages of growth and development require a mastery of new tasks. New coping styles are required at each stage. When alternate defense strategies are not developed, the person is likely to experience anxiety.

Adventitious: Result of unplanned and accidental events, such as natural disaster, national emergency, crime or violence

Risk Factors

- Impaired functioning
- Ineffective problem-solving skills
- Ineffective coping mechanisms
- Prolonged stress
- Inadequate support systems
- Anxiety, mental illness

Signs and Symptoms

- Reduced capacity for problem solving
- Inability to focus
- Severe-to-panic levels of anxiety
- Altered thought processes
- Fear
- Overwhelming sense of going crazy or losing one's mind

Assessment

- History and physical examination: Stress and anxiety can produce physical symptoms.
- Mental status examination: Assess anxiety, fear, and changes in mood, thought processes and functioning.
- Assess adequacy of support systems: Clients who have adequate support systems are less likely to inflict self-harm.
- Assess individual coping mechanisms and the client's ability to organize his thoughts, cope with the stress, and resolve the issue.

Nursing Diagnoses

- Ineffective individual coping
- Ineffective family coping
- Anxiety
- Altered thought processes
- Impaired social interaction
- Social isolation
- Self-esteem disturbance

Therapeutic Nursing Management

- Provide crisis intervention, including assessment of the crisis situation and response.
    - Identify the precipitating events, past and present, and coping mechanisms.
    - Involve the client's support systems.
    - Provide specific interventions to alleviate the perception of crisis.
    - Teach the client and family effective coping strategies.
    - Provide follow-up care.
- Provide a supportive and protected environment.
- Advise the client to avoid alcohol or other non-prescribed mind or mood-altering substances.
- Assess for suicide risk.
- Administer medications if required (e.g., antianxiety medications, antidepressants, and antipsychotic medications for more severe responses).
- Reassure the client in a therapeutic manner.

Client Outcomes

The client will:

- Experience less anxiety, as exhibited by the ability to cope with stress, appropriate sleep pattern, and participation in social activities
- Discuss feelings of anxiety; also understand behavior and situations that contribute to anxiety
- Exhibit no injury to self or others
- Identify effects of anxiety in his or her life
- Use self-monitoring methods to assess anxiety and intervene appropriately

Client and Family Education

- Phases of crisis
- Self-assessment
- Interventions to alleviate crisis and response
- Medications, if used

Complications

- Harm to self or others
- Psychological disequilibrium
- Inability to problem-solve and make decisions

Age–Related Changes—Considerations

- Impaired cognition (confusion) may hinder problem-solving skills.
- Adolescents frequently encounter crises and may respond with inappropriate behavior, such as acting out, use of alcohol and other drugs, driving recklessly, and committing suicide or violence toward others.

Critical Thinking Exercise: Crisis and Crisis Intervention

Situation: G.F. is admitted to the emergency department following a rape. She is 24 years old and lives alone. She was sexually assaulted when returning from work late at night. After she is examined, she begins to shake and cry. She will not let anyone touch her and is unable to decide what to do (e. g., call a friend to take her home, talk with a rape counselor, or agree to follow-up visit). When you try to speak with G.F., she responds rapidly and in a manner that is not clear or understandable.

1. Has G.F. experienced a crisis? And if so, how would you assess her anxiety level?

2. If you had to explain the crisis process and its phases applied to G.F., what would you say?

3. What further data about G.F. might be helpful as you plan interventions?

4. What are some consequences to G.F.'s rape and crisis?

5. Identify two interventions that you might use with G.F.

Anxiety Disorders

Key Points

- Stress can precipitate and increase anxiety.
- There are several types of anxiety disorders, but the most common are panic disorder, generalized anxiety disorder, obsessive-compulsive disorder, and post-traumatic stress disorder.
- Biological factors may affect the development of anxiety.
- There are four levels of anxiety: mild, moderate, severe, and panic.
- The goals of collaborative management include:
    - Providing a safe environment: hospital and home
    - Adhering to medication treatment
    - Ensuring that client's needs are met, especially during high levels of anxiety
    - If client protection is required, ensuring that all procedures are followed, and client is treated with respect
    - Reinforcing reality and recognize client's feelings
    - Increasing client's coping mechanisms and self-monitoring to decrease anxiety
    - Encouraging client socialization, when appropriate
    - Educating client and family about anxiety disorders and treatment
- **Key Terms/Concepts**: Anxiety, GABA neurotransmitter process, flashback

Overview

Anxiety is a normal response to threatening situations; however, it can escalate out of control. Anxiety is different from fear; a person is fearful of something specific, but anxiety is vague and diffused. An anxiety disorder is manifested feelings of apprehension and helplessness, which increases disproportionately to the situation. The anxiety response continues after the perceived risk or situation no longer exists. Anxiety is the emotional response to stress, more common in women than men. Symptoms are categorized as physiological, psychological, and behavioral. Anxiety disorders include panic disorder, generalized anxiety disorder, obsessive-compulsive disorder, post-traumatic stress disorder, somatoform disorders, and dissociative disorders. Anxiety disorders are the most common psychiatric disorders in America, affecting between 10 to 25% of the population.

Types of Disorders

Panic disorder with or without agoraphobia: Characterized by recurrent, high-intensity, anxiety episodes or panic attacks. The onset may be unpredictable. Manifestations include intense apprehension and fear or terror, often associated with feelings of impending doom, and accompanied by physical discomfort, such as chest pain, shortness of breath, anticipatory anxiety of another attack, and avoidance of situations where past attacks have occurred. Panic disorder with agoraphobia presents with the same symptoms, however, the client avoids certain situations for fear that they will have a panic attack (e.g., driving a car across a bridge).

Generalized anxiety disorder: Characterized by chronic, unrealistic, and excessive anxiety or worry. Manifestations include excessive worrying about events that are difficult to control, feeling on edge, fatigue, difficulty concentrating, muscle tension, or sleep disturbances.

Post-traumatic stress disorder: The development of certain symptoms following exposure to an extreme traumatic stressor involving a personal threat to physical integrity or to the physical integrity of others. Manifestations include re-experiencing the traumatic event or flashback, a sustained high level of anxiety or arousal, hyper-alertness, startle reflex, and a general numbing of responsiveness or depersonalization. Examples of experiences that may lead to PTSD include the experience of or witnessing such unnatural experiences as rape, assault, natural disaster, and war. The traumatic event is re-experienced in the mind, and there is an avoidance of stimuli associated with trauma.

Risk Factors

- Biochemical alterations: Depletion of norepinephrine results in increased anxiety.
- Genetics: Anxiety disorders tend to occur in families.
- Psychological influences: Ineffective coping; increased risk for depression
- Environmental stressors: Physical threats and threats to self-esteem
- Support systems: Lack of or ineffective support systems

Specific Biological Factors

- Ineffective gamma-aminobutyric acid (GABA) neurotransmitter process
- General health can affect anxiety (e.g., hypoxia, hyperthyroidism, menopause, COPD, pulmonary embolism, and pheochromocytoma).
- Fatigue can increase anxiety.

Signs and Symptoms

Physical symptoms:

- Heart palpitations
- Sweating, trembling
- Shortness of breath
- Chest and/or abdominal pain
- Nausea, diarrhea
- Dizziness
- Fatigue

- Fatigue or feeling drained
- Elevated blood pressure
- Dry mouth
- Difficulty swallowing
- Frequent urination

Psychological symptoms:

- Insomnia
- Depersonalization
- Fear of dying
- Ineffective coping
- Altered role performance
- Increase in level of apprehension
- Feelings of impending doom, fear, and hopelessness
- Fight or flight responses
- Irritability
- Impaired perceptions of others, situations, and events
- Decreased attention and concentration
- Judgment errors

Behavioral symptoms:

- Restlessness
- Rapid speech
- Withdrawal
- Pacing
- Inability to complete task
- Forgetfulness

Levels of Anxiety

Level I: Mild anxiety, which can be helpful in serving as a motivator with higher perception and ability to see the entire picture. Mild anxiety is caused by the ordinary tensions of daily life. Common coping behaviors are smoking, eating, cursing, physical exercise, sleeping, or daydreaming.

Level II: Moderate anxiety. Perception continues to be high; however, the client begins to focus only on the situation he or she is in, excluding other issues.

Level III: Severe anxiety (includes perception inaccuracies). Problem solving is drastically reduced. The client needs assistance.

Level IV: Panic with very distorted perceptions. There is a sense of awe, dread and terror. The client must have immediate intervention.

Assessment

- History and physical examination
- Family history

- Mental status examination
- Psychological testing
- Electroencephalogram (EEG)
- Psychiatric assessment and history
- Family dynamics
- Social history, including alcohol use and caffeine intake
- Interference of symptoms with functioning

Nursing Diagnoses

- Anxiety
- Powerlessness
- Ineffective individual coping
- Impaired verbal communication
- Self-esteem disturbance
- Impaired social interaction
- Risk for injury
- Sleep pattern disturbance
- Ineffective breathing pattern
- Alteration in nutrition
- Alteration in bowel and/or urinary elimination
- Knowledge deficit
- Social isolation
- Impaired adjustment

Therapeutic Nursing Management

Environment: The environment needs to be safe to prevent client injury. Reduced stimuli assists in providing a calm environment.

Psychosocial treatment:

- Individual psychotherapy may be used to assist client in identifying cause of anxiety and improving coping methods. The establishment of a trusting relationship is crucial. Listen actively and encourage open discussion of feelings.
- Cognitive behavioral therapy may include systematic desensitization, relaxation, exposure and exposure therapy, and response prevention.
- Family therapy may assist the family in coping with client's anxiety as well as encourage greater family support.
- Group therapy assists client in improving coping skills.

Psychopharmacological treatment:

- Administer and teach about medications.
- Give antianxiety and antidepressant medications as ordered.
- Monitor the client's response.

- Benzodiazepines (BZDs), monoamine oxidase inhibitors, tricyclic antidepressants, serotonin reuptake inhibitors and nonselective serotonin reuptake inhibitors are effective in treating most anxiety disorders, however, care must be taken for possible abuse potential of the BZDs.

Nursing interventions:

- Assure client that physical symptoms are related to anxiety, but only after determining that this is true.
- Support client and allow time for the client to discuss feelings. Convey a nonjudgmental attitude.
- Assist the client in understanding the anxiety process and ways to intervene. Teach client to self-monitor anxiety and reduce it.
- Guide the client in understanding the value of stress reduction, the steps that the client can take to reduce his/her stress and feelings of anxiety.
- Encourage the client to participate in hobbies, sports, recreational activities, or any healthy outlets for stress.
- Educate the client about his/her medication, as well as its administration and safe use.
- Assess the client for the inappropriate use of alcohol and/or other drugs. Intervene if necessary with appropriate treatment.
- Reinforce socially productive behavior.
- Teach progressive relaxation techniques.

Complications

- Decrease in level of functioning
- Risk to self or others, especially with a high level of anxiety and no reduction in symptoms
- Ineffective coping of individuals and families
- Altered role performance
- Depression

Client Outcomes

The client will:

- Experience less anxiety, as exhibited by the ability to cope with stress, appropriate sleep pattern, and participation in social activities
- Discuss feelings of anxiety and associate behavior and situations that contribute to anxiety
- Exhibit no injury to self or others
- Identify effects of anxiety in his or her life
- Use self-monitoring methods to assess anxiety and intervene appropriately
- Short-term: To recognize beginning signs of stress and redirect it by utilizing progressive relaxation techniques.

Adherence to treatment

- Participates in treatment planning
- Identifies dangers of alcohol and drug abuse as a method of alleviating anxiety
- Uses constructive coping methods (e.g., stress management, relaxation, exercise, imagery, and other nonpharmacologic measures)
- Adheres to medication regimen

Client and Family Education

- Discuss with the client and family the possible environmental or situational causes, contributing factors, and triggers for anxiety disorders.
- Help the client and family to identify the internal and external indicators of anxiety.
- Educate the client and family about the following issues:
  - Coping skills
  - Monitoring of symptoms
  - Stress management
  - Medication adherence
  - Risks associated with the use of alcohol and drug abuse

Age-Related Changes—Gerontological Considerations

- Many clients experience isolation related to the anxiety they feel when in social groups. Anxiety can interfere with the client's ability to interact in social situations.
- Some types of anxiety may be related to physical or sensory limitations.

Critical Thinking Exercise: Anxiety Disorders

Situation: G.L., a 44-year-old, comes to the outpatient clinic for her first appointment. She states that she has feelings of restlessness, difficulty concentrating, fatigue related to insomnia, and frequent tearfulness. G.L.'s employment status is in question due to possible downsizing at work. While waiting for the primary care provider, she is pacing and wringing her hands.

1. To fully obtain a complete history, what additional questions would the nurse ask G.L.?

2. Identify two priority problems that require nursing intervention.

3. Which medications would you expect the primary care provider to order? What effects of the medication should you expect?

Anxiety Disorders: Phobias

> ## Key Points
>
> - Three common types of phobias are:
>   - Agoraphobia without history of panic disorder
>   - Social phobia
>   - Specific phobia
> - The goals of collaborative management include:
>   - Providing a safe environment: hospital and home
>   - Adhering to medication treatment
>   - Reinforcing reality and recognizing client's feelings
>   - Gradually working with client to desensitize and decrease phobia
>   - Educating client and family about phobias and treatment
> - **Key Terms/Concepts**: Phobia, desensitization, agoraphobia, panic, stress

Overview

A phobia is an anxiety disorder characterized by obsessive, irrational, and intense fear of a specific object, an activity, or a physical situation. The fear, which is out of proportion to reality, usually results from early painful or unpleasant experiences involving a particular object or situation. A phobia may arise from displacing an unconscious conflict on an object that is symbolically related.

For example: A client with a fear of wolves may find out through analysis that this unfounded fear of wolves is based on the fear of his father.

Types of Phobias

Agoraphobia without history of panic disorder: Fear of being in places or situations from which escape may be difficult or help may not be readily available. Eventually, clients may fear leaving their own home.

Social phobia (also called social anxiety disorder): Characterized by a persistent fear of appearing shameful, stupid, or inept in the presence of others.

Specific phobia (also called simple phobia): A persistent fear of a specific object or situation, other than of the two phobias mentioned above.

- **Acrophobia**: fear of heights
- **Astrophobia**: intense anxiety during electrical storms
- **Claustrophobia**: emotional disturbance related to closed spaces
- **Glossophobia**: fear of talking
- **Hematophobia**: anxiety when exposed to blood or anticipation of a situation with blood loss.

- **Monophobia**: intense discomfort when alone
- **Hydrophobia**: fear of water
- **Mysophobia**: anxiety regarding germs
- **Pyrophobia**: fear of fire
- **Zoophobia**: anxiety related to animals
- **Aviophobia**: fear of flying

Theories of Development

Learning theory: The belief that phobias are learned and become conditioned responses when the client needs to escape an uncomfortable situation.

Cognitive theory: Phobias are produced by anxiety-inducing self-instructions or faulty cognitions.

Life experiences: Certain life experiences, such as traumatic events, may set the stage for phobias later in life.

Transactional model of stress adaption: The etiology of phobias is most likely influenced by multiple factors.

Signs and Symptoms

- Withdrawal
- High levels of anxiety
- Inability to function and meet self-care needs
- Inappropriate behavior used to avoid the feared situation, object, or activity
- Dysfunctional social interactions and relationships

Assessment

- History and physical examination
- Family history
- Mental status examination
- Psychological testing
- Electroencephalogram (EEG)
- Psychiatric assessment and history
- Family dynamics
- Social history including alcohol use, caffeine intake
- Interference of symptoms with functioning

Nursing Diagnoses

- Anxiety
- Powerlessness
- Ineffective individual coping
- Impaired verbal communication
- Altered thought processes
- Self-esteem disturbance

- Impaired social interaction
- Risk for injury
- Risk for suicide
- Ineffective breathing pattern
- Alteration in nutrition
- Alteration in bowel and/or urinary elimination
- Altered health maintenance
- Knowledge deficit
- Social isolation
- Altered role performance
- Sleep pattern disturbance

Therapeutic Nursing Management

- **Pharmacotherapy**: Administer antianxiety medication and antidepressants, as ordered.
- **Individual therapy**: Identify the nature and defining characteristics of the phobia.
- **Group therapy**: Support and reinforce appropriate behaviors.
- **Systematic desensitization**: This process of gradual exposure to phobic object or situation aimed at decreasing the fear and increasing the ability to function in the presence of phobic stimulus.
- **Supervision** for acutely anxious client.

Client Outcomes

The client will:

- Tolerate phobic object, situation, or event with a decreasing level of anxiety
- Experience decreased levels of anxiety
- Function in the presence of the phobic object or situation
- Increase socialization and relationship skills if warranted

Client and Family Education

- Discuss with the client and family the possible environmental or situational causes, contributing factors, and triggers for fears that are disproportionate to reality.
- Help the client and family to identify the internal and external indicators of a phobia or phobias.
- Educate the client and family about the following issues:
  - Coping skills
  - Monitoring of symptoms
  - Stress management
  - Medication adherence
  - Risks associated with the use of alcohol in combination with drug abuse

Critical Thinking Exercise: Phobias

Situation: J.P. has been having difficulty getting to his job. He tries to leave the house but experiences tremors, shortness of breath, and fear. He is now confined to his home and no longer able to work or maintain social activities. You ask the client what he feels like when he tries to leave, and he responds, "I feel like something awful will happen, I don't know what, but I get this overwhelming feeling of doom." J.P. has agreed to try systematic desensitization.

1. What type of phobia has been described?

2. If you had to describe his specific symptoms that support a diagnosis of phobia, what would you include?

3. What is the significance of the fact that J.P. cannot leave his home?

4. What is systematic desensitization?

Anxiety Disorders: Stress

Key Points

- All people experience stress.
- The "fight or flight" syndrome plays an important role.
- Anxiety is a component of stress.
- The goals of collaborative management include:
    - Ensuring that client does not harm self or others
    - Providing a safe environment: hospital or home
    - Adhering to medication treatment
    - Developing self-esteem and communication of needs and feelings
    - Self-monitoring of symptoms and need to seek help when needed
    - Teaching and reinforcement of stress management skills
    - Educating the client and family about stress and treatment
- **Key Terms/Concepts**: Stress, "fight-or-flight" syndrome, anxiety

Overview

Stress is a state of disequilibrium that occurs when the demands occurring within an individual's internal or external environment exceed the client's ability to initiate effective coping skills to meet those demands. Since all people experience stress, learning how to cope with stress is critical for health.

Risk Factors

- Familial tendencies: Some families are more prone to anxiety and become overwhelmed by stressful experiences.
- Past experiences: May increase anxiety and client does not feel competent to cope with stressors.
- Ineffective coping mechanisms
- Lack of or ineffective support systems
- Existing physical, emotional, mental, and cognitive conditions that make it difficult for the client to cope with stress (e.g., pain, terminal illness, physical illness in a family member; or too many life changes at one time [divorce, moving, loss of job, financial problems]).

Signs and Symptoms

- "Fight-or-flight" syndrome
- Headaches

- Anxiety
- Increased perspiration
- Inability to focus/concentrate
- Decreased gastric motility
- Increased pulse, blood pressure, and respirations
- Chest pain or tightness
- Increased or decreased eating
- Disrupted sleep

Assessment

- History and physical examination
- Mental status examination
- Developmental assessment
- Environmental assessment
- Socioeconomic assessment
- Psychiatric assessment and history
- Assessment of coping mechanisms and experience with stress

Nursing Diagnoses

- Anxiety
- Powerlessness
- Ineffective individual coping
- Impaired verbal communication
- Self-esteem disturbance
- Impaired social interaction
- Risk for injury
- Sleep pattern disturbance
- Ineffective breathing pattern
- Alteration in nutrition
- Alteration in bowel and/or urinary elimination
- Knowledge deficit
- Social isolation

Therapeutic Nursing Management

- Administer antianxiety and/or antidepressant medications.
- Teach client to understand stress and assess own stress level.
- Encourage use of stress management techniques, such as guided imagery, relaxation techniques and other methods.

Complications

- Decreased ability to handle stressors
- Withdrawal from others
- Alcohol and/or drug abuse
- Eating problems
- Impaired judgment
- Insomnia
- Hypertension
- Decreased peripheral circulation
- Harm to self or others
- Mental disorders: anxiety disorders or depression
- Myocardial infarction
- Ulcers
- Colitis
- Exhaustion
- Death

Client Outcomes

The client will:

- Experience greater ability to tolerate stressful situations
- Experience decreased anxiety
- Use stress management skills regularly and effectively

Client and Family Education

- Discuss with the client and family the possible sources of stress.
- Educate the client and family about common physical and emotional findings related to stress.
- Educate the client and family about the following issues:
  - Coping skills
  - Monitoring of symptoms for early detection of stress
  - Stress management techniques
  - Medication adherence
  - Risks associated with the use of alcohol with anxiolytics and overdose of medication to treat anxiety
  - Cognitive restructuring to reduce stress
- Teach cognitive restructuring involves helping a client realize that negative thought is trapping him in destructive behavior patterns.
- Guided imagery:
  - Guided imagery and visualization involves the therapist verbally leading a client through emotional conflicts through the use of imagination.

Age-Related Changes—Gerontological Considerations

Support systems: The older adult may feel additional stress related to the death of family and friends.

Socioeconomic factors: The older adult often worries about economic problems related to increased medical expenses, health care, and medications.

Physical health: Illnesses increase the older adult's stress levels and anxiety regarding death and dying.

Critical Thinking Exercise: Stress

Situation: You are assigned a client admitted to a medical unit for colitis. This is the client's first admission for this diagnosis. P.L. is 35 years old and appears to be uncomfortable. She is speaking rapidly throughout the interview. As you speak with her while giving her care, she comments, "This is all just because of stress. Isn't that silly? I should be able to handle my stress better."

1. What responses could you make?

2. How can you best help P.L. understand stress?

Anxiety Disorders: Somatoform Disorders

Key Points

- Somatization is the expression of psychologic stress through physical symptoms.
- Anxiety is an important factor.
- Three major types of disorders are somatization, conversion, and sleep disorders.
- The goals of collaborative management include:
  - Ensuring that the client receives a complete physical assessment
  - Providing behavior therapy and biofeedback as appropriate
  - Adhering to medication treatment
  - Development of self-esteem and communication of needs and feelings
  - Self-monitoring of symptoms and need to seek help when necessary
  - Educating the client and family about somatoform disorders and treatment
- **Key Terms/Concepts:** Somatization, conversion, biofeedback, behavior therapy, therapeutic touch, imaging, acupuncture, anxiety, hypochondriasis

Overview

Somatoform disorders are characterized by physical symptoms which suggest a medical disease(s), but without organic pathology to support that illness. It refers to all mechanisms by which anxiety is translated into physical illness. Somatoform disorders include somatization disorder, hypochondriasis, conversion disorder, and sleep disorder.

Types of Disorders

Somatization disorder: This chronic syndrome is characterized by multiple somatic symptoms that cannot be explained medically. The physical symptoms are associated with psychosocial distress. Common somatic complaints involve the neurological, gastrointestinal, reproductive, or cardiopulmonary systems.

Conversion disorder: A loss or change in bodily function is the result of psychological conflict, allowing the client to resolve the conflict through loss of a physical function. This is an involuntary reaction, and there is no organic cause. It usually suggests neurological disease and occurs following an event of severe psychological stress. The client often exhibits a lack of concern about the severity of the disease (la belle indifference).

Sleep disorder: This is characterized by difficulty initiating or maintaining sleep. Sleep disorders include hypersomnia or excessive sleepiness, narcolepsy, parasomnias, or undesirable behaviors that occur during sleep. Nightmares or sleep terror disorders may lead to an abrupt arousal from sleep. In sleep disorders, the sleep-wake schedule and circadian rhythm are disturbed.

Hypochondriasis: This is a person's unwanted fear or belief that he or she has a serious disease without significant pathology. The client pays a great deal of attention to the body and is preoccupied with bodily sensations. Symptoms are often chronic, and clients seek medical care from many providers. Hypochondriasis interferes with client's work and social relationships. Client's anxiety is marked.

Body dysmorphic disorder: The client is preoccupied with an imagined defect in appearance when there is no abnormality. Client obsesses about imagined bodily defects (facial flaws, heavy buttocks or thighs) and becomes embarrassed about them. Extreme self-consciousness about the defect may lead the client to withdraw from social activities.

Pain disorder: The pain is unrelated to a medical disease. The individual experiences severe pain that is in disproportion to the originating source.

Risk Factors

- Gender: Female
- Sociocultural: Symptoms may be influenced by the social environment.
- Age (e.g., children and older adults)
- Psychological influences: Secondary gain of attention and affection from illness learned through dysfunctional family interaction (e.g., loss of significant interpersonal relationship or separation from significant person: child from parents, move to nursing home)

Signs and Symptoms

- Pain in the absence of organic pathology
- Preoccupation with physical symptoms, diseases, physical flaws, and oneself
- Dependence on addictive substances for relief of pain that is unsubstantiated by physical findings
- Frequent visits to health care providers
- Symptoms of anxiety and/or depression
- Hypochondriasis is not a conscious decision on the part of such clients; they believe they are ill

Assessment

- History and physical examination: It is critical to rule out the physical cause of client complaints. Include self-medication information.
- Laboratory tests
- Psychiatric assessment and history
- Mental status exam
- Social assessment
- Family assessment

Nursing Diagnoses

- Impaired adjustment
- Chronic pain
- Sleep pattern disturbance

Therapeutic Nursing Management

Psychological treatment

- **Individual psychotherapy**: Insight-oriented therapy aimed at assisting the client to cope with stress by means other than preoccupation with physical symptoms.
- **Group psychotherapy**: Aimed at group interactions and helping the client associate the appearance of physical symptoms with times of stress.
- **Behavior therapy**: Applying behavioral principles to alter behavior.
- **Biofeedback**: The process of providing a client with information about the autonomic, physiologic functions of the body. By trial and error, the client can consciously control these processes, which are usually considered involuntary. Examples of conditions that may be responsive to biofeedback techniques include hypertension, migraines, and insomnia.

Psychopharmacological treatment: Administer medications (e.g., antianxiety medications, antidepressants, hypnotics, and any other medications ordered).

Nursing Interventions

- Physical follow-up is important.
- Alternative therapeutic interventions may be used, such as therapeutic touch, imaging, and acupuncture.
- Assist the client in identifying and describing stress he/she experiences.
- Assist the client in monitoring stress and knowing when to intervene.
- Teach the client about medications and to avoid alcohol and other such drugs used to alleviate stress inappropriately.
- Recognize medical problems.

Complications

- Risk to self and others
- Dependency on addictive medications
- Withdrawal symptoms related to discontinuation of sedatives, hypnotics, and narcotics
- Impairment of cognitive and psychomotor skills related to use of sedatives and hypnotics
- Alienation of client: Client may choose to seek medical advice elsewhere

Client Outcomes

The client will:

- Express feelings verbally
- Experience a decrease in somatic complaints
- Exhibit an appropriate sleep pattern
- Exhibit use of effective coping mechanisms

Client and Family Education

- Teach measures to relieve physical symptoms.

Age–Related Changes—Gerontological Considerations

- Older adults may use more dependency-causing medications.
- Older adults with somatoform disorders make numerous phone calls to health care providers, and spend increased amounts of time and money on health care visits, medications, and tests.
- The support systems of the older adult may be weary from continued physical and medical appointments.
- Older adults are at higher risk for falls and accidents caused by sedation and drowsiness. Additionally, many elderly people have physical health problems leading to decreased mobility.
- Older adults may experience drug-to-drug interactions related to decreased kidney function and the large amount of medications taken daily.

Critical Thinking Exercise: Somatoform Disorders

Situation: W.F. is a 75-year-old widow who lives alone. Her daughter lives nearby with her family. Up until this spring, W.F. had experienced few medical problems. In the last three months, she has called her primary care provider weekly with medical complaints and has had numerous appointments. She has insisted on seeing specialists. Her daughter is concerned about her mother's health and also frustrated with the frequent complaints and phone calls about medical concerns. Her mother has now decided that she must have a cardiac problem and is too weak to walk. Her primary care provider cannot diagnose any cardiac problem.

1. Given the data provided, what is W.F. experiencing?

2. Identify five interventions that may be used.

Psychotic Disorders: Schizophrenia and Other Psychoses

Key Points

- Types of schizophrenia include:
    - Disorganized schizophrenia
    - Catatonic schizophrenia
    - Paranoid schizophrenia
    - Undifferentiated schizophrenia
    - Residual schizophrenia
- Related psychotic disorders
    - Schizoaffective disorder
    - Brief psychotic disorder
    - Schizophreniform disorder
    - Delusional disorder
- Clients with schizophrenia will have periods of remission and improved functioning, but there is no cure for the disorder.
- It is theorized that biological factors play a more important role than environmental influences in the development of the disorder.
- Negative and positive symptoms are components of the disorder.
- Collaborative management is directed at:
    - A safe environment, both in the hospital and at home
    - Provision of supportive therapy
    - Development of social skills
    - Family support and education
    - Adherence to psychopharmacology and other treatments
    - Educational and vocational training
    - Development of coping skills, (e.g., coping with hallucinations and delusions, interpersonal closeness, and communication)
    - Maintenance of activities of daily living
- If client protection is required, ensure that all procedures are followed and the client is treated with respect.
- **Key Terms/Concepts:** Types of schizophrenia, dopamine and serotonin, thought processes, psychosis, hallucination, delusion, illusion, negative and positive symptoms, social skills training, medication group, tardive dyskinesia

Overview

Schizophrenia is a serious mental illness that involves disturbances in reality (psychosis), thought processes, perception, affect, social, and occupational functioning. Schizophrenia affects about 1% of the population. Treatment must be comprehensive and interdisciplinary in approach. In 75% of cases, it is diagnosed between the ages of 17 and 25 years.

Types of Schizophrenia

Disorganized schizophrenia: Characterized by flat or inappropriate affect (such as silliness, irrationality, or giggling), bizarre behavior, and social impairment.

Catatonic schizophrenia: Characterized by catatonic stupor, evidenced by extreme psychomotor retardation and posturing, and catatonic excitement, extreme psychomotor agitation with purposeless movements that may harm self or others. Echolalia and Echopraxia are also common manifestations.

Paranoid schizophrenia: Characterized by paranoid delusions in which the client falsely believes that others are out to harm him/her. The client may be hostile, argumentative, and aggressive.

Undifferentiated schizophrenia: Characterized by bizarre behavior that does not meet the criteria of other types of schizophrenia. Delusions and hallucinations are prominent.

Residual schizophrenia: Term used to describe the client who has had one major episode of schizophrenia with prominent psychotic symptoms and who has lingering symptoms.

Related Psychotic Disorders

Schizoaffective disorder: Characterized by symptoms of schizophrenia accompanied by a strong element of mood disorders, either mania or depression.

Brief psychotic disorder: Characterized by sudden onset of psychotic symptoms following a severe psychosocial stressor. Symptoms last less than one month, and the client usually returns to the premorbid level of functioning.

Schizophreniform disorder: Characterized by the symptoms of schizophrenia with the duration lasting between one month and less than six months.

Delusional disorder: Characterized by prominent, non-bizarre delusions

- **Erotomanic type**: The client believes that someone, usually of a higher status, is in love with him/her.

- **Grandiose type**: The client has irrational ideas that his or her worth, talent, knowledge, or power is immense.

- **Jealous type**: The client has irrational ideas that his/her sexual partner is unfaithful.

- **Persecutory type**: The client believes that malevolent things are happening to him/her.

- **Somatic type**: The client has an irrational belief that he/she has some physical defect, disorder, or disease(s).

- **Religious**: The client has illogical ideas about God and religion that deal with being persecuted by spirits; being saved or being damned; requiring excessive fasting, praying, or other religious rituals, which do not give release.

Risk Factors

- Biochemical factors: Neurochemical and neuroanatomical alterations
- Family genetics: Identical twins 50% risk; fraternal twins 15% risk
- Psychological influences: Stressful life events, low self-esteem, poor social skills, and demoralization
- Environmental influences: Poverty, lack of social support, hostile home environment, isolation, unsatisfactory housing, disruption in interpersonal relationships (divorce or death), job pressure, or unemployment

Specific Biological Factors

- Dopamine: Overactive
- Serotonin: Modulates level of dopamine and affects mood.
- CT and MRI studies show decreased brain volume, enlarged ventricles, deeper fissures, and a loss or underdevelopment of brain tissue. It is not clear yet what these changes mean for treatment.

Signs and Symptoms

- Disturbances in thought processes: Disorganized thinking, paranoia, blocking (loss of train of thought), echolalia (repetition of words or phrases heard), echopraxia (meaningless imitation of motions and gestures made by others), clang associations (rhyming words in sentences that make no sense), and flight of ideas (skipping from one topic to another). Thinking is often described as hazy or confused.
- Disturbance in sense of identity and self-image
- Impairment/deterioration in social and occupational functioning
- Impairment/deterioration in interpersonal functioning and relationships
- Disturbances in perception: Hallucinations, illusions, delusions
- Harm to self or others
- Self-care deficit
- Ineffective coping
- Impaired communication:
    - Loose associations—disconnected, vague, and unfocused speech, thoughts, and ideas
    - Neologisms—words created by the client that have meaning only to that person. They are often a combination of other words.
    - Tangentiality—ineffective communication pattern whereby the speaker goes off the topic and does not return
- Disturbances in emotion: Apathy, anhedonia
- Impaired relationships: Limited ability in maintaining relationships
- Hopelessness
- Depression often accompanies schizophrenia

Positive Symptoms

The assessment for schizophrenia is usually categorized in terms of negative and positive symptoms. Positive symptoms are typically identified first because they appear to be more dramatic. These symptoms include:

- Anxiety
- Bizarre behavior and inappropriate affect
- Delusions (paranoid, grandiose, broadcasting, religious, persecutory)
- Hallucinations (auditory, visual, tactile, gustatory, olfactory)
- Agitation/pacing
- Aggressiveness and hostility
- Somatic complaints
- Suspiciousness/paranoia
- Cognitive disorganization (loose associations, tangentiality)
- Speech disturbances (incoherence, word salad, random thoughts, staccato pattern, pressured speech, derailment, poverty of speech)

Positive symptoms are usually most responsive to traditional antipsychotic medications, such as Haldol, Prolixin, Thorazine, and other traditional medications that primarily block dopamine receptors.

Negative Symptoms

The negative symptoms indicate more advanced schizophrenia. These symptoms include:

- Motor retardation
- Anhedonia: absence of pleasure, inability to feel enjoyment
- Intellectual impairment: cognitive deficits
- Social withdrawal and isolation
- Depressed mood
- Apathy, a lack of motivation and disinterest
- Poor grooming and self-care
- Lack of thoughts
- Diminished thought processes
- Lack of goal-directed behavior
- Blunted affect

Treatment of these symptoms has been a problem; however, newer antipsychotic medications, seretonin-dopamine antagonists (SDAs) such as clozapine (Clozaril), risperidone (Risperdal), olanzapine (Zyprexa), and quetiapine (Seroquel), are more effective in treating these negative symptoms.

By blocking both serotonin and dopamine receptors, both the "positive" and "negative" symptoms are treated.

Assessment

- History and physical examination
- Family history
- Mental status examination
- Psychological testing
- Psychiatric assessment and history
- Social history
- CT and MRI scans to rule out other pathology
- Nutrition, fluids, sleep, exercise
- Suicidal state and harm to others
- Self-care

Assessment Guidelines

Clients with schizophrenia may not be cooperative during the initial assessment if they are experiencing symptoms such as hallucinations, delusions, and other thought process disturbances. To participate in an interview, the client must be able to concentrate, problem-solve on some level, and communicate. Pressuring the client at this time is not effective. The client needs to know that he or she will be cared for and is in a safe environment. Details about the client's history may need to be obtained later after the client has had medication and rest. Safety is also important for staff members to consider. If the nurse has limited information about the client, it is best not to be isolated with the client (e.g., keep door open, do not sit or stand in front of door). The nurse should let other staff members know where he/she is with the client; and if he/she feels insecure, another staff member should accompany him/her.

Nursing Diagnoses

- Altered thought processes
- Sensory-perceptual alterations
- High risk for violence, self-directed or toward others
- Self-care deficit
- Social isolation
- Impaired verbal communication
- Self-esteem disturbance
- Ineffective family coping
- Ineffective individual coping
- Anxiety
  - Personal identity disturbance
  - Altered role performance
  - Impaired social interaction
  - Depression/mood disturbance
  - Risk for addiction

Therapeutic Nursing Management

Environment: Provide a safe environment (hospital, home, other treatment setting). Limiting stimuli may help client cope with stress, as well as reduce the onset or intensity of hallucinations or delusions. Hospitalization may be required if the client is a danger to self or others or needs pharmacological treatment. Clients may be admitted voluntarily or involuntarily. With limitations in availability at long-term facilities today, hospitalization is generally for acute or severe psychiatric needs. It is critical that discharge planning is done early (beginning the first day of admission) to provide the best after-care treatment possible for the client.

Psychological treatment

- **Individual psychotherapy**: Long-term therapeutic approach. It may be difficult due to client's impairment in social function. This approach is used less and less frequently as it has been found that these clients respond better to a rehabilitation approach (including social skills training, self-monitoring of symptoms, and use of medication). Access to insurance affects the amount of treatment the client is entitled to receive.

- **Behavior therapy**: Behavior is modified to meet acceptable social norms in the community setting.

- **Social skills training**: May use role play in teaching clients ways to improve interpersonal skills (eye contact, posture, nonverbal cues, attention, active listening). This includes attention to ADLs, employment skills, improving communication skills, problem solving, and other techniques to improve social skills and promote interpersonal functioning.

- **Self-monitoring**: Clients become more aware of their symptoms changing, what affects them, and when to intervene to prevent further deterioration. Family and significant others are also essential in this process.

- **Behavioral contracts**: Focus on specific client needs to help the client resolve identified problems (e.g., aggressive behavior, isolation, and self-care deficits).

Social treatment

- **Milieu therapy** uses day-to-day living experiences in a therapeutic environment to affect perception and behavior. Milieu therapy is the primary role of the nurse in an effort to provide safety and promote social interaction.

- **Family therapy** is aimed at assisting the family to cope with the long-term effects of the client's illness and help the client function more effectively.

- **Group therapy** is predominately used for long-term treatment; however, client's symptoms may interfere with the client's ability to cope within a group (for example, if the client is experiencing hallucinations, delusions, or is unable to sit in one place). Until these symptoms are under control, group therapy may be difficult. Typically, this type of therapy focuses on assisting clients with communication, coping skills, and problem solving. Medication education may be effective in group settings.

Psychopharmacologic treatment

- Administer antipsychotic medications to decrease the intensity and frequency of psychotic symptoms. Antiparkinsonian medications are used to counteract the extrapyramidal symptoms associated with antipsychotic medications.

- Medication group helps the client with adherence to medication regime and provides ongoing support and education about medications and symptom monitoring.

- Medications are selected based on the target symptoms of the client.

- Psychotropic medications must be given in adequate doses and must be given adequate time to work (usually 4-6 weeks).

- Medication dosage goals are the lowest possible dose to alleviate symptoms for the client.

- As a rule, elderly clients require less medication and take longer to notice medication effects.

- Psychotropic medications should be decreased/tapered gradually to reduce the risk of rebound (temporary return of symptoms) and withdrawal (new symptom development related to discontinuation of medication) effects.

Nursing interventions

- Close interpersonal space often increases the general level of anxiety in the client with psychopathology. Maintain a comfortable distance for both the client and the nurse. It may be necessary for the nurse to verbalize any discomfort and make adjustments.

- Allow the client to make some choices.

- Nonverbal activity may assist client in stressful times.

- A client who is hallucinating or delusional may still have some concept of reality and the capacity to relate with others.

- Clients with hallucinations or thought disturbances can learn to live with such symptoms and function in society.

- Increase the type, frequency, and intensity of social interactions gradually over time.

- Reassessment of the client's mental state is critical, particularly in terms of agitation, suicidal ideation, increasing anxiety and aggression.

- Problem solving may be difficult for clients with schizophrenia. Implement a plan to help the client learn problem-solving strategies.

- Clients with schizophrenia particularly fear rejection, criticism, hostility, and depreciation. Help the client to gain insight into situations when these feelings are likely to occur and have a plan for coping with these feelings.

- Reassess for harm to self or others.

- Risk factors include past history, medication non-compliance, substance use and active psychotic symptoms.

- Use restraints (physical, chemical, seclusion/observation room) with extreme caution and only when there is risk for harm to self or others. Initiate one-to-one supervision, when appropriate, for escalating behavior or suicidal thoughts or intentions.

- Self-care needs are assessed and assistance given to the client to maintain self-care activities.

Complications

- Increase in psychotic behavior and behavior escalating to aggression
- Decrease in level of functioning
- Extrapyramidal symptoms associated with antipsychotic medications
- Risk to self or others
- Dual diagnosis: substance abuse accompanying schizophrenia
- Neuroleptic malignant syndrome (NMS): complication with use of antipsychotic medications

Client Outcomes

Outcomes must be realistic. Rehospitalization is common. Clients with schizophrenia are often characterized by low self-esteem, and may expect to be labeled the "mental patient." If staff establishes grandiose outcomes with little input or understanding from the client, the client is unlikely to feel successful in achieving his/her goals. The client will:

- Experience a reduction in symptoms
- Focus on activities in the "here and now"
- Identify problem behaviors and methods for resolving those that interfere with functioning
- Identify medications, purposes, side effects, dosage, frequency, and when to call primary care provider with problems
- Exhibit appropriate activity level, sleep pattern, eating, and independent self-care within own limitations
- Participate in treatment and treatment planning
- Exhibit coping with stress, family, and significant others
- Adhere to medication and other treatment regimens
- Exhibit no harm to self or others

Client and Family Education

- Discuss with the client and family the possible environmental or situational causes, contributing factors, and triggers.
- Help the client and family to identify the internal and external indicators of schizophrenia and other psychoses.
- Educate the client and family about the following issues:
  - Reality orientation
  - Coping skills
  - Socialization
  - Monitoring of symptoms
  - Supporting adherence to treatment
  - Medication therapy
  - Reduction of anxiety
  - Coping with hallucinations
  - Decreasing or increasing environmental stimuli

- Nutrition
- Vocation/occupational support
- Use of support groups
- Decreasing agitated behavior
- Substance abuse treatment, if needed
- Safety concerns

Age-Related Changes—Gerontological Considerations

- Cerebral changes place the older client at risk for psychopathology and may render the client unable to meet ADLs.
- Increased physical demands or difficulty with transportation may make it difficult to access health care.
- The symptoms of tardive dyskinesia may be different due to the changing metabolism in the body and the discontinuance of the antipsychotic medication.
- Drug levels must be monitored more closely due to potential changes in kidney and liver function.

Critical Thinking Exercise: Schizophrenia and Other Psychoses

Situation: A 40-year-old client is brought to the local emergency room by the police department. The client was observed shouting at customers in a local department store. He frightened many customers by talking to imaginary persons and threatening to harm anyone who attempted to console him. The client was transferred to the psychiatric unit.

On the psychiatric unit, the client keeps to himself and paces and walks away when anyone approaches him. The client talks with a flurry of ideas, laughs to himself and tilts his head to the side, as if listening. When the medical professionals attempt to talk with him, the client shouts, "Get away from me! Stay back! I know that you are one of them!" He picks up a chair, as if for his protection and appears frightened. The client's appearance is unkempt; his clothes are dirty and wrinkled, his hair straggly and uncombed, and he has body odor. The primary care provider's diagnosis is paranoid schizophrenia and the client is prescribed Cogentin and Haldol.

1. Identify assessment data from which to formulate a plan of care.

2. Prioritize the appropriate nursing diagnoses for this client.

3. List the most appropriate nursing interventions that correspond with each nursing diagnosis listed above.

Psychotic Disorders: Delusions

Key Points

- Delusions result from a thought process disorder (often called a thought disorder) and affect a client's behavior.
- Cognitive disorganization is a critical aspect of delusions.
- Types of delusions include:
  - Persecutory
  - Jealous
  - Erotomanic
  - Somatic
  - Grandiose
  - Mixed
  - Religious
  - Reference
  - Thought broadcast
- The goals of collaborative management include:
  - Providing a safe environment: hospital and home
  - Adhering to medication treatment
  - Avoiding affirming client's delusions
  - If client protection is required, ensuring that all procedures are followed, and client is treated with respect
  - Reinforcing reality and acknowledging client's feelings
  - Clarifying communication that may be confusing due to delusional thinking
  - Increasing client socialization when appropriate
- **Key Terms/Concepts**: Delusion, cognitive disorganization, fixation, types of delusions

Overview

Delusions are persistent, fixed, false beliefs or perceptions held by a client, which cannot be corrected by reasoning or social reality orientation.

Types of Delusions

Persecutory: The predominant delusional theme is that one is being subjected to some type of malevolent treatment such as spying, stalking or the spreading of false rumors of illegal or immoral behavior. This is usually seen in paranoid schizophrenia.

Jealous: The predominant theme is that the client's sexual partner has been unfaithful.

Erotomanic: The predominant theme is that a person, usually of higher status, is in love with the client.

Somatic: The predominant theme is an unshakable belief in having a physical disease or disorder.

Grandiose: The delusion involves a person of extraordinary status, power, ability, talent, etc., or having a relationship with a person with such attributes.

Mixed: There is a combination of the above, but no single theme predominates.

Religious: Illogical ideas about God and religion are exhibited by extreme or extraneous behaviors.

Reference: The false belief that casual or unrelated remarks or behavior relate to oneself, like articles in a newspaper, lyrics of songs, etc.

Thought broadcast: The belief that one's thoughts are being broadcast to the world

Thought insertion: The belief that thoughts are placed into the mind by outside persons

Signs and Symptoms

Cognitive disorganization: The inability to function on a day-to-day basis; the inability to process the information that the environment provides versus information that is not reality-based.

Fixation: Drastic distortions in viewing reality that do not waver and cannot be changed.

Childhood aloofness: Difficulty interacting with other children.

Undue suspicion: Inappropriate mistrust of others and the environment.

Assessment

- Assess for delusions related to harm to self or others
- Determine when delusions occur and note intensity
- Estimate the level of anxiety in various settings and situations, and the level of anxiety related to delusional thinking

Nursing Diagnoses

- Altered thought processes
- Anxiety
- Risk of harm, self-directed, or toward others
- Social isolation
- Ineffective individual coping
- Self-care deficit

Therapeutic Nursing Management

Environment: Safety within the environment is a primary concern for the client experiencing delusional thought disturbances. Clients may require one-to-one supervision, seclusion/ observation room, or physical restraints, but only after other measures used to provide safety are ineffective. Decrease in stimuli may also be helpful.

Psychopharmacology: Administer antipsychotic medication to enhance the client's level of cognitive functioning (e.g., haloperidol, fluphenazine, risperidone, clozapine, olanzapine).

Nursing interventions

- Staff should neither affirm the client's delusions nor argue with the client about them.
- Do not move suddenly, touch the client, or stand in the doorway, blocking client's exit.
- Reinforce reality by responding verbally to anything that is real.
- Assess the client by addressing feelings related to delusion.
  - What is the client experiencing?
  - What are the feelings associated with the delusion? The client may not be able to identify or verbalize insight about specific emotions related to the delusion. However, staff may associate the delusion with an emotion that is evident in the client's behavior and relationships with others.
- Help the client identify impersonal or universal pronouns, such as "they." Staff should use personal or proper names with the client and avoid overuse of impersonal pronouns.
- Increase type and frequency of socialization with client gradually.
- Do not insist that the client provide detail regarding the delusion. This type of action is diminutive to client as a person and may increase client's level of anxiety.
- Problem solving may be very difficult for the client with delusions.
- Assess client's anxiety level and intervene as required.
- Encourage client to participate in activities when appropriate.

Client Outcomes

The client will:

- Experience reduced delusions
- Experience reduced anxiety
- Experience increase in reality orientation
- Not harm self or others

Client and Family Education

- Discuss with the client and family the possible environmental or situational causes, contributing factors, and triggers for persistent, fixed, false beliefs or perceptions.
- Help the client and family to identify the internal and external indicators of delusions.
- Educate the client and family about the following issues:
  - Reality orientation
  - Coping skills

- Socialization
- Monitoring of symptoms
- Supporting adherence to treatment
- Medication therapy
- Reduction of anxiety
- Coping with hallucinations
- Decreasing or increasing environmental stimuli
- Nutrition
- Vocation/occupational support
- Use of support groups
- Decreasing agitated behavior
- Substance abuse treatment, if needed
- Safety

Critical Thinking Exercise: Delusions

Situation: You are making a home visit to C.K., a client who has a long psychiatric history. She has been on haloperidol (Haldol) for some time. The purpose of your visit is to follow-up about her recent surgery following a broken hip. This is your second visit in four days. On your first visit, she appeared to be pleasant and was responsive to your suggestions. As you enter the home, she seems reluctant to let you in. When you enter, you notice that she is wearing dirty clothes and appears unkempt. She looks tired, and you ask her how much sleep has she been getting. C.K. responds, "How can I possibly sleep? So much has been said about me. I have to be alert for people watching me."

1. What data do you have about this client that is important in understanding her current status?

2. What further data do you need regarding C.K.'s status?

3. You respond with, "C.K., I am sure that no one is watching you." Based on this case description, why might this response not be appropriate?

4. How can you intervene to assist C.K. at this time?

Psychotic Disorders: Hallucinations and Illusions

Key Points

- Hallucinations and illusions result from thought disorders and affect client behavior.
- Types of hallucinations include:
  - Auditory
  - Visual
  - Olfactory
  - Gustatory
  - Tactile
- Illusions can be visual or auditory. Approximately 75% of hallucinations are the auditory type.
- The goals of collaborative management include:
  - Providing a safe environment: hospital and home
  - Adhering to medication and other treatments
  - If client protection required, ensuring that all procedures are followed, and the client is treated with respect
  - Avoiding affirming client's hallucinations and illusions
  - Reinforcing reality and acknowledging client's feelings
  - Clarifying communication that may be confusing due to hallucinations
  - Increasing client socialization when appropriate
- **Key Terms/Concepts**: Hallucination, illusion, sensory-perceptual alterations

Overview

Hallucinations are false sensory perceptions that do not exist in reality. Illusions are false interpretations of external sensory stimuli and inappropriate responses to the perception.

Types of Hallucinations

Auditory: Hears voices that accuse client of an immoral act, command action, or condemn client. Voices may also be friendly and tell jokes or give information to the client. Some clients actually miss having their hallucinations when medicated.

Visual: Sees a person or object that is not present

Olfactory: Perceives an odor that actually is not present

Gustatory: Experiences a taste that is not present and frequently is bitter or strong

Tactile: Experiences the feeling of a touch (e.g., bugs crawling under the skin)

Types of Illusions

- **Visual**: Seeing an object in a different form, such as a mirage in the desert
- **Auditory**: Hearing a sound and believing that it is another type of sound, such as, hearing voices in the sound of the wind

Assessment

- Watch for client stopping to listen, or speaking to someone who is not there.
- Assess for hallucinations related to harm of self or others.
- Determine when hallucinations/illusions occur and type of hallucination/illusion.
- Estimate the level of anxiety in various settings and situations. Is the anxiety related to the hallucination?

Nursing Diagnoses

- Sensory-perceptual alterations
- Anxiety
- Risk of harm, self-directed or toward others
- Self-care deficit
- Social isolation
- Ineffective individual coping

Therapeutic Nursing Management

Environment: Safety is a primary concern for the client experiencing hallucinatory thought disturbances. Client may require one-to-one supervision, seclusion/observation room, or physical restraints, but only after other measures used to provide safety are ineffective. Restraints are rarely used, and ONLY after other measures used to provide safety are ineffective.

Psychopharmacology: Administer medication to assist with clear or cognitive functioning (e.g., antipsychotic medications of haloperidol, clozapine, risperidone, olanzapine, and quetiapine).

NursingInterventions

- Staff should not affirm the client's hallucination/illusion or argue with the client about them.
- Present reality in a non-confrontational manner ("I don't see, hear, etc., what you do, but it must be frightening," "I will stay with you," "Tell me what is happening to you.")
- Help the client to understand the triggers that most often elicit a hallucinatory experience.
- Encourage discussion of fears, anxiety, and anger as a way to deal with the emotional effects on the client.
- Do not move suddenly, touch the client, or stand in the doorway, blocking the exit.

- Reinforce reality by responding verbally to anything that is real. Identify false beliefs about real situations.
- Provide orientation cues (date, time, names, events).
- Assess the client by addressing feelings related to hallucination/illusion.
    - What is the client experiencing?
    - What are the feelings associated with the hallucination? The client may not be able to identify or verbalize insight regarding specific emotions related to hallucinations. However, the staff may associate the hallucination/illusion with a particular emotion.
    - Do not tell the client what he/she is feeling or label the emotion.
- Increase the frequency, duration, and intensity of client socialization.
- Do not insist that the client provide detail regarding the hallucination because this may increase the client's level of anxiety.
- Observe for speech that is inappropriate to the situation. There may be evidence in the word use, pattern of speech, or interpretation of the language that indicates a thought disturbance.
- Problem solving may be very difficult for the client experiencing hallucinatory thought disturbance. Help the client to use problem-solving strategies.
- Encourage the client to participate in activities that require attention or physical skills when appropriate as a distraction technique.

Client Outcomes

The client will:

- Experience reduced anxiety
- Experience reduced hallucinations/illusions
- Experience increase in reality orientation
- Not harm self or others

Client and Family Education

- Discuss with the client and family the possible environmental or situational causes, contributing factors, and triggers for false sensory perceptions that do not exist in reality.
- Help the client and family to identify the internal and external indicators of hallucinations and illusions.
- Educate the client and family about the following issues:
    - Reality orientation
    - Coping skills
    - Socialization
    - Monitoring of symptoms
    - Supporting adherence to treatment
    - Medication therapy
    - Reduction of anxiety
    - Coping with hallucinations

- Decreasing or increasing environmental stimuli
- Nutrition
- Vocation/occupational support
- Use of support groups
- Decreasing agitated behavior
- Substance abuse treatment, if needed
- Safety, particularly for those with command hallucinations

Critical Thinking Exercise: Hallucinations and Illusions

Situation: C.H. is admitted at 11 p.m. to a secured inpatient unit. The police found him wandering on the street, walking into traffic, and appearing to be talking to someone when there is no one there. He has been on your unit several times, and you know he can be very violent. He calmly enters the unit, thanks the police, and then proceeds to run down the hall screaming, "I will not do it." C.H. hits the wall with his fists. Clients come out of their rooms looking frightened. The shift is changing, and report is just about to begin.

1. Based on this description, what do you think C.H. is experiencing?

2. What is your priority at this time for C.H.?

3. From the perspective of the therapeutic milieu, why is it important for you to act quickly?

4. What interventions are the priority for C.H.?

5. What are the concerns you should have about client protection interventions?

Psychotic Disorders: Undifferentiated Type

Key Points

- Some clients with psychotic disorders may not meet the specific criteria of the other diagnoses in this category, but they do have a psychotic disorder that includes symptoms of a thought disorder.
- The goals of collaborative management include:
    - Providing a safe environment: hospital and home
    - Adhering to medication and other treatments
    - If client protection is required, ensuring that all procedures are followed, and the client is treated with respect
    - Reinforcing reality and acknowledging client's feelings
    - Clarifying communication that may be confusing due to delusions or hallucinations
    - Increasing client socialization when appropriate
- **Key Terms/Concepts**: Thought disorder, perception

Overview

The client with psychotic disorder not otherwise specified has disturbances in thought processes, perception, affect, and deterioration in social and occupational functioning. These do not fit into the categories of schizophrenia, delusional disorder, mood disorder with psychotic features, or organic mental disorder.

Risk Factors

- Biochemical factors
- Family genetics
- Psychological influences
- Environmental factors
- Drug-induced psychosis

Signs and Symptoms

- Disturbances in thought processes: disorganized thinking, paranoia, blocking, thinking is self-described as hazy and confused
- Disturbance in sense of identity and self-image
- Impairment/deterioration in social and occupational functioning
- Impairment/deterioration in interpersonal functioning and relationships
- Disturbances in perception: hallucinations, illusions, delusions, fixations

- Harm to self or others
- Self-care deficit
- Ineffective coping
- Impaired communication: associative looseness, neologisms, and tangentiality
- Disturbances in emotion: apathy, anhedonia
- Impaired relationships: limited ability in maintaining relationships

Assessment

- History and physical examination
- Family history
- Mental status examination
- Psychological testing
- Psychiatric assessment and history
- Social history
- Nutrition, fluids, sleep, exercise, enjoyment of activities
- Indications of suicidal thoughts or intentions and harm to others

Nursing Diagnoses

- Altered thought processes
- Sensory-perceptual alterations
- High risk for violence, self-directed or toward others
- Self-care deficit
- Social isolation
- Impaired verbal communication
- Self-esteem disturbance
- Ineffective family coping
- Ineffective individual coping
- Anxiety
- Personal identity disturbance
- Altered role performance
- Impaired social interaction
- Depression/mood disturbance
- Risk for addiction

Therapeutic Nursing Management

- Restructure the environment to minimize excessive sensory stimulation.
- Provide orientation cues in the surrounding area: clocks, calendars, photographs, memorabilia, seasonal decorations, and familiar objects.
- Windows are a great way to enhance the client's orientation to time. Lighting may help to decrease the "sundowning effect" and reduce hallucinations.

- Ensure safety in the physical environment.
- Minimize any sensory impairment by providing eyeglasses or hearing assistive devices, as needed.
- Allow client to care for self as much as possible.
- Administer antipsychotic or antibiotic agents as ordered.

Complications

- Increase in psychotic behavior
- Decrease in level of functioning
- Extrapyramidal symptoms or other adverse reactions associated with antipsychotic medications
- Risk to self or others
- Dual diagnosis: substance abuse with psychosis

Client Outcomes

Outcomes must be realistic. Rehospitalization is common. Clients with psychotic disorders are often characterized by low self-esteem and may expect to be labeled the "mental patient." If staff members set grandiose outcomes with little input or understanding from the client, the client is not likely to feel successful about achieving the outcomes.

Client outcomes might include:

- Experience a reduction in symptoms
- Focus on activities in the here and now
- Identify problem behaviors and methods for resolving those that interfere with functioning
- Identify medications, purposes, side effects, dosage, frequency, and when to call primary care provider with problems for all medications the client is taking
- Exhibit appropriate activity level, sleep pattern, eating, and independent self-care within own limitations
- Participate in treatment and treatment planning
- Exhibit coping with stress, family, and significant others
- Adhere to medication and other treatments
- Not harm self or others
- Have a support system with accountability

Client and Family Education

- Discuss with the client and family the possible environmental or situational causes, contributing factors, and triggers.
- Help the client and family to identify the internal and external indicators of undifferentiated psychotic disorders.
- Educate the client and family about the following issues:
  - Reality orientation
  - Coping skills

- Socialization
- Monitoring of symptoms
- Supporting adherence to treatment
- Medication therapy
- Decreasing anxiety
- Coping with hallucinations
- Decreasing or increasing environmental stimuli as needed
- Vocation/occupational training
- Use of support and psychoeducation groups
- Decreasing agitated behavior
- Nutritional considerations
- Safety

Age-Related Changes—Gerontological Considerations

- The elderly may experience inadequate support systems.
- Access to health care may affect the elderly client's ability to receive care.

Critical Thinking Exercise: Psychotic Disorders: Undifferentiated Type

Situation: You admit a new client to the Partial Hospitalization Program. E.A. is 55, diagnosed with a psychotic disorder, and was recently hospitalized for three days. When you meet with E.A. for his admission assessment, you discuss his goals for treatment and you assess his needs. E.A. tells you that he is very anxious and cannot seem to think straight. The client is taking risperidone (Risperdal) and benztropine (Cogentin). When you ask the client to tell you when and how much risperidone he takes, he cannot remember. You observe that his clothes are dirty, and he does not appear clean. In the past, E.A. has threatened others with harm and has had difficulty establishing and maintaining relationships.

1. What conclusions can you draw about E.A.'s hospital admission?

2. What outcomes would be appropriate for E.A., who will be in your day treatment program for four weeks?

3. Formulate an education plan for this client.

Mood Disorders: Major Depressive Disorder

Key Points

- A mood disorder may include symptoms of depressed mood, feelings of hopelessness and helplessness, decreased interest in usual activities, disinterest in relationships with others or cycles of depression and mania.

- Depression is often concurrent with other psychiatric diagnoses. Almost half of clients with major depressive disorders have histories of non-mood psychiatric disorders.

- A high incidence exists for persons with chronic illness or prolonged hospitalization/institutional care.

- There are important biological factors involved in the development of depression such as serotonin, norepinephrine, and acetylcholine deficiencies, the effect of light on mood as well as familial predisposition.

- The goals of collaborative management include:
  - Providing a safe environment at the treatment setting: hospital and at home
  - Ensuring that client does not harm self or others
  - Promoting an adherence to medication treatment
  - Strengthening self-esteem and communication of needs and feelings
  - Teaching self-monitoring of symptoms and encourage client to seek help when needed
  - Ensuring that client's nutritional, elimination, and sleep needs are met
  - Educating client and family about major depression and treatment

- **Key Terms/Concepts:** Neurotransmitters, psychomotor retardation, affect, suicidal

Overview

A mood disorder is characterized by a depressed mood or cycles of depressed and elated mood, feelings of hopelessness and helplessness, and a decrease in interest or pleasure in usual activities. Depression is the most common psychiatric diagnosis. Major depressive disorder is a serious depression that involves impaired functioning and often suicidal thoughts. Dysthymia is a less severe depression that lasts at least two years in adults (one year in children).

Risk Factors

- Biochemical factors
- Family genetics: Parent with depression, child 10-13% risk of depression
- Gender: Higher rate for women
- Age: Often less than 40 when begins

- Marital status: More frequently single, widowed
- Season of year: Seasonal Affective Disorder (SAD) occurs when client experiences recurrent depression that occurs annually at the same time. It is thought to be a reaction to environmental factors such as climate, latitude, and decreased light. (The use of light treatment is helpful for these clients during depression.)
- Psychological influences: Low self-esteem, unresolved grief
- Environmental factors: Lack of social support and stressful life events. (Reactive depression is in response to a specific life event, e.g., death of a spouse.)
- Medical comorbidity: Clients with chronic or terminal illness, those who are postpartum, or are currently abusing substances are especially prone to becoming depressed.

Specific Biological Factors

- Deficiency of serotonin, norepinephrine, and acetylcholine
- Effect of light on physiology (related to SAD): Neurotransmitters melatonin and serotonin may be involved.
- Neurotransmitters subsensitive to impulses

Signs and Symptoms

- Feelings of hopelessness, worthlessness, and helplessness
- Psychomotor retardation or agitation
- Affect: flat, blunted, labile
- Tearfulness, crying, melancholy
- Altered thought process: difficulty concentrating, focusing, and problem solving; may experience overgeneralization, dichotomous thinking, catastrophizing, personalization, or pessimism
- Self-destructive behavior
- Decrease in personal hygiene
- Loss of energy or restlessness
- Sexual disinterest
- Physical symptoms of discomfort/pain
- Risk of harm to self or others: suicidal ideation or thoughts, self-destructive acts, violence, overt hostility often connected with suicidal thoughts
- Weight loss or gain, overeating or anorexia
- Change in eating habits
- Insomnia or increased sleep
- Withdrawal, social isolation
- Anger, self-directed
- Loss of pleasure (anhedonia) in daily activities, interests, hobbies

Assessment

- History and physical examination to rule out medical causes for client complaints
- Mental status examination
- Family history of depression, mood disorders, medical illnesses
- Dexamethasone suppression test of serum afternoon cortisol medications and meals can interfere with results.
- Laboratory tests include sodium bicarbonate, calcium, magnesium, potassium, estrogen, progesterone levels, and thyroid-stimulating hormone test.
- Nutritional assessment, including caffeine intake and vitamin and magnesium deficiencies
- Psychiatric assessment and history
- Sociocultural history
- Suicidal ideation or history of suicidal behavior or self-harm

Nursing Diagnoses

- Risk for violence, self-directed or directed at others
- Impaired verbal communication
- Decisional conflict
- Altered role performance
- Hopelessness
- Deficit in diversional activity
- Fatigue
- Self-care deficit
- Altered thought processes
- Self-esteem disturbance
- Spiritual distress
- Anxiety
- Ineffective individual coping
- Grieving, dysfunctional
- Powerlessness
- Sexual dysfunction
- Sleep pattern disturbance
- Impaired memory
- Ineffective family coping
- Social isolation
- Impaired social interaction
- Sensory/perceptive alterations
- Constipation
- Alteration in nutrition: Less than body requirements
- Alteration in nutrition: More than body requirements

Therapeutic Nursing Management

Safe Environment: The client with severe depression and suicidal ideation may require hospitalization. Suicidal clients require one-to-one supervision until the acute threat of self-injury is resolved.

Psychological treatment

- **Cognitive behavioral therapy (CBT)**—Correcting or changing errors or distortions in thinking. Altered thinking leads to altered behavior.
- **Individual psychotherapy**—Long-term therapeutic approach or short-term solution- oriented, may focus on in-depth exploration, specific stress situations, or problem solving. Insurance coverage can affect the length of therapy that is received.
- **Behavioral therapy**—Modifying behavior to assist in reducing depressive symptoms and increasing coping skills
- **Social skills training**—Techniques include operant conditioning, shaping, prompting and fading, positive reinforcement, extinction, generalization, discrimination, and cognitive processing schedules. May use role play to teach clients ways to improve interpersonal interactions, relationships, and role-play independent living:
  - Eye contact
  - Posture
  - Attention to ADLs
  - Employment skills
  - Communication skills
  - Problem solving
- **Self-monitoring**—Clients become more aware of their symptoms and changes in symptoms, what affects them, and when and how to intervene or seek intervention to prevent further deterioration. Family and significant others are important in this process. Client feels more in control if reasonable goals are established.
- **Behavioral contracts**—Focus on specific client problems and needs to help the client resolve them, (e.g., no suicide/no self-harm contract, isolation, social interaction contract, self-care contract).

Social treatment

- **Milieu therapy**—Incorporates day-to-day living experiences in a therapeutic environment to affect perception and behavior.
- **Family therapy**—Aimed at assisting the family to cope with the client's illness and supporting the client in therapeutic ways.
- **Group therapy**—Typically, this therapy focuses on assisting clients with interpersonal communication, coping, and problem-solving skills. Some groups may involve more in-depth exploration of the nature of depression and strategies to relieve it. Access to insurance coverage affects the extent of therapy that the client may receive.

Psychopharmacologic and Somatic treatments

- Administer antidepressant medications: selective serotonin reuptake inhibitors (SSRIs) (e.g., sertraline [Zoloft], citalopram [Celexa], fluoxetine [Prozac], paroxetine [Paxil]); tricyclic (TCA) medications, (e.g., amitriptyline hydrochloride [Elavil]); monoamine oxidase inhibitors (MAOIs), (e.g., tranylcypromine sulfate [Parnate]).
- Continued assessment/monitoring of the client's mental health status is critical, particularly in terms of agitation and suicidal ideation.
- Electroconvulsive therapy
  - This therapy may be performed in inpatient or outpatient settings. The latter requires family or significant other support for aftercare in the home.

Nursing interventions

- Priority for care is always the client's safety.
- Use of behavioral contracts. Use this technique to meet outcomes relating to "no self-harm"/"no suicidal attempts," self-care, and isolation.
- Assess regularly for suicidal ideation or plan.
- Observe client for distorted, negative thinking. Do not criticize the client, but instead provide concrete strategies to the client regarding a positive attitude and outlook on life. Pace this discussion.
- Acknowledge the painfulness of depression, but do not dwell on it.
- If client exhibits withdrawn behavior, gradually work with client to increase activity one step at a time. Client needs to learn how to gradually increase social activity.
- Assist client to learn and use problem-solving and stress management skills.
- Avoid doing too much for the client, as this will only increase client's dependence and decrease self-esteem.
- It is a natural tendency to be overly cheerful to compensate for another's depression, but this approach leads to false reassurance, which can be detrimental. It is true, however, that depression usually improves with time.
- The nurse's role in the physical care of the client experiencing major depressive disorder is to provide assessment and interventions related to appropriate nutrition, fluids, sleep, exercise, and hygiene, and to provide health education.
- Explore meaningful losses in the client's life. Aid the client in resolving issues related to the grief process.
- Use a communication technique called reframing to help the client view a situation in alternative ways.
- Encourage client to practice skills learned in cognitive behavioral therapy, group and family therapies, social skills training, and symptoms management.

Complications

- Risk to self or others
- Anticholinergic and cardiovascular side effects of tricyclic antidepressants
- Sexual side effects of SSRI antidepressant

- Inability to care for self: nutrition, fluids, appropriate sleep, hygiene, exercise/rest
- Self-mutilation
- Long-term depression

Client Outcomes

The client will:

- Maintain physical safety
- Experience a decrease in symptoms of depression
- View problems realistically and situations positively
- Exhibit control of self-destructive feelings and behavior; report no thoughts/feelings of self-harm
- Use coping skills to manage stress, anxiety, and depression
- Identify problems and issues that have contributed to the depression and ways to resolve them
- Exhibit appropriate nutrition, fluids, exercise, sleep pattern, independent self-care, and hygiene
- Self-monitor depression symptoms and apply symptom management techniques
- Adhere to agreement on contracts and treatment (medication and therapy), especially cognitive behavioral therapy
- Participate in treatment planning

Client and Family Education

- Discuss with the client and family the possible environmental or situational causes, contributing factors, and triggers for serious depression.
- Help the client and family to identify the internal and external indicators of major depressive disorder.
- Educate the client and family about the following issues:
  - Suicide prevention
  - Stress management and problem solving
  - Symptoms management (e.g., positive self-talk, involvement in activities and hobbies)
  - Medications: antidepressants, antipsychotics if hallucinating
  - Family support, understanding, coping
  - Social skills strengthening
  - Self-care assistance, when needed
  - Grief resolution

Age–Related Factors—Cultural and Gender Variations

- Depression is a common disorder of youth, particularly in families with significant histories of depression.
- Irritability is seen frequently in prepubertal children with depression.

- Anger, acting-out behavior, and/or apathy are seen frequently in adolescents with depression.
- Children and adolescents are more sensitive to antidepressant medication than adults.
- Effective treatment of children and adolescents with depression involves parental supervision, education, and support.
- Depression is a common psychiatric disorder of the elderly.
- Feelings of hopelessness, helplessness, and social isolation may increase in the advanced years.
- Coping mechanisms may diminish with old age.
- Medications to treat chronic illnesses may cause unintended effects, which may intensify depression in the elderly.
- Physiological changes of aging may intensify the effects of antidepressant medications.
- Gender: Women are twice as likely to suffer depression. Culture plays a role because women are more likely to be burdened with both work and family duties. Women are more likely to have lower incomes, be single parents and more likely to have suffered physical or sexual abuse.
- Asian Pacific Islander, some cultural examples: Chinese clients may feel mental illness is a punishment for some wrongdoing by themselves, their family or ancestors. They may feel ashamed to seek treatment. In the deeply religious Korean community, some clients believe their hallucinations to be spiritual voices.

Critical Thinking Exercise: Major Depressive Disorder

Situation: A 54-year-old male is married and is an executive for a large software company. He has no history of mental illness. Lately, the client has been working overtime at the company to meet a deadline. His wife travels out of town during the weekdays. In the past two months, the client has become irritable, isolative, and withdrawn, and has started to drink more than his normal two cocktails after work each day. The client is also less attentive regarding his personal appearance. He is very concerned about the decline in sales over the last year. The client's wife suggests he see a psychiatrist and accompanies him to the appointment.

The psychiatrist's assessment findings include: a SAD affect, insomnia, weight loss, suicidal ideation, and psychomotor retardation. The client is diagnosed with Major Depressive Disorder and is prescribed sertraline (Zoloft) 50 mg. PO every morning. The client is scheduled to return to the mental health clinic in two weeks.

1. Identify the client's priority problems requiring immediate nursing intervention.

2. Provide the rationale for the priority problems.

3. Identify the appropriate nursing interventions that correspond to each problem.

Mood Disorders: Bipolar Disorder

Key Points

- Bipolar disorder is a mood disorder with recurrent episodes of depression and mania. Phases may vary depending on type of bipolar disorder.
- Biological factors are important in the development of this disorder.
- The goals of collaborative management include:
  - Providing a safe environment: hospital and home
  - Adhering to medication regimen
  - Ensuring that client's needs are met when manic or depressive (e.g., sleep/rest, nutrition and fluids, hygiene, safety)
  - If client protection is required, ensuring that all procedures are followed, and client is treated with respect
  - Reinforcing reality and acknowledging client's feelings
  - Clarifying communication that may be confusing
  - Increasing client socialization when appropriate
  - Educating client and family about bipolar disorder and treatment
- **Key Terms/Concepts**: Mania, depression, neurotransmitters, suicidal ideation, cycling, cyclothymia, hypomania

Overview

A mood disorder, formerly known as manic depression, is characterized by recurrent episodes of both depression and mania. Either phase may be predominant at any given time or elements of both phases may be present simultaneously.

Risk Factors

- Biochemical imbalances
- Family genetics: One parent, child has 25% risk; two parents, 50-75% risk
- Environmental factors: Stress, losses, poverty, social isolation
- Psychological influences: Inadequate coping, denial of disordered behavior

Specific Biological Factors

- Possible excess of norepinephrine, serotonin, and dopamine
- Increased intracellular sodium and calcium
- Neurotransmitters supersensitive to transmission of impulses
- Defective feedback mechanism in limbic system

Signs and Symptoms

- Risk to self or others
- Impaired social interactions
- Mania
  - Persistent elevated or irritable mood
  - Impulsivity: spending money, giving away money or possessions
  - Racing thoughts
  - Increase in talking and activities, grandiose view of self and abilities
  - Psychotic behavior
  - Impairment in social and occupational functioning
  - Poor judgment
  - Decreased sleep
  - Distractibility
  - Delusions, paranoia, and hallucinations
  - Neglect of ADLs, including nutrition and hydration
  - Hyperactivity, which may lead to exhaustion
  - Dislike of interference or intolerance of criticism
  - Agitation
  - Denial of illness
  - Attention-seeking behavior: flashy dress and make-up, inappropriate behavior
- Depression
  - Loss or increase in appetite or sleep, disturbed sleep
  - Psychomotor retardation or agitation
  - Affect: flat, blunted, labile
  - Tearfulness, crying, withdrawal, social isolation
  - Difficulty concentrating, focusing, problem-solving
  - Self-destructive behavior
  - Decrease in personal hygiene
  - Lack of energy
  - Physical symptoms of discomfort/pain
  - Risk to self or others
  - Anhedonia: loss of pleasure, hobbies, favorite activities

Assessment

- History and physical examination
- Mental status examination
- Family history
- Thyroid-stimulating hormone test: if elevated, increased risk of mania
- Laboratory tests, include sodium bicarbonate, calcium, magnesium, potassium, estrogen, progesterone, and level of prescribed medication, such as Lithium, to prevent toxicity

- Nutritional assessment, including caffeine intake and levels of vitamin and magnesium deficiencies
- Psychiatric history
- Social history
- Suicidal assessment

Nursing Diagnoses

- High risk for violence, directed at self or others
- Impaired verbal communication
- Anxiety
- Ineffective individual coping
- Disturbance of self-esteem
- Alteration in thought processes
- Alteration in sensory perceptions
- Self-care deficit
- Sleep pattern disturbance
- Alteration in nutrition
- Sexual dysfunction
- Knowledge deficit
- Deficit in diversional activity

Therapeutic Nursing Management

Environment: Clients who experience mania require a safe, supportive environment, which may be a hospital, a home for mild mania, or some other treatment setting. Limiting the extent or intensity of stimuli may help the client cope with manic symptoms. Hospitalization may be required if the client is a danger to self or others. Clients may be admitted voluntarily or involuntarily to begin or to adjust the pharmacologic treatment.

Psychological Treatment

- Individual psychotherapy: May be used to identify stressors and patterns of behavior. Also may be helpful as the client learns to cope with the illness and for medication monitoring.
- Group therapy: Establish a supportive environment and redirect inappropriate behavior. If the client is manic, he or she may not be able to tolerate a group or function successfully within it.
- Family therapy: Verbalize family frustrations and establish a treatment plan for outpatient use. Families may be experiencing frustration and concern about excessive behavior of the client (e.g., spending money, making poor decisions, problems with the law, etc.).

Somatic and Psychopharmacologic treatments

- Electroconvulsive therapy
- Psychopharmacology: Administer medications as ordered.

- Depression: Therapeutic effects may take two to six weeks to be noted during which time the side effects may be pronounced. Medications include: selective serotonin reuptake inhibitors (SSRIs), tricyclics.
- Mania: Drug therapy includes mood stabilizers or anticonvulsants. Lithium carbonate or Depakote (divalproex sodium) are the drugs of choice. Lab studies must be routinely monitored since the therapeutic drug level is narrow.
- Anticonvulsant medications: Tegretol, Neurontin, and clonazepam (Klonopin) have shown mood stabilization in clients with mania.
- Antipsychotics: Zyprexa (olanzapine) has received an indication for acute mania.
- Medication education: This group may be helpful in assisting the client with adherence to medication regimen and provides ongoing support and psychological education about medications and symptom monitoring.
- Reassessment of critical symptoms, such as anxiety, agitation, depression, and suicidal ideation

Nursing interventions

- Assess client's suicidal thoughts, intentions and escalating behavior regularly.
- Set consistent limits on inappropriate behavior to help the client de-escalate.
- Establish a calm environment for the client (e.g., decreased stimuli, time outs, and quiet times). Client's hyperactivity can get out of control, without intervention client can suffer exhaustion or injury.
- Reinforce and focus on reality.
- Provide outlets for physical activity, but prevent client from escalating.
- Client may be very likable during "high" periods. Staff members need to avoid participating in this behavior. At other times, client may be very irritable and staff members should approach client quietly and with limits, if necessary.
- If client cannot control self and other methods are not successful, staff may need to provide client protection if a threat of self-harm or injury to others exists (e.g., physical restraints, seclusion/observation room, or one-to-one supervision).
- Monitor client's nutrition, fluid intake, and sleep. This is critical, as the client may not be able to do this for self. Provide nutritious portable food.
- Client may be involved in schemes (e.g., spending money, financial deals, etc.). These need to be monitored as client's judgment may not be sound.
- Administer lithium carbonate (antimanic agent) and/or educate the client regarding medicating schedule.
- Educate the client regarding the adverse effects of lithium therapy. Assess for:
  - Central nervous system (CNS) changes
  - Gastrointestinal upset
  - Polyuria
  - Electrocardiogram (ECG) changes
  - Hypotension
  - Multi-organ failure (severe toxicity)

- Monitor serum levels of lithium (0.5-1.0 mEg/L). Report subtherapeutic or toxic levels to prescribing practitioner.
- Encourage liberal hydration (2,500-3,000 mL/day) during lithium therapy.
- Educate the client to consume adequate dietary salt (minimum of 2.5 gm/day).
- Therapeutic improvement takes one to three weeks after initiation of lithium treatment.
- Monitor serum levels of Depakote and Tegretol every two to four months during maintenance.

Complications

- Risk to self or others: suicide or homicide
- Lithium toxicity or toxic levels of any anticonvulsant medications
- Altered social interactions, employment difficulties
- Risk for violence
- Altered nutrition and sleep/exhaustion
- Legal problems
- Substance abuse

Client Outcomes

The client will:

- Exhibit appropriate behavior
- Provide no harm to self or others
- Exhibit appropriate levels of nutrition, fluid intake, exercise, and sleep
- Identify and use appropriate coping mechanisms
- Adhere to medication regime
- Make realistic statements about self
- Maintain interpersonal relationships
- Participate in treatment planning

Client and Family Education

- Discuss with client and family the possible environmental or situational causes, contributing factors, and triggers for a mood disorder with recurrent episodes of depression and mania.
- Help the client and family to identify the internal and external indicators of bipolar disorders.
- Educate the client and family about the following issues:
  - Self-monitoring
  - Medication therapy and importance of blood levels and other laboratory monitoring
  - Self-care, including adequate nutrition, hygiene, and sleep
  - How to decrease stimuli and use other methods to control symptoms and decrease anxiety

- No harm to self or others
- Use of self-help groups

Age-Related Changes—Gerontological Considerations

- Feelings of hopelessness, helplessness, and social isolation may increase with age.
- Coping mechanisms may diminish with age, causing mood difficulties.
- Alterations in medication absorption may lead to medication toxicity.
- Support systems may diminish due to age and death of significant others.
- Access to health care becomes increasingly difficult for the elderly adult with mental health disease; therefore, appointments may not be kept.

Critical Thinking Exercise: Bipolar Disorder

Situation: D.H., a 22-year-old married female, is diagnosed with bipolar disorder. She lives with her husband and two preschool children. D.H. had numerous mental health problems as a teenager, including anorexia nervosa. She does not take her prescribed lithium on a regular basis, stating, "There's no sense taking it when I'm feeling good! That's for when I'm depressed." Frequently, she leaves her family and travels by herself to other cities to sightsee. She charges the maximum on her credit cards and buys gifts and clothes for friends and neighbors, and buys other items that she then donates to a local charity.

D.H. shows signs of increased manic type behavior. Her primary care provider recommends inpatient admission for assessment and stabilization. She refuses admission and threatens to kill herself if she is admitted. The psychiatrist authorizes an emergency involuntary admission to the hospital for her and she is admitted to the acute psychiatric unit. Admission orders include lithium carbonate 1 gm PO bid.

1. Write the interventions necessary to care for D.H. in the manic phase of the disorder.

2. Write the interventions necessary to care for D.H. in the depressive phase of the disorder.

3. Identify the effects and side effects of lithium therapy.

Suicidal Ideation

Key Points

- Suicide is a major public health problem.
- Many factors affect a person's decision to commit suicide.
- The goals of collaborative management include:
    - Presenting no harm or danger to client or others
    - Providing a safe environment: hospital and home
    - Adhering to medication treatment
    - If client protection is required, ensuring that all procedures are followed, and client is treated with respect
    - Reinforcing reality and recognizing client's feelings
    - Clarifying communication that may be confusing
    - Increasing client socialization when appropriate
    - Educating client and family about suicide prevention
- **Key Terms/Concepts:** Suicidal ideation, theories of suicide, suicidal plan/ assessment, "no suicide/harm" contract

Overview

Suicidal symptoms relate to behavior rather than a specific disorder. It is a leading cause of death among adults, teens, and college students. The occurrences may actually be higher because of under-reporting. Ninety percent of individuals who commit suicide have some form of mental or mood disorder. Suicide among the elderly is a concern. Although the rate of suicide among children ages 5-14 is rare, an alarming number of children are hospitalized every year for self-destructive behavior. Teen suicide began to drop steadily since 1995, but has flattened out in the last few years.

Risk Factors

- Marital status: The suicide rate for single persons is twice that of married persons. The risk of suicide is also higher for divorced or widowed persons.
- Gender: Women attempt suicide more often than men; however, men succeed more frequently and use more lethal methods.
- Age: The suicide rate increases with age, especially among elderly men with medical problems. Suicide is the third leading cause of death in adolescents. The rate of suicide has tripled in the last 30 years.
- Socioeconomic status: Individuals in the very highest and lower economic status are at higher risk.

- Ethnicity: Caucasians are at the highest risk, followed by Native Americans, African Americans, and Hispanic Americans.
- Diagnosed psychiatric illnesses, such as major depression, schizophrenia, and bipolar disorder
- Alcoholism and drug abuse
- Homosexuality
- Medical illness that is associated with pain and/or disability
- Family history of suicide
- Loss of a loved one
- Lack of employment
- Living alone and/or lack of social supports
- Sudden lifestyle changes (fired from job, divorce, retirement)
- Anniversary of death of loved one
- Command hallucinations to harm self or others
- Presence of a suicide plan

Theories of Suicide

Psychological theories:

- Anger turned inward: Anger that was previously directed at someone else is turned inward.
- Hopelessness, depression, and guilt: Desperate feelings of the client.
- History of aggression and violence: Rage and violent behavior is correlated with suicides.
- Shame and humiliation: Suicide viewed as a "saving face" or saving the family name following a social defeat.
- Developmental stressors: Certain life stressors at developmental stages have been identified as precipitating factors to suicide.

Sociological theories:

- **Egoistic suicide**: Client feels separated and apart from society.
- **Altruistic suicide**: Client is integrated into a group and is governed by cultural, religious, and political ties.
- **Anomic suicide**: Client experiences a disruption in normal behavior and fears separation from a cohesive group.

Biological theories:

- Genetic tendency: Twin studies have indicated a predisposition toward suicidal behavior.
- Neurochemical factors: Postmortem studies have revealed a decreased serotonin level in the brainstem and spinal fluid.

Signs and Symptoms

- Anxiety
- Depression
- Low self-esteem
- Isolation and withdrawal, decreased social interaction
- Decrease in daily functioning
- Destructive coping mechanisms
- History of psychiatric treatment or mood disorder or demential confusion in the elderly
- History of alcohol and/or drug abuse
- Previous suicide attempts
- Family history of suicidal behavior
- Verbalization of suicidal wishes, thoughts or plans
- Non-verbal clues such as giving away possessions
- Sudden relief of depression: During severe depression, client does not have the energy to plan and carry out a suicide plan
- Inability to discuss the future
- Self-mutilation
- Expresses anger toward self
- Feels he or she is dying or dead; does not want to wake up
- Self-directed anger

Assessment

- Psychiatric assessment and history
- Mental status exam
- Social history
- Suicidal assessment: Questions to ask the client directly to assess if his/her plan is realistic.
  - Do you have thoughts of harming or killing yourself?
  - Do you have a plan to harm or kill yourself?
  - What is the plan?
  - Is it possible to implement the plan?
  - When do you plan to do it?
- A person is considered at a high-risk for suicide if the plan could be carried out within 24 to 48 hours. Other issues in determining risk include the lethality of the method and the plan for discovery after death.

Nursing Diagnoses

- High risk for violence, self-directed or directed at others
- Risk for self-mutilation
- Ineffective individual coping

- Ineffective family coping
- Spiritual distress
- Anxiety
- Self-esteem disturbance
- Impaired verbal communication
- Impaired adjustment
- Self-care deficit

Therapeutic Nursing Management

- Establish a therapeutic relationship.
- Talk directly with the client about suicide and plans.
- Communicate the potential for suicide to team members and family.
- Stay with the person.
- Accept the person and communicate in a nonjudgmental manner.
- Listen to the person.
- Secure a "no suicide/harm" contract.
- Give the person a message of hope based on reality.
- When client is able, encourage gradual increase in activities.
- Maintain suicide precautions; be particularly concerned with personal items the client may use to harm self, remove all dangerous and potentially dangerous items (belts, glass, sharp implements).
- Maintain a safe environment; remove potential means of harm.
- Do not keep secrets with the client about the client's safety.
- Documentation is critical. Include suicidal assessment, description of plan, and adherence to suicide precaution procedure. Describe client's feelings and behavior. Indicate when client's primary care provider was notified and his/her response. Include all safety procedures followed.

Client Outcomes

The client will:

- Not harm self or others
- Self-monitor symptoms and identify interventions to take to get help when needed
- Adhere to treatment

Client and Family Education

- Discuss with the client and family the possible environmental or situational causes, contributing factors, and triggers for suicidal thoughts.
- Help the client and family to identify the internal and external indicators of suicidal thoughts.
- Educate the client and family about the following issues:

- Self-monitoring
- Interventions to prevent harm to self or others
- Coping skills
- Adherence to medication regimen

Age-Related Factors—Cultural and Gender Variations

- Feelings of helplessness, hopelessness, and social isolation may increase with age.
- Risk for suicide is increased in older adults, widowed males, and older homosexual males.
- Poor physical health and pain increase the risk for suicide in the older populations.
- Males are less likely to attempt, but more likely to succeed at suicide.
- Suicide is growing in the African-American community.

Critical Thinking Exercise: Suicidal Ideation

Situation: A roommate found M.B. in her apartment after an overdose of aspirin. She was taken to the emergency department and then admitted to the psychiatric unit. M.B. is 35 years old. She recently lost her job. When her roommate was asked about the overdose, she guessed that M.B. took approximately 30 pills and assumed that her roommate knew that she would be home within the hour. The nurse's physical assessment revealed that she was quiet and responded slowly to questions. She denied wanting to kill herself and stated that she just wanted some peace. She had never tried to harm herself before. M.B. cried through most of the interview. The client said that she had only slept a maximum of four hours per night in the last month or two and had lost 15 pounds. When M.B. was told she would receive one-to-one supervision, she became angry and shouted, "I am not a prisoner."

1. Based on these data, what is the level of risk for M.B.'s suicidal act? Provide your rationale.

2. What impact might the job loss have had on M.B.?

3. What data are provided that indicate M.B. is depressed?

4. How would you respond to M.B.'s outburst about one-to-one supervision?

5. What other intervention is often used with suicidal clients to focus on their responsibility for their own actions? Describe the intervention.

Cognitive Disorders

Key Points

- Cognitive disorders are a group of conditions characterized by the disruption of thinking, memory, processing, and problem solving.
- Organic disease is part of this disorder, which can include a response to an exogenous substance.
- Types of cognitive disorders include: delirium, dementia, and memory loss disorders (amnesia or dissociative fugue).
- The goals of collaborative management include:
  - Determining the cause of the disorder
  - Ensuring that all ADL and nutritional needs are met
  - Adhering to medication treatment for physical problems
  - Ensuring safety with no harm to self or others
  - Providing a safe environment: home, hospital, and long-term care
  - Optimizing functioning in daily living
- **Key Terms/Concepts:** Organic disease, exogenous substance, cognition, confabulation, thought processes, reality orientation, delirium, dementia, aphasia, agnosia, apraxia

Overview

Cognitive mental disorders are a group of conditions characterized by the disruption of thinking, memory, processing, and problem solving. Organic disease affects the brain tissue producing a chronic and often permanent deficit in cognition. The etiology of cognitive mental disorders is primarily biological. An abrupt withdrawal of an exogenous substance may also trigger the disorder. Types of cognitive disorders include delirium, dementia, and amnesic disorders.

Risk Factors

- Physiological changes: Neurological, metabolic, and cardiovascular diseases
- Cognitive changes
- Family genetics
- Infections
- Tumors
- Sleep disorders
- Substance abuse
- Drug intoxications and withdrawals

Signs and Symptoms

- Irritability: Mood most frequently seen in organic brain disorder
- Change in level of consciousness
- Difficulty thinking with sudden onset
- State of awareness ranging from hypervigilance to stupor or coma
- Impairment in cognition and thought process, particularly short-term memory
- Anxiety
- Confabulation: Use of imaginary experiences or made-up information to fill in gaps of memory loss
- Perceptual disturbances: Hallucinations, illusions
- Disturbance in sleep-wake cycles

Nursing Diagnoses

- Altered thought processes
- Anxiety
- Self-care deficit
- Impaired home maintenance management
- Impaired verbal communication
- Ineffective family coping
- High risk for violence directed at others
- Altered family processes

Assessment

- History and physical assessment data may provide a clue to the cause of changes in the client's level of cognition. This is important because altered mental function may be a symptom of an underlying physical problem that may respond to medical treatment.
- Psychiatric assessment and history
- Electroencephalogram (EEG)
- Computerized Tomographic Brain Scan (CT Scan)
- Magnetic Resonance Imaging (MRI)
- Sleep studies

Therapeutic Nursing Management

Environment

- The nurse plays a primary role in providing a safe environment for the client and others.
- Exogenous stimuli in the environment can intensify the client's level of disorientation.
- Cognitive changes often include a period of confusion and forgetfulness. Maintaining a structured and consistent environment with routine patterns helps to reduce the client's level of anxiety and confusion for the client.

- The nurse may encourage family members to bring photographs or familiar items as a strategy to orient the client.

Psychological treatment

Psychological treatment may focus more on the family to offer them support during this stressful time. Individual and group therapy are not helpful for the client.

- Cognitive changes affect the family and care providers. Cognitive decline often means a change in the family roles and activities of daily living.
- Therapy helps the family verbalize feelings of frustration when the client becomes cognitively impaired.
- Support of the family member who is the caregiver is important.

Psychopharmacologic treatment

- Pharmacologic therapy is implemented to reduce or alleviate the associated symptoms (e.g., antianxiety medications, antidepressants, and antipsychotics).
- Calcium channel blockers may be used with clients who have Alzheimer's disease.
- The elderly usually require lower doses and may have idiosyncratic responses to medications.

Nursing interventions

- Determine the cause and treatment of the underlying causes.
- Remain with client, monitoring behavior, providing reorientation, and assurance.
- Provide a room with a low level of visual and auditory stimuli.
- Provide palliative care with focus on nutritional support.
- Reinforce orientation to time, place, and person.
- When speaking with the client, make sure you have eye contact and use short, simple sentences to enhance comprehension.
- Establish a routine.
- Client protection may be required.
- Have client wear an identification bracelet, in case he/she gets lost.
- Client should not be left alone at home.
- Day care program may be helpful.
- Break tests into small steps, giving one instruction at a time.

Complications

- Harm to self or others
- Alteration in role responsibilities
- Alteration in social interactions
- Self-care deficits
- Caregiver stress

Client Outcomes

The client will:

- Demonstrate behaviors indicating a decreased level of anxiety
- Experience improved orientation
- Not harm self or others
- Maintain self-care needs
- Improve verbal communication within client's ability
- Participate in appropriate social activities

Client and Family Education

- Discuss with the client and family the possible environmental or situational causes, contributing factors, and triggers for cognitive disorders.
- Help the client and family to identify the internal and external indicators of cognitive disorders and encourage routine medical care.
- Educate the client and family about the following issues:
  - Reality orientation
  - Coping skills
  - Family coping skills and stress management
  - Self-care needs
  - Medication therapy
  - Nutrition
  - Monitoring of symptoms
  - Respite care/relief for caregiver(s)

Age-Related Changes—Gerontological Considerations

- The elderly adult may experience vascular changes within the brain, including cerebral thrombosis, atherosclerosis, and arteriosclerosis.
- Elevated pressure in the arterial system causes severe headaches and changes in the cognitive status of the elderly adult.
- The client's support system is usually the first to recognize changes in cognition, personality, and mood.
- The elderly client commonly disguises cognitive deficits from family and friends. Therefore, access to health care may be delayed because of this fear of discovering cognitive deterioration.

Critical Thinking Exercise: Cognitive Disorders

Using the information in the chapters on cognitive disorders and any additional resources necessary, fill in the following table:

Cognitive Disorder	Cognitive Disorder Brief Description	Signs and Symptoms	Nursing Interventions
Delirium			
Dementia			
Alzheimers			
Amnesia/Fugae			

Cognitive Disorders: Delirium

Key Points

- Delirium is a condition with a rapid onset, involving disorientation, impaired memory, changed personality, and misperceptions of the environment.
- The goals of collaborative management include:
  - Determining the cause of the disorder and treating accordingly
  - Ensuring that all ADL and nutritional needs are met
  - Adhering to medication treatment
  - Providing assessment and treatment for physical problems
  - Ensuring safety with no harm to self or others
- **Key Terms/Concepts:** Delirium, distractibility, disorientation, misperceptions, psychomotor activity, intoxication, withdrawal, disorganization, memory impairment, sundowning effect

Overview

Delirium is characterized by a disturbance of consciousness and a change in cognition that develops rapidly over a short period. Delirium usually begins abruptly following head trauma or a seizure; however, the onset may be slower if the etiology is metabolic. Duration is usually brief and subsides upon recovery from the underlying condition.

Risk Factors

- Medical condition: Delirium may be due to a general medical condition, such as systemic infection, metabolic disorder, fluid and electrolyte imbalance, hepatic or renal disease, etc.
- Substance induced: Symptoms may be attributed to side effects of medications or drugs of abuse.
- Substance intoxication: Symptoms may occur following high doses of cannabis, cocaine, hallucinogens, alcohol, anxiolytics, or narcotics.
- Substance withdrawal may occur after the reduction or termination of a substance.
- Delirium due to multiple etiologies may be related to more than one condition or illness.
- Delirium is a common postanesthesia event.

Signs and Symptoms

- Difficulty sustaining and shifting attention
- Extreme distractibility
- Disorganized thinking
- Speech that is rambling, irrelevant, pressured, and incoherent
- Impaired reasoning and goal-directed behavior
- Disorientation to time and place
- Impairment of recent memory
- Misperceptions of the environment, including illusions and hallucinations
- Interruption of sleep-wake cycle
- Psychomotor activity that fluctuates between agitation and a vegetative state
- Emotional instability

Nursing Diagnoses

- Altered thought processes
- Anxiety
- Self-care deficit
- Impaired home maintenance management
- Impaired verbal communication
- Ineffective family coping
- High risk for violence directed at others
- Altered family processes

Therapeutic Nursing Management

- Restructure the environment to minimize excessive sensory stimulation.
- Provide orientation cues in the surrounding area: clocks, calendars, photographs, memorabilia, seasonal decorations, and familiar objects.
- Windows are a great way to enhance the client's orientation to time. Lighting may help to decrease the "sundowning effect" and reduce hallucinations.
- Ensure safety in the physical environment.
- Minimize any sensory impairment by providing eyeglasses or hearing assistive devices as needed.
- Allow clients to care for self as much as possible.
- Administer antipsychotic or antibiotic agents as ordered.

Client Outcomes

The client will:

- Experience a decreased level of anxiety
- Experience improved orientation
- Not harm self or others

- Maintain self-care needs
- Improve verbal communication (within client's ability)
- Participate in appropriate social activities

Client and Family Education

- Discuss with the client and family the possible environmental or situational causes, contributing factors, and triggers.
- Help the client and family to identify the internal and external indicators of delirium.
- Educate the client and family about the following issues. Teach:
  - Reality orientation
  - Coping skills
  - Family coping skills and stress management
  - Self-care needs
  - Medication therapy
  - Nutrition
  - Monitoring of symptoms
  - Respite care/relief for caregiver(s)

Critical Thinking Exercise: Delirium

Situation: E.L. is a client admitted to a medical unit of an acute care facility because of pneumonia. She lives alone and is 80 years old. Due to her illness and limited mobility, she has not taken in an adequate amount of food or fluid. When you enter her room, you notice that E.L. cannot follow your questions. She rambles and speaks incoherently. You ask her today's date and her response is July, when it is December.

When E.L.'s daughter and son come to visit, they express concern about their mother. The daughter says, "Mom is seeing things in the room. We thought she had pneumonia. Our mother has always been a clear thinker. What is wrong with her?"

1. What can you tell the family about E.L.'s symptoms?

2. How does delirium differ from dementia?

3. Based on the symptoms and probable etiologic factor, what is the prognosis for E.L.'s psychological status?

Cognitive Disorders: Dementia

Key Points

- Dementia is a condition marked by a gradual deterioration of cognitive function, language, personality, and memory.
- Typical dementias are those of Alzheimer's, HIV, Parkinson's, Huntington's, and Pick's disease.
- The goals of collaborative management include:
  - Determining the cause of the dementia
  - Ensuring that all activities of daily living (ADL) and nutritional needs are met
  - Adhering to medication treatment
  - Providing assessment and treatment for physical problems and illnesses
  - Ensuring safety with no harm to self or others
  - Providing a safe environment: home, hospital, and long-term care
- **Key Terms/Concepts**: Visuospatial, aphasia, wandering, apraxia, agnosia

Overview

Dementia is a syndrome of acquired, persistent intellectual impairment with compromised function in multiple spheres of mental activity, such as, memory, language, visuospatial, emotion, personality, and cognition. Dementia may also occur with many other medical illnesses, such as pulmonary, hepatic, cardiopulmonary, and nutritional, as well as substance-induced.

Types of Dementia

Dementia of the Alzheimer's type: Insidious and progressive deterioration in function due to neurotransmitter deficiency

Vascular dementia: Due to significant cerebrovascular disease, caused by multiple infarcts in the cortex

Dementia due to HIV: Related to brain infections with a range of symptoms from acute delirium to profound dementia

Dementia due to head trauma: Intellectual and memory difficulties due to post-trauma

Dementia due to Parkinson's disease: Caused by a loss of nerve cells and a decrease in dopamine activity

Dementia due to Huntington's disease: Damage from this disease occurs in the areas of the basal ganglia and cerebral cortex. A profound state of dementia and ataxia occurs within five to ten years of onset

Dementia due to Pick's disease: Atrophy in the frontal and temporal lobes of the brain

Dementia due to general medical diseases:
- Endocrine disorders
- Pulmonary disease
- Hepatic or renal failure
- Cardiopulmonary insufficiency
- Fluid and electrolyte imbalances
- Nutritional deficiencies
- Frontal/temporal lobe lesions
- Central nervous system (CNS) or systemic infections

Substance-induced dementia: Dementia related to the persistent use of:
- Alcohol
- Inhalants
- Sedatives, hypnotics, and anxiolytics
- Medications, such as anticonvulsants
- Toxins such as lead, mercury, carbon monoxide, insecticides, and industrial solvents

Signs and Symptoms in the Early Phase
- Impairment of abstract thinking, judgment, and impulse control
- Disregard for rules of social conduct
- Neglect of personal appearance and hygiene
- Altered language pattern
- Personality change

Symptoms in the Progressive Phase
- Aphasia
- Irritability and moodiness with sudden outbursts over trivial issues
- Inability to care for personal needs
- Wandering away from home
- Incontinence
- Impaired remote memory

Nursing Diagnoses
- Altered thought processes
- Anxiety
- Self-care deficit
- Impaired home maintenance management
- Impaired verbal communication
- Ineffective family coping
- High risk for violence directed at others
- Altered family processes

Therapeutic Nursing Management

Environment: The nurse plays a primary role in providing a safe environment that is free of excess stimulation. Cognitive changes often include a period of confusion and forgetfulness. Maintaining a structured and consistent environment with routine patterns helps to reduce the level of anxiety and confusion for the client. The nurse may encourage family members to bring photographs or familiar items as strategy to orient the client.

Psychological treatment: May focus more on the family to offer support during this stressful time. Individual and group therapy are not helpful with the client. Cognitive changes affect the family and its daily activities. Cognitive decline often means a change in the family roles. Therapy helps the family verbalize feelings of frustrations when the client becomes cognitively impaired. Support of the family member who is the caregiver is important.

Psychopharmacologic treatment: Medications are used that treat the specific causes of a cognitive disorder. Pharmacologic therapy is implemented to reduce or alleviate anxiety or psychotic symptoms. Calcium channel blockers may be used with clients who have Alzheimer's. The elderly usually require lower doses and may have idiosyncratic responses to medications.

Client Outcomes

The client will:

- Demonstrate behaviors consistent with a decreased level of anxiety
- Experience improved orientation
- Not harm self or others
- Maintain self-care needs
- Improve verbal communication within client's ability
- Participate in appropriate social activities

Client and Family Education

- Discuss with the client and family the possible environmental or situational causes, contributing factors, and triggers.
- Help the client and family to identify the internal and external indicators of dementia.
- Educate the client and family about the following issues. Teach:
  - Reality orientation
  - Coping skills
  - Family coping skills and stress management
  - Self-care needs
  - Medication therapy
  - Nutrition
  - Monitoring of symptoms
  - Respite care/relief for caregiver(s)

Critical Thinking Exercise: Dementia

Situation: B.C. is an elderly male diagnosed with dementia five years ago. He lives with his wife, who is also an elderly person. B.C.'s wife is concerned about his behavior and deteriorating mental status, and is finding it increasingly difficult to care for him at home. He wanders out of the house, is disoriented to time and place, and is unable to dress and groom himself. B.C.'s primary care provider encourages placement in a nursing home, but his wife resists. The primary care provider then arranges for a home health nurse to visit B.C. and his wife.

1. Identify the pertinent client and caregiver information requiring nursing intervention.

2. What instructions regarding B.C.'s safety should be given to his wife?

Cognitive Disorders: Alzheimer's Disease

Key Points

- Alzheimer's disease is the most prevalent form of dementia and is characterized by memory loss, deficits in thought processes, and behavioral changes.
- Onset is insidious and course of disease progresses through four stages:
  - **Stage I:** Forgetfulness
  - **Stage II:** Confusion
  - **Stage III:** Ambulatory dementia
  - **Stage IV:** End stage
- The goals of collaborative management include:
  - Ensuring that all ADL and nutritional needs are met
  - Adhering to medication treatment
  - Providing assessment and treatment for physical problems
  - Ensuring safety with no harm to self or others
  - Arranging for a safe environment: home, hospital, and long-term care
- **Key Terms/Concepts:** Alzheimer's disease, attention span, cognitive deficits, sundowning, spatial orientation

Overview

Alzheimer's disease is the most prevalent form of dementia characterized by memory loss, deficits in thought processes, and behavioral changes. The onset is insidious and course of disease progressive. Physiologic studies indicate pathologic degeneration of cholinergic neurons and biochemical deficiencies in the neurotransmitter system.

Risk Factors

- Advanced age: One in twenty-six at age 65, two out of five after age 85
- Female
- Head trauma
- Family history of Alzheimer's and/or trisomyal (Down's syndrome)

Signs and Symptoms

Memory disturbance is the classic sign:

Stage I: Lasts 1-3 years

- Short-term memory loss
- Decreased attention span

- Subtle personality changes
- Mild cognitive deficits
- Difficulty with depth perception

Stage II: Lasts 2-10 years

- Obvious memory loss
- Confusion
- Wandering behavior
- Sundowning: Behavior changes as sun goes down; grows more confused
- Irritability and agitation
- Poor spatial orientation
- Impaired motor skills
- Impaired judgment
- Covers up memory loss through confabulation
- Symptoms intensify when stressed, fatigued, or removed from familiar environment
- Depression related to awareness of reduced capacities

Stage III: Lasts 5-15 years

- Increasing loss of expressive language
- Loss of ability to care for self in activities of daily living (ADLs)
- Becomes more withdrawn
- Loss of reasoning ability

Stage IV: Lasts 8-10+ years

- Absent cognitive abilities
- Disoriented to time and place
- Absent communication skills
- Impaired or absent motor skills
- Bowel and bladder incontinence
- Does not recognize family members, or self in mirror

Nursing Diagnoses

- Altered thought processes
- Anxiety
- Self-care deficit
- Impaired home maintenance management
- Impaired verbal communication
- Ineffective family coping
- High risk for violence directed at others
- Altered family processes

Therapeutic Nursing Management

- The client in the later stages of the disease will probably require long-term, protective care and assistance with ADLs and other activities.
- Families or caregivers also require support during this time.

Complications

- Injury to self, related to wandering
- Injury to others, related to aggression
- Medical problems
- Complete dependence on others

Client Outcomes

The client will:

- Experience a decreased level of anxiety
- Experience improved orientation
- Not harm self or others
- Maintain self-care needs
- Improve verbal communication within client's ability
- Participate in appropriate social activities

Client and Family Education

- Education for client is more appropriate in earlier stages while client can understand information. Focus is on families and caregivers, especially during later stages.

Critical Thinking Exercise: Alzheimer's Disease

Situation: J.L. is a 72-year-old male with Stage II Alzheimer's disease. He lives with his wife. During a routine clinic visit, J.L.'s wife verbalizes concern about her husband's violent, angry behavior and irritability. She tells the primary care provider that her husband often tells her that something is "crawling on the wall" when in reality there is nothing there. He wanders out of the house, is disoriented to time and place, and is unable to dress and groom himself. The client's wife is having difficulty caring for him at home. The primary care provider encourages placement in a nursing home, but J.L.'s wife refuses. The primary care provider then arranges for a home health nurse to visit J.L. and his wife.

1. Identify the pertinent information requiring nursing intervention.

2. Identify appropriate nursing diagnoses that pertain to the case study.

3. Prioritize the nursing interventions based on the information acquired above:

_____ Provide safety, keeping harmful objects away from the client.

_____ Orient client to time and place using posters and signs.

_____ Assess the client's abilities to dress himself.

_____ Provide structure to the daily routine.

_____ Schedule rest periods throughout the day.

_____ Provide the caregiver with relief by using local support groups and government agencies.

_____ Keep environmental stimuli to a minimum.

Dissociative Disorders: Fugue and Amnesia

Key Points

- A dissociative fugue (flight) involves sudden travel away from home with confusion about one's identity.
- Dissociative amnesia is the inability to recall an extensive amount of personal information: often triggered by physical or psychological trauma.
- Memory loss is the defining characteristic, often precipitated by a traumatic event.
- Most clients recover.
- Types of fugue or amnesia are local, selective, general, continuous, or systematic.
- The goals of collaborative management include:
    - Determining the cause of the disorder
    - Ensuring that all ADL and nutritional needs are met
    - Assessing for injuries/trauma
    - Ensuring safety with no harm to self or others
    - Providing support to decrease anxiety and stress
    - Helping the client reorient
- **Key Terms/Concepts**: Amnesia, dissociative, fugue, stress, anxiety

Overview

A fugue is a rare type of dissociative disorder that involves sudden travel away from home. The client has confusion about his/her identity and may adopt a new one. The client with dissociative fugue has memory loss about many aspects of the past, often precipitated by a traumatic event, such as war, conflicts, natural disaster, or criminal behavior. It is not the result of an organic disorder. Recovery can be rapid, spontaneous, and complete.

Risk Factors

Psychodynamic theory: Behavioral theory and biological theory offer the same explanations as dissociative amnesia.

Theory of family dynamics: Unsatisfactory parent/child relationship, with subsequent internalization of an inner loss has been associated with dissociative fugue. Also unfulfilled separation anxiety, defects in personality development, and unmet dependency needs are thought to contribute to this disorder.

Transactional model of stress/adaptation: Etiology is due to multiple factors.

Traumatic event: war, severe conflicts, criminal behavior, natural disasters, or any significant loss. Child abuse may trigger a dissociative episode. Event precipitates the fugue, or flight.

Signs and Symptoms

- Types of Dissociative Amnesia
    - Local amnesia—The inability to recall the incidents associated with a traumatic event for a specific period following the event
    - Selective amnesia—The inability to recall certain incidents associated with a traumatic event for a specific period of time
    - General amnesia—The inability to recall anything that has happened to the client during the client's life, including personal identity
    - Continuous amnesia—The inability to recall events from a specific time through the present
    - Systematized amnesia—The client cannot remember events that relate to a specific category of information such as to one's family, or to one particular person or event
- Anxiety
- Relocation to a geographic area, and inability to recall personal identity (dissociative fugue only)

Assessment

- History and physical examination
- Family history, or look for clues as to the client's identity
- Mental status examination
- Psychological testing
- Psychiatric assessment and history
- CT and MRI scans to rule out other pathology of brain

Nursing Diagnoses

- Anxiety
- Impaired social interaction
- Ineffective individual coping
- Impaired adjustment
- Self-esteem disturbance
- Personal identity disturbance
- Hopelessness
- Impaired memory
- Altered role performance
- Altered family processes

Therapeutic Nursing Management

Psychological treatment

- Individual therapy may be useful in providing psychosocial support and understanding of the illness process as well as a therapeutic plan. Insurance plan or managed care may limit the length of treatment.

- Hypnotherapy may be used to enhance client's memory.
- Psychopharmacologic treatment.
- Administer anxiolytic agents for symptoms; however, there is no specific medication to treat a dissociative fugue.

Nursing interventions

- Supportive care, as required until memory returns.
- Assist client in coping with stress and periods of severe anxiety via intervention.
- Teach the client about anxiety and use of interventions, such as stress management relaxation and other methods used to decrease anxiety.
- Family support without pressure to remember, if available.
- Nutritional support.

Client Outcomes

The client will:

- Experience decreased anxiety
- Use stress management methods
- Identify medications and relevant information about their use
- Recall information about self and life
- Adhere to treatment
- Participate in treatment planning

Client and Family Education

- Discuss with client and family the possible environmental or situational causes, contributing factors, and triggers.
- Help the client and family to identify the internal and external indicators of dissociative disorders.
- Educate the client and family about the following issues. Teach:
  - Coping skills
  - Monitoring of symptoms
  - Self-care
  - Anxiety reduction strategies
  - Medication therapy

Critical Thinking Exercise: Fugue and Amnesia

Situation: M.L. is admitted to the surgical unit following a fall from a building. He is alert but is unable to remember his name. His wife comes to visit him and he does not recognize her. M.L. becomes agitated and yells out, "I can't remember who I am. What is going on?" At the time of his discharge from the surgical unit three days later, he is still unable to remember anything about himself or his accident. His family takes him home, but he is reluctant to go with them because he perceives them as strangers.

1. What type of amnesia does M.L. have?

2. What can be done to assist M.L.?

3. Identify three nursing diagnoses that might be applied to M.L.

Eating Disorders

| Key Points |

- Anorexia is an eating disorder that is characterized by voluntary refusal to eat. Alterations in body weight occur as a result of the consumption of fewer calories than needed for metabolic needs.
- Bulimia is characterized by recurrent episodes of eating volumes of food, which may be followed by self-induced vomiting, laxative or diuretic abuse, or excessive exercise.
- Obesity is the consumption of more calories than needed for metabolic needs.
- Clients may require extensive physical assessment, intervention, and reassessment.
- The three major types of eating disorders are anorexia, bulimia nervosa, and obesity (with and without binge eating).
- Eating disorders are predominately found in females.
- Family interaction patterns that are identified in persons with eating disorders are enmeshment, rigidity, overprotectiveness, and lack of conflict resolution.
- The goals of collaborative management include:
  - Providing a safe environment: hospital and home
  - Ensuring adequate intake of nutrition
  - Setting limits as required for client's safety and well-being
  - Increasing client's self-esteem, communication, and appropriate expression of feelings
  - Providing medical care for all physical problems
  - Adhering to medication treatment
  - Educating client and family about eating disorders and treatment
- **Key Terms/Concepts:** Anorexia nervosa, bulimia nervosa, amenorrhea, hypokalemia, hypothermia, binging, purging

Overview

Disordered eating patterns occur in persons who fluctuate between food restriction and episodes of excessive caloric or fat intake. Clients with eating disorders hide their problem.

Specific Types of Eating Disorders

Anorexia nervosa: The morbid fear of obesity, characterized by a refusal to maintain a minimally normal body weight in the absence of a physical cause. The condition occurs most often in the adolescent and young adult.

Bulimia nervosa: An episodic, uncontrollable, compulsive, rapid ingestion of large quantities of food over a short period of time (binging), followed by inappropriate compensatory behaviors to rid the body of the excess calories such as self-induced vomiting (purging), misuse of laxatives, diuretics, or enemas. Most bulimics maintain a weight within a normal range.

Obesity: An eating disorder in which the client consumes a large amount of food but does not attempt to prevent weight gain. Some obese clients binge and others do not.

Risk Factors

- Gender: Predominately females
- Age: Most common from 12-30, although obesity occurs at any age
- Family genetics: More commonly seen in families with sisters and mothers with eating disorders
- Biological: Hypothalamic, neurotransmitter, hormonal, or biochemical imbalance
- Interpersonal relationships: Influenced by parental pressure and the need to succeed
- Distorted body image
- Psychological influences: Rigidity, ritualism, separation and individuation conflicts; feelings of ineffectiveness, helplessness, and depression
- Environmental factors: Pressure from society to have the "perfect body," culture of abundance
- Family eating patterns
- Dysfunctional family with controlling parent(s)
- Female athletes, particularly at elite level of a sport

Theories Regarding Influences on the Development of Eating Disorders

Biological influences: Genetics, hereditary predisposition is likely. Anorexia is more common among mothers/daughters and sisters, and those with neuroendocrine abnormalities.

Psychodynamic influences: It is suggested that in rare instances, eating disorders result from very early and profound disturbances in mother/infant interactions.

Family influences:

- Conflict avoidance may be used by families, which promote and maintain psychosomatic symptoms and avoid their true conflicts.
- Families may also use power and control to override elements of conflict.
- Parental criticism can lead to an increase in obsessive and perfectionistic behavior on the part of the client, who continues to seek love, approval, and recognition.
- Ambivalence toward the parents develops, and distorted eating patterns may represent a rebellion against the parents, which is a way to gain control.
- Some theorize that a father's lack of connection to his daughter may be a contributing factor.

Social influences: Social influences are powerful and difficult to resolve. The covert message displayed in the media and society is the importance of having a "perfect body," or the "perfect image."

- Athletics: A sport may require a very thin body, which is achieved through unhealthy eating patterns.

Special Biological Factors

- Neurotransmitter dysregulation, particularly serotonin, may be related to the occurrence of an eating disorder. High levels of serotonin may affect anorexia; low levels are related to bulimia.

- Endorphin levels may also be associated with the occurrence of eating disorders. Low levels may lead to decreased food intake and depressed moods.

- Excessive levels of the brain hormone vasopressin are associated with eating disorders and other obsessive-compulsive behaviors.

Signs and Symptoms

- Distortion in body image
- Marked weight loss (may be more than 20% of expected weight), weight gain, or fluctuating weight
- Electrolyte imbalance
- Abdominal distention
- Refusal to eat
- Obsession with food (e.g., talks about recipes and food)
- Depression and anxiety, insomnia
- Perfectionism and obsessive thoughts
- Abuse of laxatives, diet pills, diuretics, and steroids, but also may have constipation
- Vomiting following food intake (bulimia nervosa)
- Nutritional intake limited to low-calorie foods; may consume as little as 500 calories per day (anorexia)
- Exercise to excess (particularly in anorexia)
- Extreme motivation to please others. Anorexics typically are over-achievers.
- Secretive fasting and binging after eating high-calorie foods (particularly bulimia). Caloric intake may be as much as 20,000 calories per day.
- Anorexics may engage in starvation as a mechanism of control for other factors in life.
- Manipulative social behavior
- Lanugo (fine body hair), hypotension, hypothermia (particularly with anorexia)
- Symptoms of medical problems
- Suicidal ideation
- Psychotic symptoms
- Self-mutilation
- Substance abuse

- Brittle, dry hair and nails; gaunt appearance (anorexia)
- Calluses on fingers related to self-induced vomiting (bulimia)
- Tooth decay (bulimia)

Assessment

- **History and physical examination**: Baseline weight and height to determine the extent of weight gain or loss and to rule out underlying pathology. May need family's help to determine extent of gain/loss. Questions to ask may include:
  - Do you think about food often throughout the day?
  - Do you have regret after eating?
  - Do you use laxatives, diuretics, or diet pills to control your weight?
  - Do you vomit after eating certain foods?
  - Do you eat uncontrollably?
  - Do you feel hungry most of the time?
  - Do you feel anxious when you are unable to exercise?
  - Are your menstrual periods regular?
- **Mental status examination**: Identification of inappropriate coping and abnormal eating patterns
- **Nutritional assessment** to assess eating habits and caloric intake
- **Social history**: Interaction and relationships in family
- **Family history**: Assess influences and cultural patterns of eating behaviors.
- **Routine height and weight comparisons**

Nursing Diagnoses

- Anxiety
- Alteration in nutrition: Less than body requirements, or more than body requirements
- Body image disturbance
- Alteration in thought process
- Impaired social interaction
- Risk of harm to self
- Powerlessness
- Self-esteem deficit
- Ineffective individual coping

Therapeutic Nursing Management

Environment

- Safety and structure within the environment are important for the client with an eating disorder.
- Hospitalization is often required for the client whose weight loss poses an

imminent threat to the physical function of the individual. Client protection may be required in the form of one-to-one supervision particularly around meal times and to prevent the client from vomiting and/or using exercise to diminish weight.

Psychological treatment

- Individual therapy may be used to improve client's self-esteem, coping mechanisms, and resources for problem solving. Insurance factors may impact the availability, extent, and duration of the treatment.
- Behavior modification: Inpatient treatment programs are used to shape the desired behavior into daily living. Privileges are given on the basis of weight gain or loss and adherence to the mutually-established plan for care.

Social treatment

- Group therapy: Support groups are important in assisting the client to recognize his/her own patterns of fasting, binging, eating, or exercise.
- Family therapy: The family is a vital link in assisting this client with treatment. The target of family therapy is to improve the effectiveness of communication and enhance the understanding of the impact of interpersonal relationships within the family. Problem-solving techniques and strategies for conflict resolution are addressed.

Psychopharmacology

- There is no specific medication available to treat eating disorders, although antidepressants and anti-anxiety medications (e.g., clomipramine [Anafranil], and fluoxetine hydrochloride [Prozac]), have been used with success.
- Appetite stimulants/depressants, as indicated
- Stool softeners/bulking agents for constipation

Nursing interventions

- Priority intervention is to correct nutritional and electrolyte imbalance, which can result in death.
- The client is secretive and manipulative in attempting to control weight. The nurse's role is to obtain an accurate health history, including dietary patterns.
- Eating patterns are elicited and goals are mutually developed with the client. Behavioral contracts are used to assist the client in maintaining an appropriate weight. Supervision is required. Dietitian is consulted to develop the appropriate diet.
- One-to-one supervision may be necessary if client does not adhere to the plan or has a high risk for suicide. Supervision for designated amount of time after eating helps to ensure that the client does not purge. Plan for meals needs to consider the diet, amount of time client will have to eat, how staff will respond to client during meals, follow-up after meals, and how staff will respond if client does not complete meal requirement. All staff must follow this plan consistently.
- Suicidal assessment
- The client with anorexia nervosa may engage in "water loading" (excessive drinking of water) prior to weighing to conceal weight loss. For an accurate weight, the nurse must prevent this activity.

- Weigh the client at the same time each day with same amount of clothing. Avoid telling client current weight.
- Staff needs to maintain close communication and provide consistent care.
- Perform a thorough physical assessment; clients with anorexia nervosa can develop acute life-threatening complications.
- Enteral nutrition (tube feeding) is used only in life-threatening situations. The decision to use these interventions must be made carefully with interdisciplinary consultation that includes the family and the client.
- Work with client to adopt a realistic view of his/her body and to improve self-esteem.
- Assist the client in increasing health coping mechanisms and stress tolerance.

Complications

- Dehydration
- Electrolyte imbalance (particularly note hypokalemia)
- Seizures
- Constipation
- Amenorrhea
- Loss of enamel on the teeth
- Irritation or scarring of the esophagus from self-induced vomiting
- Cardiac dysrhythmias
- Hypotension
- Hypothermia
- Renal dysfunction
- Death
- Emaciation

Client Outcomes

The client will:

- Maintain weight in safe range
- Adhere to treatment (medication, individual, family, and group therapies)
- Exercise appropriately
- Demonstrate improved family interactions and communication
- Verbalize less fears, cognitive distortions, and decreased need to please others
- Experience decreased anxiety
- Exhibit improved physical status
- Participate in treatment planning

Client and Family Education

- Discuss with the client and family the possible environmental or situational causes, contributing factors, and triggers for eating disorders.

- Help the client and family identify the internal and external indicators of eating disorders.
- Educate the client and family about the following issues:
  - Coping skills
  - Problem solving
  - Body image
  - Communication skills
  - Monitoring of symptoms
  - Medication adherence
  - Supporting adherence to treatment
  - Decreasing anxiety
  - Nutrition and exercise
  - Use of support group
  - Individual and family therapies

Age-Related Changes—Gerontological Considerations

- The elderly and especially elderly men are prone. Triggers include personal losses that impinge on identity, retirement, loss of spouse or a child leaving home.

Critical Thinking Exercise: Eating Disorders

Situation: K.T. has been admitted to the inpatient psychiatric unit. She is 16. Her height is 5' 6", and she weighs 75 pounds. This is her first psychiatric hospitalization, but she was admitted last year to the medical unit when she had pneumonia and her weight could not be maintained at home. As you begin the admission assessment, she immediately complains that she is overweight. She asks questions about the calories in the meals and alternate choices. She complains of being tired; however, later you find her exercising in her room with the door shut. You have already told her that the door must remain open. You notice that she has unpacked and neatly arranged all of her clothing and personal items. Her lab work indicates that she has hypokalemia. As you ask about her menstrual cycle, she tells you she has not had her period for one year. Her parents seem over-attentive, but of course, her condition is unstable at this time. You decide to explore more about their relationship later, after K.T. has settled in more on the unit. You do notice that the parents are thin, but not unhealthy in appearance. K.T. has no siblings. She has been unable to attend school in the last two weeks due to her weakness, although she is an excellent student. She expresses concern about getting behind in her schoolwork. You reassure her that a teacher is available who will help her maintain her studies, and this seems to relieve some of her anxiety.

1. What further data do you need to determine if K.T. has anorexia nervosa or bulimia? Describe the difference between the two conditions. What is the similarity?

2. When you conduct further assessment of the family, what factors might have predisposed K.T. to an eating disorder?

3. What type of behavior would you expect from K.T. regarding food use on the unit?

4. Identify three complications that K.T. might experience that require monitoring. Identify one she now has.

5. Describe the interventions that might be considered for mealtimes.

6. What is the significance of K.T. wanting to know how many calories are in each of the items on her tray?

Personality Disorders

Key Points

- Personality disorders concern maladaptive personalities in which there is an enduring pattern of perceiving, relating to, and thinking about the environment and oneself.
- Personality disorders are chronic disorders, marked by deviations in cognition, affect, impulse control, and interpersonal functioning.
- Types of personality disorders include:
  - Paranoid personality
  - Borderline personality
  - Antisocial personality
  - Schizoid personality
  - Dependent personality
  - Compulsive personality
  - Passive-aggressive personality
- The goals of collaborative management include:
  - Ensuring that client does not harm self or others
  - Development of self-esteem and communication of needs and feelings
  - Self-monitoring of symptoms and need to seek help when necessary
  - Development of problem-solving skills
  - Assisting client to identify triggers of maladaptive behaviors
  - Educating client and family about personality disorders and treatment
- **Key Terms/Concepts**: Personality, manipulation, self-mutilation, splitting

Overview

Personality is defined as the totality of a person's unique biopsychosocial and spiritual traits that consistently influence behavior. When an individual's personality and functioning are maladaptive and deviate markedly from the culture, the designation of a personality disorder is assigned. This is a disease process in which the pattern of perceiving, relating to, and thinking about the environment and oneself are exhibited in a wide range of social and personal contexts. The following traits are likely in individuals with a personality disorder: 1) interpersonal relations that range from distant to overprotective, 2) suspiciousness, 3) social anxiety, 4) failure to conform to social norms, 5) self-destructive behaviors, and 6) manipulation and splitting of staff. Prognosis is poor, clients experience long-term disability and may have other psychiatric disorders.

Common Types of Personality Disorders

Paranoid personality disorder: Represents a pattern of behavior arising from pervasive distrust and suspiciousness of others. These suspicious motives are interpreted as malevolent. Clients are hypervigilant and prepare for any real or imagined threat. Clients can be insensitive to the feelings of others.

Borderline personality disorder: Characterized by behavior that is impulsive and manipulative. Includes a combination of almost all of the perceptual, cognitive, affective, and behavioral disturbances present in other personality disorders. Clients are irritable, sad, and self-centered. Self-mutilation for attention-seeking reasons is sometimes present.

Antisocial personality disorder: Previously termed sociopathic or psychopathic, is most frequently found in criminals and highly manipulative persons. Clients have few boundaries and do not respect others.

Schizoid personality disorder: Characterized by a profound deficit in the ability to form personal relationships or respond to others in a meaningful way. Clients may appear indifferent, aloof, and/or unresponsive to praise or criticism. They typically have no close friends and prefer to be alone.

Dependent personality disorder: Marked by a pattern of relying on others excessively for emotional support, advice, and reassurance. This disorder more commonly occurs in the youngest child of a family with older children. Clients have a notable lack of self-confidence and avoid positions of responsibility. They are easily hurt by criticism or disapproval.

Compulsive personality disorder: Characterized by inflexibility about the way things must be done with a devotion to productivity to the exclusion of personal pleasure. Organization and efficiency are matters of concern. On the surface, the client typically appears to be calm and controlled, while underneath this exterior there is a great deal of conflict and anxiety.

Passive-aggressive personality disorder: Marked by a pervasive pattern of negative attitudes and passive resistance to demands for adequate performance in social and occupational situations. Clients passively resist demand by authority with behaviors such as dawdling, procrastination, or "forgetting." Clients often do not express their anger, and instead, express it through resistant or negativistic behavior.

Risk Factors

Family genetics: Genetic links are implicated in the disorder.

Altered personality development: Alterations in the deeply rooted personality traits that are largely unconscious.

Environmental factors: Personality disorders have been linked to childhood experiences or early family dysfunction. The child may develop maladaptive patterns to meet their needs. Maladaptive patterns become a deeply ingrained part of the personality and continue into adulthood.

Altered social interaction patterns: Social interactions may modify feelings of self-esteem or ideas of worth.

Personality characteristics: Tendencies toward aloofness that make social settings and interactions difficult, clients tend to avoid social gatherings.

Psychological influences: Influences from a combination of events may lead to dysfunction.

Signs and Symptoms

- Inappropriate response to stress and inflexible approach to problem solving
- Long-term difficulties in relating to others, in school and in work situations
- Demanding and manipulative
- Ability to cause others to react with extreme annoyance or irritability
- Poor interpersonal skills
- Anxiety
- Depression
- Anger and aggression
- Difficulty with adherence to treatment
- Harm to self or others (suicidal ideation, self-mutilation, violence toward others, or threats)
- Egocentric
- Overwhelming fears of abandonment
- Pessimistic, immature, lonely, impulsive, hostile, and suspicious

Assessment

- **History and physical examination**: Baseline assessment to rule out any physical abnormalities
- **Family assessment**: Family patterns of behavior or childhood experiences are assessed for patterns associated with dysfunction.
- **Mental status examination**: Provides information about current mental functioning
- **Psychological tests**: Specified by the psychiatrist after completion of the baseline assessment
- **Legal history**: May have a legal history of breaking the law, aggression, or violent behavior
- Suicidal ideation and violence toward others

Nursing Diagnoses

- Ineffective individual coping
- Social isolation
- Impaired social interaction
- High risk for violence to self or others
- Anxiety
- Fear of abandonment
- Depression
- Cognitive disturbance

Therapeutic Nursing Management

Environment: When safety is a concern, the client may require hospitalization. Physical restraints, seclusion/observation room, or one-to-one supervision may be necessary if imminent threat of harm to self or others is an issue. The nurse must remember to use the least restrictive environment or measure to meet the needs of the client. Always document the necessity for a more restrictive environment or measure.

Psychological treatment

- **Individual therapy** is used to assess anger and help client learn to express feelings. Insurance is a major factor in the length of treatment.
- **Behavior therapy** focuses on helping the client to develop appropriate responses to stressful situations. This may reduce the frequency of self-destructive behavior, length or frequency of hospitalization, and help the client to meet important clinical goals for improved quality of life.
- **Group therapy** provides feedback from others in a controlled, safe environment. It may be difficult for the client due to his/her illness to continue treatment. Insurance factors may impact the duration and extent of treatment.
- **Psychopharmacological treatment**: There is no specific medication for personality disorders; however, symptoms of anxiety or depression may be treated with related medications, and in some cases, antipsychotic medication may be used.

Nursing interventions

- Work with client to increase coping skills and identify need for improved coping.
- Respond to client's specific symptoms and needs.
- Keep communication clear and consistent.
- Client may require physical restraints, seclusion/observation room, or one-to-one supervision. Follow policies and procedures.
- Keep client involved in treatment planning.
- Behavior contract may be used for anger and aggression, suicidal ideation, manipulation, or isolation.
- Do not become victim to the client's maladaptive behavior.
- Limit-setting is important for interactions with a client who is manipulative or acts out.
- Encourage the client's involvement in appropriate self-help groups.
- Require that the client take responsibility for his/her own behavior and the consequences for actions.

Client Outcomes

The client will:

- Exhibit a decrease in anxiety and/or depression
- Exhibit a decrease in suicidal ideation or violence
- Eliminate self-mutilation
- Verbalize loss of control

- Experience improved coping and problem solving
- Experience improved social interaction
- Experience improved appropriate communication

Client and Family Education

- Discuss with the client and family the possible environmental or situational causes, contributing factors, and triggers.
- Help the client and family to identify the internal and external indicators of personality disorders.
- Educate the client and family about the following issues:
  - Coping skills
  - Anger management
  - Stress management
  - Problem solving
  - Medication adherence

Age-Related Changes—Gerontological Considerations

- Family and friends must know how to relate to the client. This may cause increasing concerns as the years progress and family members are no longer present or become tired of the required interpersonal support. With normal aging, many elderly persons tend to engage in this type of behavior more often.
- Older clients may feel that no further therapy is needed, especially if it has become difficult to access health care due to transportation or other health needs.

Critical Thinking Exercise: Personality Disorders

Situation: You have been told that you must meet with the parents of R.H., who has recently been diagnosed with a personality disorder. You arrange for an appointment with the parents, who tell you they are very concerned and confused about their son's diagnosis and treatment.

1. Describe five traits that are frequently found in persons with personality disorders. These traits may be helpful as you talk with the parents about their son's behavior.

2. The parents want to know how long will it take to cure their son. How do you respond to this?

Personality Disorders: Borderline Personality Disorder

Key Points

- Borderline personality disorder includes almost all of the perceptual, cognitive, affective, and behavioral disturbances present in personality disorders.
- Anxiety and maladaptive coping behaviors, particularly manipulation, regression, and splitting are important in this disorder.
- Clients with this disorder experience major problems with unstable relationships.
- The goals of collaborative management include:
  - Ensuring that client does not harm self or others, including self-mutilation
  - Development of self-esteem and communication of needs and feelings
  - Setting limits on inappropriate behavior and avoiding power struggles
  - Development of problem-solving skills
- Treatment is aimed at reducing the presenting symptoms.
- Intensive psychotherapy may be necessary to change behavioral, affective, or cognitive function.
- **Key Terms/Concepts**: Manipulation, splitting, regression, self-mutilation, impulsivity, projection, identification

Overview

An individual with a borderline personality disorder exhibits a combination of almost all of the perceptual, cognitive, affective, and behavioral disturbances present in other personality disorders. A diminished tolerance for anxiety and maladaptive coping behaviors is exhibited. This disorder is characterized by a pervasive pattern of unstable interpersonal relationships, self-image, and affects, as well as marked impulsivity beginning by early adulthood. These clients are most easily identified by their intensity or instability of affect or behavior.

Risk Factors

- Intensity or instability of affect or behavior
- Genetic predisposition
- Dysfunctional family life

Signs and Symptoms

- Chronic depression
- Inability to tolerate being alone
- Clinging, distracting, and erratic behaviors
- Splitting

- Manipulation
- Mistrust, blaming
- Difficult interpersonal relationships
- Self-destructive and self-mutilation behaviors
- Impulsivity and exaggerated mood swings
- Rage reactions
- Substance abuse
- Inappropriate sexual behavior
- Frequent hospitalizations
- Common violent outbursts
- Overwhelming fear of abandonment
- Low self-esteem, self-pity, and apathy

Assessment

- History and physical examination: Baseline assessment to rule out any physical abnormalities
- Family assessment: Family patterns of behavior or childhood experiences are assessed for dysfunctional patterns.
- Mental status examination: Provides information about current mental functioning
- Psychological tests: Specified by the psychiatrist after completion of the baseline assessment
- Legal history: May have a legal history of breaking the law, aggression, or violent behavior
- Suicidal ideation and violence toward others

Nursing Diagnoses

- Ineffective individual coping
- Social isolation
- Impaired social interaction
- High risk for violence to self or others
- Anxiety
- Fear of abandonment
- Depression

Therapeutic Nursing Management

- Protect the client from self-mutilation and suicide.
- Setting limits is the most effective method for dealing with manipulation. Manipulation and passive aggression are primary traits displayed by the client with borderline personality disorder. Assist the client in the development of personality by confronting the client's issues and feelings.

- Avoid power struggles with the client by having clearly defined, consistent treatment approaches with clear communication among all caring for the client. The client's divisive actions are used to split staff, particularly over discrepancies in the treatment plan and implementation.
- Help the client identify his/her own use of projection, splitting, manipulation, regression, and inappropriate response to rejection with anger.
- Hospitalization may be required to keep client safe; however, long hospitalization often leads to further regression for the client with borderline personality disorder.
- Staff usually perceives that the client is demanding and judgmental in interpersonal relationships, which can lead to difficult nurse-client rapport.

Client Outcomes

The client will:

- Experience reduced anxiety and decreased impulsivity
- Not harm self or others
- Improve communication and interpersonal relationships
- Improve problem solving and use of appropriate coping mechanisms
- Not report fear of abandonment

Client and Family Education

- Discuss with the client and family the possible environmental or situational causes, contributing factors, and triggers for borderline personality disorder.
- Help the client and family to identify the internal and external indicators of borderline personality disorder.
- Educate the client and family about the following issues:
  - Coping skills
  - Anger management
  - Stress management
  - Problem solving
  - Medication adherence
- Home safety

Critical Thinking Exercise: Borderline Personality Disorder

Situation: S.T. has been admitted to the hospital four times within one year. She is 29 years old. Typically, she is admitted after threatening suicide and has been found to burn herself with cigarettes. On the unit, she has complimented one staff member and told that nurse that she is the best nurse and all other staff is awful. This nurse has defended S.T. during team meetings. Other staff members are now angry with this nurse. During group meetings, S.T. has convinced other clients that the staff is incompetent.

1. Describe the data that indicate S.T. may have a borderline personality disorder.

2. What risks are involved in caring for S.T.?

3. What is your initial impression for S.T.'s effect on the staff and the unit as a whole?

Personality Disorders: Paranoid Personality Disorder

Key Points

- Delusions of grandeur or persecution are often present.
- Paranoia develops slowly.
- The goals of collaborative management include:
  - Ensuring that client does not harm self or others
  - Avoiding affirming delusions while recognizing client's feelings
  - Adhering to medication treatment
  - Developing problem-solving skills
  - Educating client and family about paranoid personality disorder and treatment
- **Key Terms/Concepts:** Delusion, grandeur, persecution

Overview

This disorder is characterized by extreme suspiciousness and distrust of others to the degree that the client blames others for his/her own mistakes and failures. The client goes to abnormal lengths to validate prejudices, attitudes, or biases. Delusions of grandeur or persecution are often centered on one major theme, such as a financial matter, job situation, spouse, or other problem. The paranoia may develop slowly and progressively over years until it is an intricate, logical, highly organized delusion that is believable.

Signs and Symptoms

- Hypersensitivity
- Rigidity and stubbornness
- Hostility and envy
- Exaggerated self-importance
- Extreme argumentativeness
- Lack of sentimental or tender feelings
- Grandiose attitudes and unrealistic expectations
- Blaming others
- Suspiciousness and distrust
- Inability to reach out to or connect with others

Nursing Diagnoses

- Ineffective individual coping
- Social isolation
- Impaired social interaction
- High risk for violence to self or others
- Anxiety
- Fear of abandonment
- Depression

Therapeutic Nursing Management

Psychological treatment

- Individual therapy: Helps the client explore problem areas realistically and define options; however, client's mistrust may make it difficult for the client to maintain treatment.
- Behavior therapy: Focus on behavior that manifests underlying problems. Caution is warranted because of the intrusive nature of behavior therapy. Interventions should be directed toward stabilizing the dysfunctional behavior.

Social treatment

- Group therapy: Group members help the client to see how the client's behavior impacts others. Insurance may impact the availability, extent, and duration of treatment.

Psychopharmacologic treatment

- Administer medications (e.g., antianxiety medications, antipsychotics).

Nursing interventions

- Keep communication clear and consistent.
- Do not argue with client about his/her delusions, but try to refocus on reality.
- Client may require physical restraints, seclusion/observation room, or one-to-one supervision for safety of self or others. Follow policies and procedures for treatment. Respect for human rights and personal integrity must be maintained.
- Adherence to treatment may be difficult due to paranoia and delusions.
- Be firm and not overly friendly.

Critical Thinking Exercise: Paranoid Personality Disorder

Situation: J.E. works in a factory, where he has been employed for three years. His supervisor has noticed over the years that he has certain characteristics. He takes criticism poorly and can become overtly angry and hostile. He tells his peers that he knows the best approach to all problems that they encounter during work and refuses to acknowledge a mistake. His peers do not like working with him. His supervisor has decided to watch J.E. more closely as he is concerned about his behavior. In the last month, the supervisor has overheard J.E. making comments such as, "You don't trust me and are out to get me," and "Get out of my face. I am the only one who knows what to do and who will be successful." The supervisor has been called to the work area because a fight has broken out between J.E. and one of the employees.

1. How can the supervisor best intervene at this time?

2. If the supervisor requires that J.E. see a counselor, what data would be important for the counselor to know about? What data might support that he has a paranoid personality disorder?

3. Will it be easy to involve J.E. in treatment? Provide your rationale.

Personality Disorders: Antisocial Personality Disorder

Key Points

- Antisocial persons generally believe the world and people within it are essentially evil. This antagonistic attitude in life drives their malicious behavior.
- Criminals and highly manipulative persons often exhibit antisocial personality disorder.
- Diagnosis usually occurs in late teens to early adulthood due to person's antisocial behavior.
- The goals for collaborative management include:
  - Ensuring that client does not harm self or others
  - Providing a safe environment: hospital and home
  - Development of self-esteem and communication of needs and feelings
  - Setting limits on inappropriate behavior
  - Development of skills for controlling inappropriate behavior
  - Teaching importance and value of following rules and being sensitive to feelings of others
  - Developing problem solving and communication skills
  - Educating client and family about antisocial personality disorder and treatment
- **Key Terms/Concepts**: Exploitation, manipulation, lack of remorse

Overview

Antisocial behavior, previously termed sociopathic or psychopathic, is an aggressive personality type that is most frequently exhibited in criminals and highly manipulative persons. Manifestations of the disorder include hostility toward others, a low tolerance for frustration, inconsistent work or academic performance, and the inability to form lasting relationships with spouse or children. Examples of antisocial behavior typically include stealing, vandalism, school or work problems, substance abuse, fighting with others, and legal problems.

Risk Factors

- Possible genetic influence
- Conduct disorder as a child, evidenced by truancy, shoplifting, or bullying
- Parental deprivation for the first five years of life
- History of physical abuse
- Poverty
- History of parent(s) with alcoholism or antisocial behaviors

Signs and Symptoms

- Exploitation and manipulation of others for personal gain
- Lack of remorse
- Belligerence and argumentativeness
- Failure to conform to social norms
- Impulsiveness and recklessness
- Indifference to the feelings of others
- Lack of regard for rules, regulations, or laws

Nursing Diagnoses

- Ineffective individual coping
- Social isolation
- Impaired social interaction
- High risk for violence to self or others
- Anxiety
- Fear of abandonment
- Depression

Therapeutic Nursing Management

Psychological treatment

- Individual therapy: Focuses on identifying abnormal behavior and helps client to use other coping methods in order to avoid aggression and hostility. Insurance factors may impact the availability, extent, or duration of treatment.
- Behavior therapy: Seeks to help the client delay gratification by setting limits on inappropriate behavior. Provide positive feedback when tasks are completed per guidelines.

Social treatment

- Group therapy: May be used to accomplish same goals as individual therapy.

Psychopharmacological treatment

- Administer antianxiety, antidepressant, or antipsychotic medication.

Nursing interventions

- Demonstrate the use of stress management, problem solving, and new coping methods.
- Set consistent limits on client's inappropriate behavior.
- Protect others from client's inappropriate behavior.
- Be aware of client's ability to manipulate others.

Client Outcomes

The client will:

- Exhibit a decrease in anxiety and/or depression
- Exhibit a decrease in suicidal ideation or violence
- Verbalize loss of control
- Experience improved coping and problem solving
- Experience improved social interaction
- Experience improved appropriate communication

Client and Family Education

- Teach the value of rules and sensitivity to other people's feelings.
- Bring to conscious awareness the effect of their aggressive or harmful behavior on others.

Critical Thinking Exercise: Antisocial Personality Disorder

Situation: A 20-year-old male, T.J., has no history of mental illness. As a child, he was abandoned by his mother and physically abused by his father. He currently lives with an older sister, but spends most of his time with gang members. He has developed a pattern of altercations with the law, reckless driving, carrying concealed weapons, forging signatures on checks, and theft from neighborhood homes. Recently, he has been involved in more fights. T.J. is presently unemployed and depends on his sister and friends for money. His sister makes excuses for his behavior, stating he had a "rocky start in life."

Recently, T.J. was arrested for theft. During the arrest, he became aggressive and assaulted one of the police officers. Due to his extreme rage, he was taken to the psychiatric hospital for evaluation. He refused to be admitted, and the psychiatrist petitioned for an involuntary admission. The admitting diagnoses are mood disorder and antisocial personality disorder.

1. Based on available assessment information, identify the immediate nursing actions.

2. Write an expected outcome for each of the following nursing diagnoses:

   a. Risk for violence to self and others related to aggressive behavior and rage, as evidenced by a history of aggression and association with gang members.

      Expected Outcome:

   b. Ineffective individual coping related to irresponsible behavior as evidenced by illegal actions and sister making excuses for his behavior.

      Expected Outcome:

Personality Disorders: Obsessive-Compulsive Disorder

Key Points

- Anxiety is a major factor in the development of obsessive-compulsive disorder (OCD).
- OCD is a serious mental illness.
- Types of behavior include:
  - Obsessions
  - Ruminations
  - Cognitive rituals
  - Compulsive motor rituals
- The goals of collaborative management include:
  - Protection of the client if OCD behavior is harmful to health
  - Adherence to medication treatment
  - Development of self-esteem and communication of needs and feelings
  - Self-monitoring of symptoms and ability to seek help when needed
  - Educating client and family about obsessive-compulsive disorder
- **Key Terms/Concepts**: Obsession, compulsion, ritualistic behavior, anxiety

Overview

Obsessive-compulsive disorder (OCD) is characterized by persistent thoughts and urges to perform repeated acts or rituals, usually as a means of releasing tension or anxiety. The frequency and intensity of the ritualistic behaviors, such as hand washing, ordering, or checking, are time consuming and cause marked distress, significant impairment, or interfere with daily living. The client realizes that these thoughts and actions are excessive or unreasonable. Preoccupation and ritualistic behavior are commonly related to the following:

- Hair pulling (trichotillomania)
- Food
- Physical appearance
- Clean and tidy environment
- Illicit substances
- Sexual urges or fantasies
- Guilt feelings
- Germs and personal hygiene
- Personal safety

Obsessions and compulsions need NOT both be present for the diagnosis to be made.

Obsession and Compulsion DSM IV Diagnostic Criteria

Obsession:

- The person experiences recurrent and persistent thoughts, impulses, images that are intrusive, disturbing, inappropriate, and are usually triggered by anxiety.
- The thoughts, images, and impulses are not simply excessive worries about real-life problems.
- The person attempts to ignore or suppress the thoughts, images, and impulses and neutralize them with other thoughts or actions.
- The person recognizes the thoughts, images, and impulses are from within his/her own mind.

Compulsion:

- Repetitive behaviors or mental acts that a person feels driven to perform, which usually adhere to a rigid and specifically defined routine.
- The behaviors and ideations are typically aimed at reducing anxiety or preventing some dreaded situation from occurring. However, they may not be connected in a realistic way to the source of stress.

Risk Factors

- Anxiety
- Biochemical factors
- Family history of OCD

Specific Biological Factors

- There is some evidence that indicates OCD is linked to a deficiency in serotonin.
- Clients have also been shown to have abnormalities in frontal lobes and basal ganglia; however, it is unclear what the implications are for clinical care.

Signs and Symptoms

Obsessions: Recurrent, persistent ideas, thoughts, images, or impulses that involuntarily come to awareness.

Ruminations: Forced preoccupation with thoughts about a particular topic, associated with brooding, doubting, and inconclusive speculation.

Cognitive rituals (compulsion): Elaborate series of mental acts the client feels compelled to complete; termination of the action depends on proper performance.

Compulsive motor rituals: Elaborate rituals of everyday functions such as grooming, dressing, eating, washing, cleaning, counting, or checking (doors, appliances).

Compulsive avoidances: Substitute actions performed instead of appropriate behavior that induces anxiety.

Other symptoms: Chronic anxiety, low self-esteem, difficulty expressing positive feelings, depressed mood, judgmental attitude toward self and others, focus on details, rigid and perfectionist traits, tendency to be very productive, and suicidal thoughts.

Nursing Diagnoses

- Anxiety
- Powerlessness
- Ineffective individual coping
- Impaired verbal communication
- Self-esteem disturbance
- Impaired social interaction
- Risk for injury
- Sleep pattern disturbance
- Ineffective breathing pattern
- Alteration in nutrition
- Alteration in bowel and/or urinary elimination
- Knowledge deficit
- Social isolation

Therapeutic Nursing Management

Psychopharmacological treatment

- Administer medications, such as selective serotonin reuptake inhibitors (SSRIs), or antianxiety medications, such as sertraline (Zoloft).

Psychological treatment

- Individual therapy assists the client in maintaining anxiety at a manageable level without having to resort to ritualistic behavior.
- Cognitive behavioral therapy helps the client understand OCD, its symptoms, and how to deal with obsessive thoughts and compulsive actions. One approach is *Thought stopping*. Thought stopping is a gradual challenging of irrational behaviors, systematic desensitization to decrease reaction to stressful triggers, tracking and monitoring of thoughts, feelings, and actions.
- Group therapy involves the use of a group setting to model adaptive methods of coping with anxiety.

Nursing interventions

- Limit, but do not interrupt, the compulsive acts. Client may experience panic if he/she cannot complete acts. Negotiate with the client for a time to perform ritual, possibly after grooming or eating.
- Teach client to use alternate coping methods to decrease anxiety.
- Client's behavior can be frustrating to staff and family. Power struggles often result. Be clear on goals and outcomes. Consistency in the approach to care is critical.
- Nutrition, sleep, activities of daily living, and exercise need to be maintained at appropriate levels.
- Assess client's physical needs carefully, as problems may develop, related to compulsive acts (e.g., compulsive washing of hands, which may lead to skin problems).

- Provide an environment that has structure and predictability as a strategy to decrease anxiety.

Client Outcomes

The client will:

- Experience less need to use compulsive acts or obsessions
- Experience decreased anxiety and depression (if the latter is a problem)
- Increase self-care activities
- Report less frequent, less intense obsessions and compulsions

Client and Family Education

- Discuss with the client and family the possible environmental or situational causes, contributing factors, and triggers for obsessive-compulsive behavior.
- Help the client and family to identify the internal and external indicators of obsessive-compulsive disorder.
- Educate the client and family about the following issues:
    - Coping skills
    - Monitoring of symptoms
    - Stress management
    - Medication adherence
    - Risks associated with the use of alcohol and drug abuse

Critical Thinking Exercise: Obsessive-Compulsive Disorder

Situation: L.G. is married and has three children. She has always been a very neat and organized person. After the birth of her third child, she wanted to go back to work; however, she could not find adequate childcare, mostly due to her demands of the caretaker. Her husband began to notice that she was more and more concerned about cleaning the house. She developed an elaborate schedule and procedures, which she had to follow. Eventually, the schedule and procedures became so important that if she was interrupted she had to begin all over again. This began to consume more of her time, and she was less able to care for her children. Her husband would come home from work in the evening and find L.G. cleaning while the children were dirty, running wild throughout the house, having not been fed lunch. The husband took L.G. to their family primary care provider.

1. What is happening to L.G.?

2. What is the significance of anxiety to L.G.'s problems?

3. What factors may have predisposed L.G. to a phobic response?

4. Describe the impact of biochemical factors on the anxiety L.G. is experiencing.

5. How can you best intervene to assist L.G.?

Behavioral Disorders: Child or Adolescent with Attention-Deficit/Hyperactivity Disorder (ADHD)

Key Points

- Attention-deficit hyperactivity disorder (ADHD) is a syndrome with a developmentally inappropriate, persistent pattern of behavior that includes inattention, impulsivity, distractibility, and hyperkinetic motor activity (hyperactivity).
- It is found in children, typically beginning before age seven.
- The symptoms lead to problems in school and in social interactions with peers and family.
- Low self-esteem is common. Other mental disorders may result, such as depression and oppositional defiant disorder.
- The goals of collaborative management include:
  - Providing assessment to identify the needs of the child
  - Ensuring safety with no harm to the child and others
  - Fostering an environment where the child can develop positively to his/her maximum potential
  - Adhering to medication treatment; adjusting medication regimen as needed
  - Implementing supportive therapy
  - Providing education and support to family and teachers
- **Key Terms/Concepts:** Hyperactivity, hyperkinetic activity, attention deficit, impulsivity, distractibility, constructive feedback

Overview

Attention-deficit hyperactivity disorder (ADHD) is a syndrome referring to a developmentally inappropriate, persistent pattern of behavior that includes inattention, impulsivity, distractibility, and hyperkinetic motor activity. The symptoms of ADHD typically appear before age seven, cannot be accounted for by another learning or mental disorder, and have persisted for at least six months. The condition occurs more often in boys. Boys typically exhibit more behavioral problems, while girls demonstrate poor academic performance. Children with ADHD often have average or above-average intelligence. Every aspect of the child's life is affected. Socially, they have difficulty forming and maintaining relationships. In school, their inattention (and perhaps hyperactivity) prevents them from learning and being successful in the structured environment. The repeated maladaptive behavior leads to negative reactions from others, and the development of low self-esteem in the child.

Risk Factors

- Family Genetics: ADHD is more prevalent in first cousins of children with ADHD. Many studies report familial tendencies.
- Biochemical Factors: Studies for the markings of biochemical factors on ADHD implicate a deficit of dopamine, norepinephrine and serotonin as well as decreased glucose metabolism in the brain.
- Environmental Influences: Structured environments with appropriate limits can be comforting and instructive to the child. Consistent patterns of discipline are likely to result in improved self-control, which leads to feelings of self-worth.

Signs and Symptoms

- **Inattention**: An inability to focus for periods of time and ready distractibility
  - Fails to pay close attention to details
  - Frequent, careless mistakes in schoolwork or other activities
  - Often does not listen when spoken to directly
  - Loses things necessary to complete tasks or activities
  - Easily distracted by extraneous detail
  - Forgetful
  - Avoids activities that require concentration
  - Poor handwriting
- **Hyperactivity and impulsivity**: Excessive or exaggerated motor movements with an inability to control impulses or delay gratification
  - Fidgets and squirms
  - Excessive talking
  - Inappropriate or exaggerated motor movement
  - Difficulty remaining seated or quiet
  - Interrupts and intrudes on others
  - Difficulty waiting
  - Often blurts out answers inappropriately
- **Impaired social interactions**: Children with ADHD are often labeled as "bad" by other children, parents, and teachers. They may have trouble relating to peers or making friends.
  - Child often engages in dangerous activities with little to no consideration of the consequences
  - Anxiety
  - Depression
  - Difficulty in school and/or with the law
  - Impaired verbal communication
  - Lack of academic success; poor academic progress

Assessment

History and physical examination: To establish a baseline and rule out biological factors of a disease process that may be influencing behavior

Mental status examination: Concentration, feelings of self worth

Family: Familial tendencies or personality disorder

Social history: Assesses the behavioral structure of the environment that may affect the child's behaviors

Cognitive assessment: Provides data regarding the cognitive level of the client for formulation of an appropriate learning plan

Psychological testing: Identifies needs and treatments that may be beneficial based on the psychosocioemotional development of the child, which may also rule out learning disabilities

Academic history: May reveal poor progress

Data from teachers and other sources: May indicate inattention, impulsivity, distractibility, hyperactivity, aggression, and level of frustration

Nursing Diagnoses

- Anxiety
- Self-esteem disturbance
- High risk for violence, self-directed or directed at others
- Impaired verbal communication
- Altered family processes
- Impaired interaction with others
- Caregiver role strain
- Social isolation
- Academic difficulties

Therapeutic Nursing Management

Psychological treatment

- The goal of group therapy is to provide support and learning experiences through socially appropriate and structured activities.

Social treatment

- Family education therapy assists family members in learning to cope with the demand of ADHD. Information and instruction about the importance of clarity, structure, consistent discipline, and other aspects of treatment is provided to the family.
- Social skills training is behavior therapy that uses positive reinforcement for goal attainment.

Academic modification

- A kinesthetic learning approach should be integrated into the classroom experience.
- Child/teen should sit in front of classroom to decrease distractions.
- The child will need to have opportunities to release energy.

Psychopharmacologic treatment

- Psychostimulants may be used for the treatment of symptoms of attention disorders. The nurse providing care to the client with ADHD should monitor the appetite, weight, and height, as this information is important for correct dosing of medication. Evaluate the effectiveness of medication. Specific medications that might be ordered include:
  - Psychostimulants (Ritalin, Adderall, Dexedrine, Concerta) improve attention and focus while decreasing hyperactivity and impulsivity. Side effects include: nervousness, unstable mood, insomnia, and slowed physical growth.
  - Clonidine decreases impulsivity and hyperactivity.
  - Antidepressants (Wellbutrin, Effexor) improve mood and decrease impulsivity.

Nursing Interventions

- Behavioral contracts may be used to help the child gain control and use appropriate behavior.
- Consistent, clear communication is one of the most important aspects of care for the child with ADHD.
- Encourage the child to openly discuss feelings and behavior. Listen.
- Provide constructive feedback. Avoid false reassurance. Children are perceptive and know when praise is not authentic.
- Assist the child to learn new, more effective ways to cope and relate to others.
- Teach parents to create a structured home environment with limit-setting and consequences to inappropriate behavior.
- Encourage the family to seek the support of family, friends, or support groups.
- Methylphenidate (Ritalin) should never be given to a child with a tic disorder.

Complications

- Injury to self or others due to overactive and impulsive behavior
- Exhaustion from increased activity and trying to focus on tasks
- Inability to fulfill role responsibilities, especially in school
- Alteration in social interactions, related to impulsive and aggressive behaviors which may interfere with or annoy peers
- Low self-esteem related to poor interpersonal relations, difficulties at home and school, and a negative response from others
- Anorexia, related to medication side effect
- Risk of physical abuse, related to inability of caregiver to cope with child's behavior
- Diminished physical growth, related to medication

Client Outcomes

The client will:

- Exhibit a decrease in anxiety
- Experience improvement in social interactions
- Experience improvement in academic performance
- Experience improvement in self-esteem

Client and Family Education

- Discuss with the client and family the possible environmental or situational causes, contributing factors, and triggers for ADHD.
- Help the client and family to identify the internal and external indicators of ADHD.
- Educate the client and family about the following issues:
  - Coping skills
  - Problem solving
  - Stress management
  - Discipline
  - Communication
  - Medication adherence
  - Support groups for parents and child/teen
  - Academic assistance and modifications

Age-Related Considerations—Children

- ADHD is a disorder that affects all aspects of life throughout the lifespan. Even without treatment, hyperactive behavior tends to diminish by the time the client reaches the teen years or early twenties. However, it is noted that many children with ADHD have more social and emotional problems that persist into adulthood. Health care providers need to gather assessment data to develop an appropriate therapeutic plan to maximize the child's level of functioning within the family, school, community, and society at large.
- Positive feedback is very important throughout the lifespan. Constant social support is needed in childhood and adulthood as well. Studies have shown that hyperactivity is associated with poor social relationships as the child with ADHD ages.
- Since the child's self-image and esteem are greatly influenced by academic performance, involvement and a personal relationship with teachers is essential. Academic support may be provided through tutors at home or school. Parents should participate in "504" meetings at school to recommend or approve academic modifications.

Critical Thinking Exercise: Child or Adolescent with Attention–Deficit/Hyperactivity Disorder

Situation: You are a school nurse in an elementary school. You receive a call from a mother who wants to come in and talk with you about her son who is seven years old. When you meet with the mother, she tells you that her son has been put on Ritalin for attention-deficit hyperactivity disorder. The mother is concerned about her son's behavior in school and at home. Her primary care provider has given her little information about this type of behavioral disorder or the medication that has been prescribed for her son. You tell her that there are other children in the school with this problem and that you will help her gain some understanding.

1. What symptoms would you expect this mother to describe?

2. How would you describe the purpose of Ritalin to the mother?

3. Why would you suggest that the mother use behavioral contracts with her son?

Behavioral Disorders:
Anger with Aggressive and Violent Behavior

> **Key Points**
>
> - Anger is an emotional response which can be expressed in healthy or dysfunctional ways.
> - Psychotherapy, behavioral modification, and pharmacotherapy may be used for treatment of aggression or violent behavior.
> - A conduct disorder is a repetitive and persistent pattern of behavior whereby a person violates the basic rights of others.
> - The goals of collaborative management include:
>   - Ensuring safety with no harm to self or others
>   - Adhering to medication treatment and other forms of treatment
>   - Providing assessment of other possible psychiatric disorders
> - **Key Terms/Concepts**: Anger, aggression, behavioral modification, operant conditioning, behavioral contract, biofeedback, triggers and stimuli, de-escalate

Overview

Anger is an emotional response, which can be expressed assertively in a positive manner to solve problems and make decisions. Alternatively, a client's response to a situation may be expressed by aggression, a behavior that is intended to threaten or injure the victim's security or self-esteem. It may be displayed by impulsive acts, such as fighting with damaging words or weapons. The defining characteristic of dysfunctional anger or aggressive behavior is the intentionality of damage or personal injury.

Risk Factors

Role-modeling: Primary caretakers are the earliest role models for anger management or mismanagement.

Operant conditioning: This is the act of positive or negative reinforcement of a behavior. A positive reinforcement is a response to a specific behavior that is pleasurable or produces a desired response. A negative reinforcement is a response to a specific behavior that prevents an undesirable result from occurring.

Socioeconomic factors: Aggressive behavior is found more often in persons living in conditions of poverty. The influence of financial stress, deprivation, unemployment, substandard housing, crowding, excessive noise, and other factors often contribute to violence.

Environmental factors: Factors that are associated with aggressive behaviors include physical crowding of people, discomfort associated with elevated environmental temperature, use of alcohol or drugs, and the availability of weapons with aggression used as a coping method.

Biological factors: Chemical imbalances and neurophysiological conditions play a role in perception, cognition, and mood.

Past history of violent behavior

Diagnoses of mental health disorders: Persons with a history of substance abuse dependency, paranoia, psychosis, schizophrenia, post-traumatic stress disorder (PTSD), or organic brain disorder may be more prone to aggressive and escalating behaviors.

Specific Biological Factors

- **Neurophysiological disorders**: Several disorders within the brain are implicated in episodic aggression and violent behavior, including temporal lobe epilepsy, brain tumors, brain trauma, encephalitis, end-stage AIDS and mild to severe mental retardation.

- **Biochemical factors**: Aggressive behaviors may be associated with certain biochemicals, such as hormonal dysfunction associated with hyperthyroidism or alterations in the neurotransmitters (epinephrine, norepinephrine, dopamine, acetylcholine, and serotonin).

Signs and Symptoms

- Intense distress
- Pacing
- Clenched fists
- Change in tone of voice and/or body posturing
- Threatening behavior
- Suicidal or homicidal ideation or threats
- Self-mutilation
- Substance abuse
- Paranoia
- Carrying a weapon

Assessment

- **History and physical examination**: The history and physical assessment aid in establishing the severity of the condition. Organic brain disease and temporal lobe disorders are common findings for clients with a pattern of aggressive or violent behavior.

- **Mental status examination**: Aggression is commonly seen in individuals with schizophrenia and post-traumatic stress disorder.

- **Family and social history**: A person's response to stress, disorganization, threat, or deficit is learned from the modeled behavior of family and friends.

- **Psychological and emotional testing**: Reveals a person's inclination toward aggression

- **Laboratory data**: Urine testing for drugs

Nursing Diagnoses

- Anxiety
- Impaired verbal communication
- Impaired social interaction
- Social isolation
- Altered family responses
- Ineffective individual coping
- Self-esteem disturbance
- Personal identity disturbance
- Powerlessness
- Altered thought processes
- Risk for violence directed at self or others
- Self-mutilation

Therapeutic Nursing Management

- Psychopharmacologic treatment
- Pharmacologic agents: There is no specific medication for anger control; however, some medications are effective to assist with management of symptoms (e.g., mood stabilizers, antipsychotic medications).

Nursing Interventions

- **Behavioral contracts** may be helpful by outlining the expectation and strategies to control aggression and prevent escalation of the behavior.
- **Behavior modification** and biofeedback focuses on biological responses to anger.
- The client may require **physical restraints** or a seclusion/observation room; however, these interventions should be implemented only after other less restrictive interventions have been tried without success. Adhere to the policies and procedures of the institution for safety, client rights, respect, and privacy.
- **Decreasing stimuli** may assist client in controlling anger.
- Assist the client in identifying the **triggers** for his/her anger. Work out a plan to monitor and intervene with coping methods (e.g., relaxation, seeking someone to speak with, and removing self from situation).
- Use appropriate **physical activities** as an outlet for anger control (e.g., exercise, sports, music, or other hobbies).
- Discuss with the client the differences between appropriate and inappropriate anger and responses to anger.
- Use **consistent interventions**.
- Manage the situations with a positive approach. Tell the client what he/she can do rather than what the client cannot do.
- Provide **appropriate choices** for the client, providing some control for the client.

- Avoid threatening **body language**, verbal language, touching the client, standing in the doorway, or isolating self with an angry client.
- **De-escalate** client with a calm voice. Avoid arguing and give client some choice.
- When two or more clients have conflict with one another, the first intervention is to separate them.
- **Document incidents** in an objective manner, stating factual information only.
- **Alert security** personnel if an episode occurs that poses actual or potential harm to self or others.
- Family and friends may be unwilling to assist the client due to fear of the client's behavior. Discuss this with client at an appropriate time. Client will need to understand how his/her behavior affects others.

Complications

- Violence to self or others
- Alterations in role responsibilities
- Impaired social interactions
- Problems with the law
- Lack of family support

Client Outcomes

The client will:

- Display less inappropriate anger and control aggression
- Experience decreased anxiety
- Self-monitor escalation and use coping methods to prevent escalation or ask for help
- Use appropriate coping mechanisms
- Increase appropriate communication with family, significant others, and in social, school, and/or work situations
- Adhere to treatment plan
- Participate in treatment planning

Client and Family Education

- Discuss with the client and family the possible environmental or situational causes, contributing factors, and triggers for anger and aggressive behavior.
- Help the client and family to identify the internal and external indicators of aggressive behavior.
- Educate the client and family about the following issues:
  - Self-monitoring of anger and escalation
  - Problem solving
  - Coping methods
  - Stress management

- Communication skills
- Medication therapy
- Differentiation between appropriate and inappropriate anger and response to anger

Critical Thinking Exercise: Anger with Aggressive and Violent Behavior

Situation: You are working on the evening shift. The psychiatric unit has been fairly calm, but you do notice that two clients seem to be irritating each other. One of them, E.M., has a history of aggressive behavior and has a diagnosis of paranoid schizophrenia. The other client was admitted for a suicide attempt and will be discharged within two days. E.M. was admitted 12 hours ago. You do not know him. You recognize that both clients are having problems managing their anger. During team meeting, the staff members discuss interventions that need to be taken.

1. How might the anger that is felt by these two clients differ?

2. What will the client who will be discharged in two days need to know about self-monitoring his anger?

3. What needs to be done to assist the new admission, E.M., with his anger?

Substance Abuse Disorders

Key Points

- There are two major types of substance abuse: substance use disorders and substance-induced disorders.
- Dependence and tolerance are major factors in substance abuse.
- Substance withdrawal can lead to major medical problems.
- The goals of collaborative management include:
    - Maintaining abstinence from drugs/alcohol
    - Ensuring safety with no harm to self or others
    - Adhering to medication treatment that might be used to maintain abstinence or to treat withdrawal symptoms
    - Assessing for physical problems
    - Developing coping, problem-solving, and communication skills
    - Adhering to supportive treatment, such as Alcoholics Anonymous (AA), Narcotics Anonymous (NA)
    - Educating client and family about substance abuse and treatment
- **Key Terms/Concepts**: Abuse, dependency, physical dependence, psychological dependence, tolerance, withdrawal, blood alcohol level and levels for other substances, AA, NA, abstinence

Overview

Substance abuse is the use of chemicals or materials for non-medical purposes with the intention of producing an altered state of consciousness, sensorium, heightened sensory perception, or change in self-image. It is manifested by repeated use of the substance and/or cognitive, behavioral, and physiological symptoms of intoxication, withdrawal, anxiety, and delirium. Substance abuse and substance dependence are related to the use of alcohol, CNS depressants, CNS stimulants, opioids, hallucinogens, and cannabinoids.

Types

Substance use disorders

- Abuse
- Dependency

Substance-induced disorders

- Intoxication and withdrawal
- Delirium and dementia

- Amnesia and psychosis
- Mood and anxiety disorders
- Sexual dysfunction and sleep disorders

Substance Use Disorder Criteria

- Recurrent substance use resulting in the failure to fulfill role responsibilities
- Recurrent substance use in situations that are physically dangerous
- Recurrent substance use that produces financial or legal problems
- Recurrent substance use that causes or intensifies problems with interpersonal relationships

Substance Dependency/Tolerance

Physical dependence is marked by a need for increasing amounts of the drug to produce the desired effects. A syndrome of withdrawal occurs upon cessation of the drug.

Psychological dependence occurs when a client feels that the substance is needed to maintain an optimal state of well-being, interpersonal relationships, or skill performance.

The **substance-specific syndrome** causes clinically significant distress or impairment in social, occupational, or other important areas of functioning.

Substance Withdrawal Criteria

- The development of specific symptoms is caused by the cessation or reduction of heavy or prolonged substance use.
- The symptoms are not caused by another medical disorder.

Classes of Psychoactive Substances

- Alcohol
- Amphetamine-type stimulants (ATS)
- Caffeine
- Cannabinoids
- Cocaine
- Hydrochloride and crack
- Hallucinogens
- Inhalants
- Nicotine
- Opioids
- Phencyclidine (PCP) and related substances
- Sedatives, hypnotics, and anxiolytics

Risk Factors

Biological factors

- Genetics: Heredity factors play a role, especially in alcohol abuse.
- Biochemical: Alcohol may produce morphine-like substances in the brain leading to alcohol addiction.

Psychological factors

- Developmental influences: May relate to severe ego impairment and disturbances in the sense of self
- Personality factors: Certain personality traits have been suggested to play a part in both the development and maintenance of dependence. They include impulsivity, negative self-concept, weak ego, social conformity issues, and introversion.

Sociocultural factors

- Social learning: Children are more likely to use substances if their parents do so, modeling their behavior. Peer pressure also promotes substance abuse.
- Conditioning: Pleasurable effects from substance use act as a positive reinforcement for their continued use.
- Culture and ethnic influences: Some ethnic groups are more susceptible to substance abuse, due to cultural acceptance.
- Mental illness: Clients with certain mental illnesses (e.g., bipolar disorder, schizophrenia) are vulnerable to substance abuse.

Assessment

- History and physical examination
- CAGE Questionnare
    - The CAGE is a brief, relatively non-confrontational questionnaire for detection of alcoholism.
        - Have you ever felt you should CUT down your drinking?
        - Have people ANNOYED you by criticising your drinking?
        - Have you ever felt bad or GUILTY about your drinking?
        - Have you ever had a drink first thing in the morning to steady your nerves or get rid of a hangover (EYE-opener)?
    - Alcohol dependence is likely if the client gives two or more positive answers.
- Psychiatric assessment and history
- Family history of addiction and mental illness
- Blood alcohol level
- Blood or urine level (UA) for presence of illicit or addictive substances
- Legal history
- Social assessment
- Suicidal ideation

Nursing Diagnoses

- Powerlessness
- Risk to self or others
- Spiritual distress
- Ineffective denial
- Ineffective individual coping
- Altered thought processes
- Anxiety
- Disturbance in self-esteem
- Altered role performance
- Ineffective family coping

Therapeutic Nursing Management

Environment

- Some clients may seek an inpatient treatment program for substance abuse and dependence. These are highly structured, intensive programs, which are often the most successful methods of treatment. Insurance support may play a role in the availability, type, and duration of treatment.

Psychological treatment

- **Group therapy**: Substance abusers are forced to confront their usage and recognize the serious consequences that their use has on their body systems, family, and friends.
- **Behavioral therapy**: Includes avoidance of the abused substance. Stress management and behavioral modification using positive and negative reinforcement are commonly employed techniques.
- **Counseling**: The goal of counseling or individual therapy is to alleviate or reduce a client's aversive life situation and to assist the client in putting the pieces of his/her life back together. Regression or relapse is a frequent problem because often the underlying problem is not resolved.

Social treatment

- Support group: The goal of this type of social treatment is to decrease co-dependent behavior and reinforce appropriate behavior for the client and family. Clients attend support groups such as Alcoholic Anonymous (AA) or Narcotics Anonymous (NA), and family members may participate in the Al-Anon group. There are other support groups available in many communities. Members of these groups are asked to share their experiences and give support without advice/judgment to other members during times of crisis or relapse.

Psychopharmacologic treatment: Many approaches to substance abuse treatment do not recommend the use of any drugs, even if prescribed. There are times, however, when they are prescribed.

- Benzodiazepine agents to manage withdrawal symptoms
- Multivitamins, folic acid, thiamine, and narcotic antagonist agents

- Narcan for acute narcotic depression
- Disulfiram (Antabuse) is used to discourage impulsive alcohol use. Clients will become very ill when ingesting substances containing any alcohol, including cough syrup, fruitcake, even cooking wine.
- If the symptoms of narcotic withdrawal are severe, methadone hydrochloride (Dolophine) is used to achieve narcotic abstinence. Treatment is usually 10-40 mg in a single daily dose. Restricted use of methadone during pregnancy and lactation is a key consideration.
- Anxiolytic agents, such as chlordiazepoxide (Librium), are the drugs of choice for alcohol withdrawal.
- Anticonvulsant drugs, particularly phenytoin (Dilantin), or phenobarbital (Luminal) are given for alcohol and sedative-hypnotic drug withdrawal seizures.

Therapeutic Nursing Interventions

- Conduct a comprehensive health history with physical assessment.
- Monitor vital signs during the withdrawal period. For example, in the client with alcohol withdrawal, monitor blood pressure every two hours for first 12 hours, then every four hours for the next 24 hours, followed by every six hours unless it is unstable. Early signs of withdrawal are anxiety, anorexia, tremors, and insomnia and may begin within eight hours after last intake of alcohol.
- Protect the client from injury.
- Assess for seizures and hallucinations. Approach client calmly, using soft voice, keep lights dim, and allow a family member or friend stay with the client. Reduce environmental stimulation and noise.
- Assist the client with learning new problem-solving methods.
- Educate the client about stress reduction techniques and alternative coping mechanisms.
- Encourage client to participate in support groups, such as AA or NA.
- Determine the need for occupational or vocational therapy and consult with collaborative team members as needed.
- Assess client's nutritional status and intervene with appropriate diet.

Complications

- Overdose
- Risk to self and others
- Withdrawal symptoms
- Impairment in decision-making
- Peripheral neuropathy
- Korsakoff's psychosis
- Alcoholic cardiomyopathy
- Esophagitis
- Gastritis
- Pancreatitis

- Alcoholic hepatitis
- Cirrhosis of liver
- Criminal behavior to finance the substance(s) abused

Client Outcomes

The client will:

- Not experience complications of withdrawal
- Improve level of problem solving and communication
- Recognize destructive behavior and inadequate coping
- Seek support when needed
- Remain sober
- Avoid situations and people who tend to increase risk of substance abuse
- Identify triggers to relapse
- Adhere to treatment and support groups (AA, NA)
- Participate in treatment planning

Client and Family Education

- Discuss with the client and family the possible environmental or situational causes, contributing factors, and triggers for substance abuse.
- Help the client and family to identify the internal and external indicators of substance abuse.
- Educate the client and family about the following issues:
  - Coping skills
  - Problem solving
  - Substance abuse triggers
  - Seeking help
  - Relapse
  - Family support and coping
  - Support groups (AA, NA)
  - Reality orientation
  - Nutrition
  - Vocational and occupational support

Age-Related Changes—Gerontological Considerations

- In the elderly, there is a greater risk for substance abuse related to altered mentation and increased usage of over-the-counter medications and prescription drugs. Loneliness in elderly people is another factor. Substance abuse is frequently overlooked in this age group.

Gender-Related Factors

- Women possess greater sensitivity, have greater likelihood of becoming addicted and develop related health problems sooner than men.

- 70% of women in alcohol treatment come from sexually abusive homes.
- 12% of men in alcohol treatment come from sexually abusive homes.

Critical Thinking Exercise: Substance Abuse Disorders

Situation: You are the nurse admitting a new client to the mental health unit of your facility. Your assessment reveals a client with hand tremors, diaphoresis, and agitation. The client reports long-standing relationship problems, depression with thoughts of suicide, and mentions concurrent use of alcohol, cocaine, and nicotine.

1. Would you classify this as a substance-use disorder, and/or a substance induced disorder? Why?

2. Provide three examples of therapeutic interaction that you could offer this client to build trust and rapport during the initial stages of the admission process.

3. What discharge needs do you anticipate for this client?

Substance Abuse Disorders: Alcohol Abuse and Dependence

Key Points

- Alcohol abuse and dependency can lead to major physical, psychological, and social/economic problems for the client and the client's family/significant others.
- There is no cure for the disease. When sobriety is achieved, the client is referred to as a recovering alcoholic.
- The goals of collaborative management include:
    - Maintaining sobriety
    - Adhering to treatment plan to ensure sobriety
    - Providing assessment and treatment for physical problems
    - Ensuring safety with no harm to self or others
    - Supporting long-term behavior changes
    - Educating client and family about alcohol abuse, dependence, and treatment
- **Key Terms/Concepts:** Withdrawal, sobriety, Wernicke's encephalopathy, Korsakoff's psychosis, esophagitis, cirrhosis, alcohol myopathy, peripheral neuropathy, detoxification

Overview

Alcohol intoxication typically occurs when the alcohol blood level exceeds 80 mg/dL. Common withdrawal symptoms include elevated vital signs, tremors, increased psychomotor hyperactivity, insomnia, nausea, vomiting, abdominal cramping, seizures, or hallucinations. Physical symptoms occur within four to twelve hours after cessation or reduction in heavy and prolonged abuse. Disulfiram (Antabuse), a drug that causes violent vomiting and hypotension when followed by the ingestion of alcohol, may be administered to discourage a client from returning to alcohol consumption. Naltrexone (ReVia) is also used to reduce craving for alcohol. The client, to cope with stress, often uses alcohol. When sobriety is achieved, the client is referred to as a recovering alcoholic; there is no cure for the disease.

Effects on the Body

Peripheral neuropathy: Neurological condition resulting in pain and decreased sensation in the legs

Alcohol myopathy: Characterized by sudden leg cramps

Wernicke's encephalopathy: Inflammatory, hemorrhagic degenerative condition due to thiamine deficiency. Lesions in the cerebrum cause vision, memory, and coordination changes.

Korsakoff's psychosis: Degeneration in the thalamus due to vitamin B1 (thiamine) deficiency; characterized by short-term memory loss, the inability to learn new skills, falsification of memory, and peripheral neuropathy.

Alcoholic cardiomyopathy: Diminishes the strength and contractility of the heart

Esophagitis, pancreatitis, gastritis, hepatitis, and ascites: Irritation of the lining of the digestive tract from alcohol ingestion

Cirrhosis of the liver: Chronic condition of the liver that interferes with liver function. Elevated ammonia levels cause alteration in mentation

Nutrition deficiencies: Poor intake, decreased vitamins A, D, and K, decreased B vitamins. Anemia due to decreased RBCs, WBCs, and abnormal marrow functioning.

Early Symptoms of Alcohol Withdrawal

Withdrawal symptoms from alcohol may begin as soon as four hours after the last ingestion and may last weeks. Symptoms typically include anxiety, anorexia, tremors, and insomnia. Staff members need to assess clients for symptoms on a regular basis so that appropriate interventions can be made.

Detoxification

- Detoxification is the first step in recovery.
- Medication may be necessary to help ease the withdrawal symptoms associated with certain drug or alcohol use.
- The major objective of detoxification is to safely detoxify the client from mood-altering substances so that treatment can begin.

Treatment for Alcoholism

- Treatment usually consists of both counseling/support and medications that help individuals to stop drinking.
- Medications used to treat alcoholism such as benzodiazepines (Valium or similar drugs) are sometimes used during the first days after drinking stops to help a patient safely withdraw from alcohol. These medications are not used beyond the first few days because they may be very addictive.
- Other medications can help a person remain sober, such as naltrexone. When combined with counseling, naltrexone can reduce the craving for alcohol and help prevent a person from returning to heavy drinking. Disulfiram (Antabuse) also helps to discourage drinking by making the client extremely nauseous and may produce vomiting if the client drinks alcohol.

Critical Thinking Exercise: Alcohol Abuse and Dependence

Situation: A 45-year-old male was admitted to the hospital at 2 a.m. after vomiting a large amount of blood. In the initial interview, the nurse documents the following data:

The client's father died of complications related to alcoholism two years ago. The client's mother, who is still living, has a past history of substance abuse (Valium). The client relates that he had his first drink as a young teenager when he secretly took it from his parents' stock. He has continuously used alcohol since that time. The client smokes three packs of cigarettes a day, and tells the nurse that he would like to quit smoking, however, does not feel that he can.

The client is married with two teenage children. He has had marital problems but is currently living with his wife. They are having financial problems. His work history is varied and he is unable to hold a job for a long period of time. He has difficulty arriving to work on time and has frequent absences, and asks that his wife call in sick for him. He blames his boss and coworkers for his difficulties at work. Yesterday, he was fired from his job and spent the night at the bars drinking. He was drinking when his hematemesis began.

The client states he was diagnosed with an ulcer three months ago and he has been noncompliant with his medications because he is unable to afford them.

1. Identify the predisposing factors that influence the client's behavior.

   a. Genetic influences:

     1.

     2.

   b. Past experiences:

     1.

     2.

     3.

     4.

     5.

   c. Existing conditions:

     1.

     2.

     3.

     4.

2. Identify the expected outcomes for the following nursing diagnoses:

a. Chronic low self-esteem as evidenced by self-destructive nature of alcohol abuse and inability to take responsibility for self.

Expected outcome:

b. Risk for injury as evidenced by central nervous system agitation and withdrawal.

Expected outcome:

Substance Abuse Disorders:
Central Nervous System Depressant Abuse and Dependence

Key Points

- Central nervous system (CNS) depressants create a feeling of relaxation and sleepiness and impair general functioning.
- Abrupt withdrawal is not advised. Detoxification should be supervised.
- Combining barbiturates with alcohol can lead to a profound depressant effect due to cross-tolerance and additive effects when taken together.
- Withdrawal delirium usually occurs within one week of cessation of barbiturate or alcohol. Persons may experience seizures and/or delirium during this period.
- The goals of collaborative management include:
    - Maintaining abstinence from drugs
    - Providing assessment and treatment for physical problems
    - Ensuring safety with no harm to self or others
    - Educating client and family about dependence on CNS depressants and treatment
- **Key Terms/Concepts**: Withdrawal, abstinence, disinhibition, intoxication, withdrawal, delirium

Overview

Central nervous system (CNS) depressants include a variety of sedative, hypnotic, and anxiolytic drugs. Drugs in this category include barbiturates, non-barbiturates, and alcohol. They create a feeling of relaxation and a reduction in levels of anxiety. Consequently, general functioning is impaired. The effects of CNS depressant intoxication range from disinhibition and aggressiveness to coma and death. The duration of withdrawal symptoms depends on the half-life of the ingested drug.

Effects on the Body

Sleeping and dreaming: Clients may experience a deep sleep or "wild" dreams due to alteration in Rapid Eye Movement (REM)/Non-REM cycle description.

Respiratory depression: Respiratory rate and depth decrease.

Cardiovascular effects: Heart rate may slow and cardiac arrest may occur.

Renal function: Renal function may be impaired, allowing toxins to build in the system.

Hepatic effects: Metabolism may be slowed, allowing drug levels to remain high in the system.

Body temperature: Body temperature may be decreased.

Sexual function: Sexual functioning may be impaired (premature ejaculation or impotence).

Gastrointestinal function: Gastric motility is decreased, causing anorexia and constipation.

Neurovascular impairment: Leads to altered judgment and decreased motor coordination.

Amnesic disorder: Impaired short-term memory occurs with heavy ingestion.

Consequences of Overdose

- Central nervous system (CNS) depression
- Respiratory depression
- Coma
- Death

Critical Thinking Exercise:
Central Nervous System Depressant Abuse and Dependence

Situation: P.T. is admitted to the substance abuse treatment program from the emergency department. She is 40 years old and has never received treatment for substance abuse. In her admission assessment she reports that she has been taking barbiturates for three years. Her admission was precipitated when she drank alcohol in large quantities and also took barbiturates.

During the assessment, P.T. says she does not know why she had a "bad reaction" to the drugs this time. She has been having more problems holding a job but needs money to buy drugs.

1. Describe the effects that central nervous system depressants may have on P.T.'s body.

2. How would you respond to P.T.'s comment about her bad reaction?

Substance Abuse Disorders:
Central Nervous System Stimulant Abuse and Dependence

Key Points

- Central nervous system stimulants can lead to a strong psychological dependence.
- Acute intoxication with these drugs can lead to violent, aggressive behavior or psychotic episodes.
- Withdrawal from amphetamines is characterized by dysphoria. Depression and irritability can last for months.
- The goals of collaborative management include:
  - Maintaining abstinence
  - Providing assessment and treatment for physical problems
  - Providing safety with no harm to self or others
  - Involvement in support groups (e.g., CA [Cocaine Anonymous])
  - Educating client and family about dependence on CNS stimulants and treatment
- **Key Terms/Concepts:** Withdrawal, euphoria, psychological dependency, paranoia

Overview

Central nervous system (CNS) stimulants include amphetamines, non-amphetamine stimulants, cocaine, caffeine, and nicotine. These substances are used to reduce fatigue, combat mild depression, and bolster self-confidence. Intoxication produces euphoria, impaired judgment, confusion, and changes in vital signs. Psychological dependence is strong. Acute intoxication can lead to violent, aggressive behavior or psychotic episodes, characterized by paranoia, uncontrollable agitation, and restlessness. Caffeine intoxication occurs with the ingestion in excess of 250 mg; restlessness and insomnia are the most common symptoms. Withdrawal from caffeine may include fatigue, headache, anxiety, nausea, and vomiting. CNS stimulant withdrawal from amphetamines and cocaine may include dysphoria, fatigue, sleep disturbances, and increased appetite. Withdrawal from nicotine may include dysphoria, anxiety, difficulty concentrating, restlessness, and increased appetite.

Effects on the Body

CNS stimulation: Pupillary dilation, chills, and increased body temperature. Hallucinations and delusions occur with cocaine use.

Cardiovascular/pulmonary effects: Heart rate and respiratory rate increase.

Gastrointestinal and renal effects: Symptoms include decreased hunger and increased urination.

Sexual functioning: May be impaired.

Psychological manifestations: Agitation, grandiosity, talkativeness, elation, anxiousness, hypervigilance, combative behavior, impaired judgment, and interference with social and occupational functioning

Nursing Diagnoses

- Alteration in thought process
- Risk to others

Therapeutic Nursing Interventions

- Implement safety measures.
- Obtain vital signs.
- Assess for withdrawal symptoms.
- Assess anxiety level.
- Reduce environmental stimuli.

Critical Thinking Exercise:
Central Nervous System Stimulant Abuse and Dependence

Situation: The same day that P.T. is admitted, another client is admitted three hours later. He is experiencing hallucinations and believes that everyone is out to get him. This client, R.G., is 22. His family gave a history of drug abuse over the last five years with no treatment. R. G. arrives wearing dirty clothes and appears to have lost weight, as his clothes are too big on him. Staff members are told he has been abusing amphetamines and cocaine. He has dropped out of college.

1. You are told to develop a plan for his initial care. What interventions need to be considered initially for R.G.?

2. Identify two nursing diagnoses that apply at this time and the rationale for them.

Substance Abuse Disorders: Opioid Abuse

Key Points

- Dependency on opioids (narcotics) can lead to major medical problems that may result in death.
- Withdrawal is difficult with major medical problems.
- The goals of collaborative management include:
    - Maintaining abstinence
    - Adhering to medication treatment
    - Providing assessment and treatment for physical problems
    - Ensuring safety with no harm to self or others
    - Educating client and family about opioid abuse and treatment
- **Key Terms/Concepts:** Withdrawal, methadone

Overview

Opioids include: opioids of natural origin, opioid derivatives, and synthetic opiate-like drugs. Opiates are used for the analgesic, mood-calming, and sedative effects. Morphine is the best known of this classification. Other opioid derivatives include heroin, codeine, and Dilaudid. Synthetic opioids include meperidine (Demerol) and propoxyphene (Darvon), oxycodone (Percocet), codeine, and hydrocodone (Vicodin). Naloxone (Narcan) is administered intravenously to treat an opioid overdose. Methadone therapy may be used for withdrawal. Tolerance and physical dependence develop rapidly. Withdrawal symptoms may occur within six to 24 hours, peak in one to three days, and decrease in two weeks.

Effects on the Body

Central nervous system (CNS) depression: Dilated pupils, slurred speech, drowsiness, impaired memory, apathy

Gastrointestinal effects: slowed digestion and peristalsis

Cardiovascular effects: Decreased heart rate and respiratory rate

Impaired judgment: Impaired social or occupational functioning

Sexual dysfunction and/or sexually deviant behavior

Withdrawal symptoms: Sweating, vomiting and diarrhea, weakness, tremors, tearing, runny nose, fever, irritability, depression, hallucinations, illusions, grandmal seizures, hypoactivity, and personality changes

Medical complications: HIV, hepatitis, ulcer disease, tuberculosis, anemia, nutritional disorders, heart arrhythmias, and many other serious side effects

Musculoskeletal effects: Dysarthia

Critical Thinking Exercise: Opioid Abuse

Situation: The substance abuse unit team meeting is discussing its treatment program for opioid dependent clients. There are a number of new staff members who need to be oriented to the different types of clients and drugs abused, as well as to the treatment program offered. You have been assigned the job of providing this orientation. You make up a list of critical questions that you think new staff might ask. Then, you prepare for your session by answering them.

1. "What are opioids? It sounds exotic but I have no idea what drugs are included."

2. "How does tolerance develop and what are possible complications?"

3. "Withdrawal is an important topic for us as we are treating clients who are experiencing it. What data are important as the clients are monitored for withdrawal and how long does withdrawal take?"

4. "Are there any medications used to treat opioid dependence?"

Substance Abuse Disorders: Hallucinogen Abuse

Key Points

- Hallucinogens lead to perceptual alterations, depersonalization, and derealization.
- Intoxication and withdrawal can lead to major health problems.
- The goals of collaborative management include:
    - Maintaining abstinence from abused substance
    - Adhering to medication treatment
    - Providing assessment and treatment for physical problems
    - Ensuring safety with no harm to self or others
    - Educating client and family about hallucinogen abuse and treatment
- **Key Terms/Concepts:** Withdrawal, intoxication, perceptual alterations, depersonalization, derealization, grandiosity, synesthesia, flashbacks

Overview

Hallucinogens are mind bender psychedelic drugs that alter perception or consciousness. Hallucinogens include naturally-occurring hallucinogens, such as mescaline and psilocybin. Synthetic compounds include LSD (lysergic acid diethylamide), STP, dimethyltryptamine (DMT), phencyclidine (PCP), and "designer drugs." Symptoms occur within a few hours of taking the drug and may include perceptual alterations, depersonalization, and derealization. Symptoms of PCP intoxication may include belligerence, combativeness, and progression to seizures and coma. Withdrawal symptoms include hallucinations, nausea, and vomiting. Persisting perception disorder (flashbacks) are recurrences of hallucinations when the drug is not being used, which may occur at unpredictable times and for years following cessation of the drug. Not all clients taking hallucinogens actually hallucinate, there are a number of additional problems resulting from usage.

Effects on the Body

Cardiovascular system: Tachycardia and palpitations may occur. Elevated blood pressure is common.

Mental status: Hallucinations and delusions may occur along with paranoia, ideas of reference, anxiety and/or depression, and impaired judgment, mood swings, and altered sense of time and space.

Grandiosity: Inflated self-esteem

Central nervous system (CNS) symptoms: Dilated pupils, tremors, incoordination, euphoria, sweating, fever, synesthesia (seeing noise), seizures, temperature instability, fever, confusion, suspiciousness, paranoia, and coma

Respiratory symptom: Irregular respiration

Gastrointestinal symptom: Nausea and diarrhea

Self-control: Mixed speech, loss of muscle control, meaningless movements, and aggressive/ irrational behavior

Therapeutic Nursing Interventions

- Monitor vital signs.
- Implement safety measures during perceptual alterations and hallucinations. Self-injury can occur during periods of delusions.
- Decrease visual and auditory environmental stimuli.
- Perform neurovascular checks.
- Implement close observation (one-to-one supervision may be necessary).

Critical Thinking Exercise: Hallucinogen Abuse

Situation: M.H. is admitted to the substance abuse unit from the emergency department, after he was found walking down the street with no clothes on and yelling that he was being chased. He was not being chased. After he became lucid, M.H. admitted to taking PCP at a party. M.H. admits to a long history of PCP use.

1. How can you best intervene at this time?

2. What potential medical problems can occur while you are monitoring M.H.?

3. How might the drug affect him psychologically?

Substance Abuse Disorders: Cannabis Abuse

Key Points

- The active ingredient in marijuana is tetrahydrocannabinol (THC).
- Cannabis, particularly marijuana, is a commonly abused drug.
- It is controversial whether marijuana use may lead to the abuse of more potent drugs. Withdrawal does occur with the use of cannabis.
- The goals of collaborative management include:
  - Maintaining abstinence
  - Providing assessment and treatment for physical problems
  - Ensuring safety with no harm to self or others
  - Educating client and family about cannabis abuse and treatment

Overview

Cannabis comes from the hemp plant. Tetrahydrocannabinol (THC) is the active ingredient in marijuana and hashish. Symptoms include impaired motor coordination, euphoria, anxiety, a sensation of slowed time, and impaired judgment. Impaired motor skills last for eight to 12 hours. Withdrawal symptoms may include headache, fatigue, or restlessness, hyperhidrosis and loss of appetite.

Effects on the Body

Cardiovascular: Moderate tachycardia, increase in heart rate and cardiac output, bloodshot eyes, and increased appetite

Central nervous system (CNS): Slowing of reaction time, lethargy, and passivity

Sexual function: Pleasurable experiences, such as sexual intercourse, are thought to be enhanced with the use of cannabis.

Reproductive: Marijuana use is associated with infertility, fetal loss, and congenital anomaly.

Mental: Euphoria, paranoia, anxiety, and heightened sensitivity to external stimuli.

Critical Thinking Exercise: Cannabis Abuse

Situation: You have been assigned a clinical rotation with a school nurse in a middle school. During your clinical rotation in a drug rehabilitation unit, you presented an inservice program for new staff. The clinical instructor was very impressed with the information and style of your program. Now he tells you he has a bigger challenge for you. You are to present an educational program to the students on cannabis, which is used by many of the students. You know as much about this topic as you did about opioid abuse, so you approach it in the same way, by asking yourself questions and answering them.

1. What are the typical drugs that are used? What is the active ingredient that causes the physical and mental effects?

2. If I wanted to tell the students about the impact that these drugs have on their bodies, what would I tell them?

Homeless Mentally Ill

Key Points

- Homelessness is a major social problem in this country.
- One-fourth to one-half of the homeless population has mental illness.
- There are three types of immobility in homeless, mentally ill people:
  - Episodic periods of homelessness
  - Seasonal mobility and within defined geographic region
  - Migratory movements in wider geographic areas
- There are inadequate funding and treatment sources for this population.
- Many of the population have chronic medical problems.
- Adherence to long-term treatment is difficult to accomplish.
- The goals of collaborative management include:
  - Providing assessment and treatment for physical and psychiatric illness
  - Providing safety with no harm to the client and others
  - Ensuring that basic needs (nutrition, housing, clothing) are met
  - Providing supportive therapy
  - Adhering to medication treatment
- **Key Terms/Concepts:** Residential instability, interdisciplinary staff, and treatment

Overview

Individuals with mental illness account for one-third to one-half of the homeless population. Approximately half of the total homeless population exhibits signs of depression and/or schizophrenia. Changes in the treatment philosophy, mental health laws, and reduced federal funding have led to shortened hospitalization and mental health services for clients with varying degrees of mental illness. Therefore, the many chronically ill persons who are unable to adequately care for themselves and their families are contributing to the growing social and health problems of homelessness.

Risk Factors

Age: Homeless clients can range in age from runaway children to the deinstitutionalized, poor elderly with no support systems.

Socioeconomic status: The homeless are clients of low socioeconomic status who often cannot maintain a job due to mental disorders.

Support systems: Support systems are usually absent or are distant with dysfunctional family relationships.

Mental health care: Access to hospitalization for the mentally ill has been decreased over recent years, leaving mentally ill persons living on the streets. Homeless shelters become havens for the mentally ill and often leave few beds for acute need. Mental health care in the outpatient setting is not routinely accessed, resulting in fragmented health care.

Residential instability: Residence may be established, but often the finances are insufficient, forcing the client to return to the street. Because mental health care is not available, the client may have disorganized thinking and inability to maintain a residence. High mobility may be related to a feeling of restlessness common in homeless, mentally ill people.

Physical, mental, and cognitive health status: All aspects of the client's general health are impacted by unmet basic needs. Limited access to pharmacologic therapy or poor compliance to a medication regimen compromises the mental and physical well-being of the client. Typical health problems include liver disease, trauma-related problems, seizure disorders, and nutritional deficiencies.

Substance abuse: High incidence of alcohol and drug abuse is often a contributing factor to homelessness in the mentally ill population. Many spend their limited funds on these substances instead of on housing, food, or clothing.

Community resources: Are available, if qualifications are met. Frequently, attendance and compliance in social programs are poor. Community resources may be the last effort to help homeless clients meet the social standards of the community.

Signs and Symptoms

- Note: Any of the signs and symptoms of psychiatric illnesses may be found in this client population.
- Transient residential stability
- Untreated physical and mental disorders
- Self care deficits

Assessment

History and physical examination: Assess physical changes as a result of homelessness and review the past medical history, including medication regimen.

Mental status examination: Assess for mental illnesses, which may interfere with the client's ability to function and perform ADLs.

Nutritional assessment: regarding the adequacy, type, and amount of food ingested, eating behaviors, food preparation and safety, and attitude regarding food and timing of meals in accordance with the medication regimen is necessary. Develop an appropriate nutritional plan for the client according to the assessment data.

Socioeconomic assessment: Assess whether the client can meet basic needs with available resources. Determine the client's knowledge of community resources and ability to obtain necessary services.

Environmental assessment: Assess the living arrangements of the client. Include factors such as:

- Fire safety
- Exposure to toxic chemicals, pollutants, or disease

- Number of persons and their relationships within the environment
- Access to food, heat, clothing, water, and light
- Exposure to domestic violence or street crime
- Presence of disease-carrying insects, rodents or animals
- Safety in the environment for children (play equipment, electrical outlets, poison)

Assess potential factors that prevent access to help:

- Lack of insurance
- Lack of knowledge about available services and how to access care
- Lack of transportation
- Suspiciousness about the system and fear of reporting to protective services for child abuse or neglect
- Language barriers
- Loss of personal identification (driver's license, social security card, etc.), which may be necessary to qualify for services
- Eligibility criteria may also require an address
- Poor decision-making and priority-setting capacities
- Unrealistic life goals for their circumstances, skills, and resources

Nursing Diagnoses

Note: Any of the diagnoses for psychiatric illnesses may be found in this client population.

- Altered thought processes
- Risk for violence
- Powerlessness
- Altered family process
- Social isolation
- Ineffective individual coping
- Self-esteem disturbance
- Risk for injury
- Risk for infection
- Altered growth and development
- Anxiety and fear
- Impaired communication

Therapeutic Nursing Management

- Ensure that client has a stable, safe environment if or when he/she needs intensive treatment.
- Encourage participation in group therapy or support group for social interaction.
- Teach appropriate self-care, performance of activities of daily living.

- Assess the need for job skills training to allow the client the opportunity to be self-sufficient. Provide occupational/vocational therapy, as required.

- Provide individual supportive therapy. Concentrating on the needs of the client will make a difference.

- Promote holistic care, with a positive regard of the client.

- Administer medication specific to disease processes and assessment findings. Ensure that client is able to obtain and comply with the pharmacologic regimen.

- These clients require the nurse to work closely with interdisciplinary staff and agencies to obtain the services clients require. Case management is important to the client's overall health and needs.

- Medical psychiatry is often necessary to help the client obtain care for the complex physical and mental health needs.

- Many homeless persons with mental illness refuse medical and psychiatric treatment. Ensuring compliance with care is a key.

- Some homeless persons fear staying in shelters because of threats of violence among the residents.

Complications

- Chronic cognitive deficits
- Nutritional deficiencies
- Multi-system physical deficits and diseases
- Psychosocial deficits and poor support systems
- Harm to self or others
- Victims of crime

Client Outcomes

Planning care for the homeless client and family must include individualizing the intervention plan and developing outcome criteria that are reasonable and attainable. Clearly, a reasonable goal may be to increase the safety and stability in the environment. Improved access to supportive services for medical and mental health, nutrition, and social problems is needed to promote higher-level functioning.

Client and Family Education

Client and family education about available support services should include concise information describing the services and ways to get assistance.

Topics that may be beneficial include personal hygiene, immunizations, substance abuse help, dental care, cancer risks, sexually transmitted disease information, infestation, and mental health issues. Public resources on homelessness include:

- National Resource Center on Homelessness
- Bureau of Primary Health Care for the Homeless
- National Coalition for the Homeless
- National Volunteer Clearinghouse for the Homeless

- Health Care for the Homeless Information Resource Center
- Housing Assistance Council, Inc.
- Home Base: The Center for Common Concerns
- National Alliance to End Homelessness
- Interagency Council on the Homeless

Critical Thinking Exercise: Homeless Mentally Ill

Situation: A volunteer at a homeless shelter brought the client, a 35-year-old homeless person, to the psychiatric hospital. The client reportedly had been rocking back and forth on his cot, yelling loudly and hitting himself in the head. The workers at the shelter were afraid for the client's safety.

Upon admission to the psychiatric unit, the client was oriented to time, place, and person and knew identifying information about himself. He told the nurse that he has been homeless for 20 years and stated, "My family thought that there was something wrong with me and sent me away. I wandered from place to place for a while and finally I found a place to stay in a junk yard where the workers would bring me food. The junk yard closed last month. I came to the shelter because I don't have anywhere else to go. I can't stand the noise of the radio. The radio plays in my head all the time and I wish that it would stop."

1. Identify the client's immediate needs.

2. Write the most relevant nursing diagnoses.

3. Identify the realistic outcome criteria for the client.

4. List the community resources available for the homeless client.

Victimization: Child Abuse or Neglect

Key Points

- Child abuse is a non-accidental physical or emotional injury usually inflicted by a parent or other caregiver.
- Types of child abuse include physical neglect and abuse, emotional neglect and abuse, sexual abuse, and verbal abuse.
- Federal law requires the reporting of all suspected child abuse to child protective services.
- A family history of abuse is common.
- The goals of collaborative management include:
    - Providing assessment and treatment for physical and emotional problems
    - Ensuring a safe environment, which may mean removing the abused or neglected child from his/her home
    - Implementing supportive therapy
- **Key Terms/Concepts**: Abuse, neglect, vulnerability

Overview

Child abuse is a non-accidental physical or emotional injury usually inflicted by the parent or caregiver. Maltreatment is exhibited in a variety of ways: physical harm, sexual abuse, mental maltreatment, educational neglect, emotional harm and neglect. Neglect is the failure on the part of the parent or caregiver to provide for the child's basic needs of food, clothing, shelter, medical/dental care, or supervision. Emotional abuse is defined as a chronic failure by parents or the caretaker to provide the child with the love and support necessary for the development of a sound, healthy personality. Sexual abuse involves sexually explicit activity that ranges from sexual play to intercourse and is imposed upon a child by an adult who has greater power, knowledge, and resources. Verbal abuse may be defined as the assault on the child that is verbally degrading, such as comfort ridicule. Federal law requires the reporting of all suspected child abuse to child protective services.

Risk Factors

Vulnerability: Children are the most vulnerable group within our society. They can be coerced into keeping the incident(s) a secret or forced to engage in acts that are harmful. Children are usually trusting and willing to please.

Family history: Often adults who abuse were victims of abuse themselves. Patterns of dysfunctional discipline or abuse are commonly passed through generations.

Age: Abuse may begin as early as the newborn period (e.g., shaken baby syndrome), and continues throughout childhood. Children under the age of three are at higher risk for fatal abuse secondary to head trauma, burn injury, drowning, shaking syndrome, neglect, or any number of various causes of abuse.

Gender: Studies suggest that boys are more often abused than girls; however, with more than two million children abused, both boys and girls suffer at an alarming rate.

Signs and Symptoms

Non-accidental physical injuries of the child:

- Bruises in various stages of healing, bite marks, skin welts, burns
- Fractures, lacerations, unusual bleeding
- Bald spots
- Sexual trauma
- Malnutrition
- Infected sores
- Physical injuries inconsistent with the caregiver's history
- Sexually transmitted disease
- Pregnancy
- Urinary tract infections (chronic) in young children
- Old, healing fractures on x-ray

Behaviors of the child

- Fear of caretaker
- Wary of physical contact with adult
- Rage or withdrawal
- Verbal reporting of abuse
- Self-injury
- Running away from home
- Continued hunger, poor hygiene, unsupervised activity
- Poor school performance
- Sexual promiscuity
- Unusual sexual knowledge
- Sexual abuse of others
- Anxiety
- Depression
- Withdrawn affect, even during a painful procedure
- Constant fatigue, listlessness, or falling asleep in class

Assessment (child)

History and physical exam: The abused victim's examination is performed for documentation. Outward physical and behavioral signs of abuse or neglect are reported.

Mandatory reporting: of any suspected incidences of physical, sexual, or emotional abuse exists for health care providers.

Investigation of home environment and caretakers: referral to social service agency when child abuse or neglect is suspected

Psychiatric assessment of child: A psychiatric evaluation may be necessary for the child with a significant history of child abuse, due to the potentially profound effects on the child's psychosocial and personality development.

Growth assessment: Failure to thrive can result in the child with a history of recurrent abuse and/or neglect.

School attendance record: Frequent absences, poor academic performance, or diminished ability to concentrate in the classroom setting

Assessment (abuser)

Family history of the abuser: A pattern of abuse is noted in some families. It is thought that learned behavior increases the risk for abuse of subsequent generations. Persons physically abused as children are more likely to behave in an abusive manner to their own children.

Mental status examination for the abuser: Aimed at identifying psychiatric disorders, such as psychosis, bipolar personality disorders, depression, postpartum psychosis or schizophrenia that would be associated with abusive behavior.

Psychological testing for the abuser: Identifies patterns of behavior and thought processes to help redirect abusive behavior.

Behavioral assessment:

- Lack of concern about the child
- Attempt to conceal the child's injuries
- Impulsive behavior with poor anger management skills, often followed by a feeling of remorse
- Routine use of harsh, inappropriate and age-inappropriate punishment
- Unreasonable expectations that the child will feel the abuser's emotional needs

Nursing Diagnoses

- Anxiety
- Fear and mistrust
- Impaired communication
- Ineffective individual coping skills
- Ineffective family coping skills
- Altered family processes
- Social isolation
- Altered growth and development

Therapeutic Nursing Management (child)

Environment

- Child needs to be in a supportive, protective environment, removed from the abusive or neglectful persons and environment. This may be a foster home, with another relative, or brief hospitalization for more intensive support or care of the related injury. Child may be admitted to hospital for medical problems.

Psychological treatment

- **Individual psychotherapy**: Counseling on an individual basis is necessary to address the child's feelings and self-esteem needs. The type of insurance or managed care is a major factor in the duration and extent of treatment.
- **Play therapy**: Children find play therapy helpful to express internally disturbing feelings. Puppet play is frequently used as a method for role play or conflict resolution.
- **Art therapy**: Children who have been sexually abused commonly exaggerate the genitals of the figure in drawings, while physically abused children often exaggerate the hands of the person in the picture.
- **Group therapy**: Group interactions coupled with emotional support provided in a protective environment with participants who have had similar experiences often increases coping skills and improves esteem.
- **Family therapy**: May be useful in alleviating abusive behavior within families and dealing with the underlying issues. Individual therapy may be needed for some persons within the family group. Support groups may be useful for family members.

Psychopharmacologic treatment

- Administer medications for specific symptoms (e.g., antianxiety, antidepressant).

Nursing interventions

- Treat physical injuries, malnutrition, or physical diseases.
- Document assessment findings clearly, objectively, and with descriptive detail.
- Report child abuse to state protective services.
- Provide safe environment: The abuser (parents or others) will need to be kept from child, in accordance with legal requirements.
- Gradually assist child in discussing feelings and fears. Provide opportunities to express feelings nonverbally.
- Child may be fearful and anxious with physical touch or during physical examinations. Respect of the child's interpersonal space is key to the development of a trust relationship with the health care provider. A calm, gentle approach with direct eye contact and caring attitude is very important to the establishment of a therapeutic relationship.

Complications

- Continued abuse and neglect
- Psychological stress lasting through years of abuse, which can lead to major mental illness (e.g., depression, anxiety, multiple personality disorder)

- Feelings of worthlessness and low self-esteem
- Physical injuries and disease from prolonged abuse
- Abused children may become abusers in adulthood
- Unable to maintain relationships
- More prone to substance abuse
- Death

Client Outcomes

The client will:

- Experience no further evidence of physical, sexual, emotional abuse, or neglect
- Experience decreased anxiety and fear
- Display more effective coping behaviors
- Maintain a physically stable status
- Exhibit appropriate behavior, play, and functioning for age
- Maintain personal relationships

Client and Family Education

- Discuss with the client and family the possible environmental or situational causes, contributing factors, and triggers.
- Help the client and family to identify the internal and external indicators of child abuse or neglect.
- Educate the client and family about the following issues:
  - Coping skills
  - Communication skills
  - Problem solving
  - Medication therapy
  - Support group for child and other family members
  - Supportive interaction with abused child or children

Age-Related Factors—Cultural and Gender Variations

- Mothers are more likely to be abusive than fathers (58%):
  - Mothers spend more time with children
  - Mothers struggle with the stressors of work and home responsibilities
  - Mothers are likely to be the head of single parent families
  - More likely to live in poverty

Critical Thinking Exercise: Child Abuse or Neglect

Situation: You have taken a new position in an outpatient unit that provides services to children who have experienced abuse or neglect and their families. You know little about child abuse and neglect. On the first day you sit in on a team meeting and hear about abuse and neglect, the family history of abuse, play therapy, and complications from abuse and neglect. When you leave the meeting, you are even more confused about these topics. Now you must get yourself prepared to help the children and their families.

1. How would you describe the differences between child abuse and neglect?

2. What does Federal law have to do with child abuse?

3. You understand the importance of getting a family history, but you are not sure what important data might be obtained. What would you be looking for?

4. You are going to observe a play therapy session, but what is it?

5. As you assess children, you need to be aware of complications that they might experience. Identify what these might be.

Victimization: Physically/Emotionally Abused Adult

Key Points

- Physical abuse is the purposeful maltreatment of one person (child, adult, elderly) by another.
- Family violence occurs most often in families with poor communication among the members, and a lack of emotional support.
- Federal law requires the reporting of all suspected child abuse to child protective services.
- The goals of collaborative management include:
  - Providing assessment and treatment for physical and emotional problems
  - Providing a safe environment, which may mean removing the abused client from his/her home
  - Providing supportive therapy
- **Key Terms/Concepts**: Domestic violence, cycle of abuse

Overview

Domestic violence is the most common cause of injury to women, with or without sexual assault. Abusive behavior is often the result of drug or alcohol abuse, unemployment, cycle of abuse (abuser's history of abuse as a child), low self-esteem, ineffective coping mechanisms, or poor stress management skills.

Risk Factors

- **Age**: The victim can be of any age, (child, adult, often elderly).
- **Socioeconomic status**: Persons of any socioeconomic status can be affected.
- **Support systems**: The victim often protects the abuser because of fear.
- **Environmental factors**: Individuals who are raised in an abusive home are more likely to abuse others and accept abuse as a deserved consequence. Modeling has a powerful influence on a person's coping reactions.

Signs and Symptoms

- Contusions, lacerations, abrasions, burns, fractures, and other physical problems, which many times are unexplained, or explained with unusual stories
- Alterations in sleep patterns and nutritional intake
- Humiliation, self-blame
- Panic and anxiety, fear
- Low self-esteem

- Fear of physical violence and death
- Looking to controlling person for answers to questions; over-pleasing others
- Social isolation and withdrawal
- Black eyes and facial bruises (particularly abused women)
- Broken eyeglass frames or signs of restraint (particularly with elderly)
- Bilateral upper arm bruises common in abused elderly
- Skeletal fractures in multiple stages of healing

Assessment

- History and physical examination
- Exploration of explanations for injuries
- Psychiatric assessment with mental status examination
- Assessment of social network and support system
- Family history

Screening for Domestic Violence

- All females age 14 and older should be screened.
- How should domestic violence screening occur?
  - Interview client alone
  - Use gender-neutral terms
  - Use trained non-familial interpreters when translation is necessary
  - Ask direct questions
  - Be nonjudgmental and supportive
  - Make eye contact
- Be able to identify red flag signals of domestic violence.
  - Inconsistency between history and injury
  - Frequent medical visits
  - Delay in seeking medical care
  - Partner insists on staying close and answering questions directed to the client
  - Repetitive psychosomatic complaints
  - Depression or suicidality
  - Injury during pregnancy
  - Multiple injuries in different stages of healing
  - Injuries suggestive of defensive posture (e.g., bruises on backs of forearms)
  - Injuries to head, neck, breast, abdomen
  - Pattern injuries
- Acronym for remembering stages of screening for domestic violence (RADAR)
  - Routinely screen.
  - Ask the question (e.g., "Has your partner ever physically hurt or threatened you?").

- Document (verbatim quotes, body map or photos of injuries, safety assessment)
- Assess client safety.
- Review options and make referrals.

Nursing Diagnoses

- Anxiety
- Fear and mistrust
- Impaired communication
- Ineffective individual coping skills
- Ineffective family coping skills
- Altered family processes
- Social isolation
- Altered growth and development

Therapeutic Nursing Management

- Provide a confidential environment for the disclosure of information or feelings.
- Assist victim in exploring options about future living arrangements and relationship with abuser.
- Encourage victim to locate or create a safe living environment.
- Involve victim in occupational/vocational training if needed, and encourage her/him to become knowledgeable about own and family finances.
- Respond to client's requests for legal representation.
- Encourage follow-up physical and mental health care.
- Encourage autonomous decision-making and problem-solving.
- Many communities offer abuse awareness programs to educate the community about the problem. Also, there are safe and confidential shelters for abused and battered spouses in most communities.

Complications

- Further or continued abuse
- Altered growth and development
- Multi-system physical deficits and diseases
- Psychosocial deficits
- Sexually transmitted diseases
- Pregnancy
- Harm to self or others
- Guilt and self-blame

Client Outcomes

The client will:

- Experience no further evidence of physical, sexual, emotional abuse or neglect

- Experience decreased anxiety and fear
- Display more effective coping behaviors
- Maintain a physically stable status
- Exhibit appropriate behavior and functioning for age

Client and Family Education

- Additional treatment interventions:
  - Safety concerns, including safe environment
  - Vocational/occupational counseling and training, if needed
  - Community resources deal with victim's financial and legal issues

Critical Thinking Exercise: Physically/Emotionally Abused Adult

Situation: At midnight, a 39-year-old woman is brought to the emergency department by her husband. Her lip is bleeding and she has a reddened and swollen area around her left eye. She is crying as she tells you that she fell down the stairs at her home. She has 3 children at home, ages 1, 3, and 6 years; she called her mother to stay with them while she came to the hospital. She expresses concern about her children. In the waiting room, her husband is belligerent and repeatedly asks to see his wife.

1. What assessment data do you need to collect about this woman and her injuries?

2. What concerns do you have about this woman's safety?

3. What nursing interventions are of priority concern?

Human Immunodeficiency Virus
Neuropsychological Complications

Key Points

- Human immunodeficiency virus (HIV) is a viral agent that produces immunosuppression, resulting in Acquired Immune Deficiency Syndrome (AIDS).
- Complications of AIDS include cognitive dysfunctions, dementia, and personality changes.
- Depression, anxiety, and psychosis may occur as the disease progresses.
- Treatment must include support for a terminal illness.
- The goals of collaborative management include:
  - Providing assessment and treatment for physical and psychological problems
  - Providing a safe environment
  - Adhering to medication treatment
  - Ensuring that basic needs are met (ADLs)
  - Providing supportive therapy
  - Promoting healthy grieving
  - Preventing maladaptive coping mechanisms
- **Key Terms/Concepts**: HIV, AIDS, sexual transmission, anxiety, depression, psychosis, sensory-perceptual alterations, wasting syndrome, opportunistic infections, suicidal ideation

Overview

Human immunodeficiency virus (HIV) is a viral agent that produces immunosuppression, resulting in Acquired Immune Deficiency Syndrome (AIDS). Physical manifestations of the HIV infection include cerebral atrophy, vacuole formation in the brain or spinal cord, and enlargement of the inner structure of the brain (ventricle). Neuropsychologic assessment reveals general impairment of cognitive function, dementia, and personality changes. Gross and fine motor changes are evidenced as muscle weakness, clumsiness, and difficulty performing the activities of daily living. Clients may develop secondary psychiatric disorders such as depression, anxiety, and psychosis.

Risk Factors

- Sexual transmission: Unprotected sex
- Blood-borne transmission
- Perinatal transmission
- Past psychiatric history may lead to relapse of psychiatric disorder during this time
- Substance abuse, especially IV drug use

Signs and Symptoms

Early stage—acute infection

- Acute infection, sore throat, lymphadenopathy
- Fever, malaise, nausea, vomiting

Middle stage—disease

- Persistent lymphadenopathy
- Fever
- Night sweats
- Chronic diarrhea
- Fatigue, headache
- Oral infections

Late stage—disease

- Wasting syndrome: weight loss below 10%
- Fever, weakness
- Opportunistic infections
- Altered mental status: delirium, depression, AIDS dementia complex
- Psychiatric disorders

Psychological

- Anxiety
- Depression
- Isolation and loneliness
- Stress due to loss of job, financial problems, loss of relationships or difficulties in relationships, housing
- Fear of terminal illness

Assessment

- History and physical examination
- Laboratory testing: ELISA, Western Blot, CD4 cell count
- Psychiatric assessment and history
- Mental status examination
- Suicidal assessment
- Substance abuse assessment
- CT, MRI of head and spine

Nursing Diagnoses

- Anxiety
- Altered thought process
- Sensory-perceptual alterations

- Self-care deficit
- Impaired verbal communication
- Impaired individual coping
- Self-esteem disturbance
- Sexual dysfunction
- High risk for self-directed violence
- Social isolation
- Impaired social interaction
- Risk for loneliness
- Altered role performance
- Risk for caregiver role strain
- Altered family processes

Therapeutic Nursing Management

- Universal precautions
- Supportive care: Guilt and anger are common emotions experienced by both caregivers and the client.
- Hospice care
- Pain management
- Terminal care
- Interview for sexual contacts
- Suicide precautions
- Administer antiviral agents, antibiotics, antineoplastic agents, antianxiety medications, antidepressants, antimanic medications, or antipsychotic medications as ordered.
- Spiritual care

Complications

- Wasting syndrome
- Major depression
- Harm to self
- Suicide
- Opportunistic infections
- Respiratory distress
- Fluid and electrolyte imbalance
- Death

Client and Family Education

- Discuss with the client and family the possible environmental or situational causes, contributing factors, and triggers.

- Help the client and family to identify the internal and external indicators of neuropsychologic complications of HIV.
- Educate the client and family about the following issues:
  - Coping skills
  - Stress management
  - Participation in treatment planning
  - Medication therapy
  - Support groups and other support mechanisms
  - Nutrition
  - Self-care
  - Stages of grief and loss by Kubler-Ross: Denial, anger, bargaining, depression, acceptance

Age-Related Changes—Culture and Gender Variations

- Severity of pathology increases with age.
- Elderly persons are often more susceptible to infection as a function of age.
- When general health is compromised, the risk for immunocompromise is further increased.
- The individual who is dealing with terminal illness often has a more intense need for emotional support. However, persons with HIV infection may experience isolation and rejection from family, friends, and the community due to the stigma of the disease.
- Access to health care may be limited in the middle and later stages of the disease as related to compromised mobility and deteriorating health status.
- Cultural changes: People at highest risk of HIV often live in poverty, have a history of abuse, experience forms of oppression, and lack of culturally appropriate health care.

Critical Thinking Exercise: Human Immunodeficiency Virus Neuropsychological Complications

Situation: D.K. is admitted to the medical unit for treatment of Kaposi's sarcoma. He has had AIDS for two years and has been hospitalized twice before for other complications. You know the client well, but notice major physical and psychological changes from his last admission. When you last saw him, he had complaints of chronic diarrhea, fatigue, night sweats, and was experiencing some signs of depression and anxiety. Now, his symptoms include severe weight loss, fever and weakness, and delirium. According to his significant other, D.K. seems more depressed. He talks little and sleeps most of the day. He no longer has interest in what is happening around him and appears to have given up.

1. Based on these data, what stage of illness was D.K. in when he was last admitted and how has that changed?

2. What interventions need to be considered?

Critical Thinking Exercise Answer Keys

Situation: In an outpatient treatment setting, you meet a young man who is about to undergo an initial psychiatric-mental health nursing assessment. He asks you, a student nurse, what will happen in the assessment interview.

1. How would you respond to his question?

   "In the assessment interview, the nurse will ask you about the problem you are having now and problems you have had in the past, as well as your family background. Also, we need to know about any medicine you are taking, your allergies, and any medical conditions you might have. Knowing how you coped with problems in the past will give us ideas about how to help you with this present problem."

2. After the interview, he asks you why it was necessary to know all those things about him, his family, and his job.

   "This information was necessary to determine what kind of mental health problems you are having and how to help you. The mental health team is trying to get a picture of your health, illnesses, and strengths so they can design a treatment plan that will address your needs and help you solve your problems."

Situation: Staff members working on the psychiatric unit are reviewing their policies and procedures, an annual event. Usually they are not too happy about having to do this; however, there is one particular topic of interest due to some recent incidents on the unit. Client rights have been questioned. A client was recently told that he could not receive mail. He called an attorney. When the attorney reviewed the client's medical record he noted that there was no primary care provider's order to deny the client the right of receiving mail.

1. The first task of the staff is to identify the important client rights that need to be addressed. What are these?

> **Right to receive telephone calls, mail, visits from clergy and attorneys; confidentiality and privacy maintained; and an expectation that treatment will be appropriate without experiencing verbal, physical, or sexual abuse.**

2. Why was it important to have a primary care provider's order to withhold mail?

> **Restricting rights can only be done for sound clinical reasons, which are identified by the primary care provider, ordered by the primary care provider, and documented. These orders must be reviewed periodically to ensure that they are still required clinically.**

Situation: You are working on an inpatient psychiatric unit. The telephone at the desk keeps ringing and no one is around to answer it, so you pick it up. After you identify yourself and the unit, the person asks to speak with P.B., a client admitted to the unit. You tell the person that P.B. is available but that he must be reached on the client payphone, and you give the caller the telephone number.

1. Why does the nurse manager become upset when she finds out that you have provided this information over the telephone?

> **No information should be given out on the telephone about clients who are in treatment. You do not know who is calling or if the client wants others to know he is in the hospital. It is the client's right to decide whether to share information about his mental problems with anyone.**

2. As the nurse manager speaks with you, what does she tell you is the purpose of confidentiality?

> **Confidentiality is of primary importance in establishing trust with a client. There are also legal risks if the client does not want information revealed to people who have no need for it.**

Situation: The following day you are assigned a client who requires one-to-one supervision following a suicide attempt. She tells you that she has something special to tell only you, and asks if you can keep a secret.

3. How do you respond?

> **"I know it is important for you to trust me, but I cannot keep a secret that might hurt you or others. It is important for you to talk about how you are feeling, and I am here to listen and keep you safe."**

Client Protection in the Mental Health Setting Answer Key

Situation: O.W. is admitted to the inpatient psychiatric unit. She is diagnosed with major depression. Shortly after admission, she attempts self-injury. The client requires one-to-one supervision. You have been asked to explain the supervision to a new staff member.

1. How would you describe one-to-one supervision to the new staff member?

> **One-to-one supervision is used to protect O.W. from harm. At no time should she be left alone, no matter what she promises. The client needs to receive appropriate care during this time, such as nutrition, sleep, exercise, communication with staff, and all aspects of treatment. The client's status is assessed regularly.**

Situation: You read O.W.'s medical record. It states, "10 a.m.: Client participated in group meeting. 11:30 a.m.: Client put on one-to-one supervision."

2. How would you critique this documentation? What would need to be documented after instituting the supervision?

> **The documentation does not provide a clear description of what happened prior to putting O.W. on one-to-one supervision. There needs to be a clear description of the process whenever restrictive procedures are used. What did the O.W. do? What was her medical condition and what interventions were taken? What was her psychological status? Was the primary care provider contacted? Would O.W. sign a no-harm contract? If so, is it in the record? After instituting the supervision, the documentation needs to continue to describe O.W.'s behavior and response to supervision. Interventions to meet her needs must be described. Periodic assessment for removal of supervision is described and then, when removed, the reason for removal.**

Situation: As a student nurse, you are assigned to care for G.R., a 60-year-old man of a different cultural background, who is being treated for depression. He tells you that he does not think anyone truly understands why he has suffered with his problem.

1. How should you respond to him?

> **"G.R., what can you tell me about your problems? What do you think caused your problems?"**
>
> **Ways to deliver culturally-competent care include: assessing what behavior is "normal' versus "abnormal" in the client's culture; determining the client's expectations and misconceptions about treatment; incorporating the client's cultural health practices and healers into the plan of care, and supporting the client's spiritual beliefs about the illness and treatment.**

2. G.R. says that he is being punished for the "awful things" he did when he was young. He asks you to pray for him. What should you say to him?

> **"It must be painful, G.R., to believe that you did something so awful that you have to be punished for it now. Many times, clients find that rather than being punished, they are experiencing depression due to an imbalance of chemicals in the brain and from the stresses in life. Yes, I will pray for you, that you will experience peace and comfort. Would you like me to call someone from your place of worship for support?"**

Situation: During an interdisciplinary team meeting on a medical unit, a staff member mentions that spirituality has no place in the discussion of a client's care. Several other staff members agree; however, you do not. Feeling somewhat uncomfortable, you do not say anything. Two weeks later, the team discusses a client who was admitted with multiple sclerosis. You admitted the client and indicated in the record that one nursing diagnosis for the client was spiritual distress. The team is discussing this diagnosis, and again some disagree with its use. You must defend your decision by educating the staff members about spirituality and relevant nursing care.

1. You begin by giving them a definition of spirituality, which is:

> **Spirituality is the life principle that pervades a client's entire being, integrating and transcending one's biologic and psychosocial nature. It affirms the person's unity with the environment.**

2. What data might you identify in the client's behavior to support the nursing diagnosis of spiritual distress?

- **Expresses concern about the meaning of life**
- **Verbalizes inner conflict about beliefs and may express anger toward a higher power**
- **Questions meaning of own existence**
- **Is unable to participate in usual religious practices**
- **Questions moral/ethical implications of the therapeutic regimen**

3. You anticipate that one of the client's concerns likely to be verbalized is: "What can we possibly do about this problem?" How will you answer this question?

- **Promote spiritual well-being by asking if the client would like to see the chaplain or his/her own clergy. If so, provide privacy during the visit.**
- **Be present for the client by listening and discussing concerns that client may have during this time.**

- Facilitate religious rituals and practices with client's agreement. Client may not realize that it is possible to do this in the hospital.
- Encourage the client to identify positive aspects of his/her life.

Situation: You are working for a hospice home care agency. You have been assigned a client, P.S., who has breast carcinoma. She is 42, married, and has three children, ages 14, 10, and 8. You make your first visit to her home, and her husband answers the door. He tells you that he is so glad you are there. He is very concerned about his wife. You ask him what specifically concerns him today. "My wife has always been upbeat but has had tough times too. Three weeks ago I could not get her to talk about her feelings, and she seemed to not care about anything. Before that, she would break into rages about her illness, and sometimes would say, 'I'd do anything just to live to see my children as adults.'" You ask him how his wife is responding now. He says, "That is the strange part. She seems at peace now. I don't like this and am not sure what it all means."

---

1. How would you explain P.S.'s emotions and reactions to her husband? (Apply Kubler-Ross' responses to dying.)

   When P.S. was angry (as demonstrated by her question, "Why me?") she was in the second stage of dying. She is angry at everything, and it is not unusual for her to lash out at her family. Stage 3, or bargaining, occurs when she tries to bargain and ask for more time. Depression is experienced in stage 4. She no longer denies the illness, and depression helps her begin to prepare for separation from loved ones. P.S. was experiencing depression when she withdrew. She is now in the fifth and last stage, the one of acceptance. She is at peace with what will happen, and she has had enough time and the support to prepare herself.

2. According to Colin Murray Parkes' phases of dying, which phase is P.S. experiencing?

   Recovery or readjustment to life as it is.

Situation: A newly admitted client has the following diagnoses written in the chart:
 Axis I: Alcohol dependence
 Axis II: Mild mental retardation
Axis III: Bronchitis
Axis IV: Problems related to primary support and occupational problems
 Avis V: 40/55

---

1. Which of these axes and diagnoses is the reason why this client is receiving treatment?

   Axis I, Alcohol dependence

2. The numbers, "40/55" refer to:

   The first number refers to the client's current level of functioning and the second number refers to the highest level of functioning in the past year.

3. What is identified in Axis IV in the DSM's multiaxial system?

   Axis IV lists the client's problems that affect his psychiatric illness and treatment.

Situation: The nurse working with an anxious client formulates the nursing diagnosis, "Sleep Pattern Disturbance, related to anxiety and exaggerated fears, as evidenced by subjective complaints of fitful sleep and fatigue, observed pacing at 4 a.m., lack of daytime alertness, and repeated requests for a 'stronger' sleep medication."

4. Which part of the nursing diagnosis will guide nursing interventions?

The second part of the nursing diagnosis, "anxiety and exaggerated fears," will guide nursing interventions.

5. What data could you, as a student, gather to support the nursing diagnosis of Sleep Pattern Disturbance?

Information about and observation of the client's sleep, level of energy, mood, complaints of fatigue, requests for sleep medication, complaints about stimuli such as noise.

Situation: As a student nurse, you observe the RN interacting with a severely depressed female client who sits with shoulders slumped and eyes downcast. You note that the client answers the nurse's occasional questions with one or two-word answers. The nurse sits quietly by the client's side.

---

1. Why is the nurse just sitting next to the client? How does that behavior promote a therapeutic relationship?

   The nurse is focusing on the client and her needs. To establish rapport, the nurse is following the lead of the client and adapting the pace of the interaction to the client's slow pace of responding and movement.

Situation: After weeks of meeting with two clients to discuss their problems and establish a therapeutic relationship, you meet with your nursing instructor and report the following, "M.A. and I seem to be making progress. He wants to discuss the difficulty he has with meeting new people. I taught him some social skills and he practiced them with me. M.J. and I have also met together. We talk about what she wants to accomplish in our time together."

---

2. The instructor asks you to identify which phase of the therapeutic relationship you are engaging in with each of your clients.

   M.A.: Phase II, working phase. M.J.: Phase I, orientation phase.

Situation: A 40-year-old male client is discussing his family situation with a nurse. State whether the nurse's responses are therapeutic or nontherapeutic.

---

1. **Client**: "I don't know what to do any more. My wife has left me and she took the children." **Nurse**: "Go on."

   Therapeutic

2. **Client**: "Our 15-year-old son has been smoking dope and he says it's because I don't spend enough time with him." **Nurse**: "Smoking marijuana leads to the use of other drugs. That is terrible for a 15-year-old. Why don't you put him into sports?"

   Nontherapeutic

3. **Client**: "What will I do without her?" **Nurse**: (Sits silently with him.)

   Therapeutic

4. **Client**: "I feel so lonely without her and the kids. The house is empty and there's nothing left of me." **Nurse**: "You feel sad and empty without your wife and children."

   Therapeutic

Identify the defense mechanism in each statement and indicate why the client's reasoning is not accurate.

1. P.J. is a 47-year-old smoker. She smokes three packs of cigarettes per day and claims that many people who smoke do not get lung cancer. In fact, she says, smokers can be some of the healthiest people you meet.

    Defense mechanism: Denial of reality

    Explanation: P.J. does not face the reality that statistics indicate that smoking puts her at risk of developing lung cancer and other serious illnesses.

2. A little league baseball coach becomes excessively demanding with his young players. When asked why he acted this way, he responded that he had a football coach who was extremely tough and the football team won the conference. He added that the football team was the "talk of the town."

    Defense mechanism: Rationalization

    Explanation: The coach wants to feel worth by being associated with a successful team, and can rationalize his behavior because of past successes.

3. A man who is troubled by his attraction to gambling begins a campaign to force a casino out of town.

    Defense mechanism: Reaction formation

    Explanation: The man denies his feelings about what he perceives as an unacceptable behavior (gambling) by acting the opposite way.

4. A boy does not make the soccer team so he puts all of his energy into academics.

   Defense mechanism: Overcompensation

   Explanation: The boy knows he will not do well in sports, so he focuses on school work.

5. L.K. is an unmarried 47-year-old who continues to rely on his 77-year-old mother to meet his basic needs.

   Defense mechanism: Dependency

   Explanation: L.K. is attaching himself to his mother in an unreasonable manner by not taking responsibility for his own life. L.K. is relying on his mother as though he were still in childhood.

6. A woman who is harassed by her boss at work initiates an argument with her husband.

   Defense mechanism: Displacement

   Explanation: This woman displaces her anger related to her boss onto her husband. To her, he is a "safer" target.

7. An emotionally distraught mother of three teenage boys cannot recognize individual qualities of her children. Instead, she views them all as either all good or all bad.

   Defense mechanism: Splitting

   Explanation: This mother cannot appreciate the personal attributes and abilities of her children. Instead, she characterizes them as all good or all bad.

Hospitalization and Milieu Therapy/Outpatient Treatment Answer Key

Situation: The staff team on a new psychiatric inpatient unit is meeting to discuss the purposes of therapeutic milieus. The criteria for admission to the unit must also be identified. The unit is a 25-bed unit in an acute care hospital. It is a locked unit. Most staff members have little psychiatric experience. You are one of the more experienced nurses; therefore, the staff seeks your advice and help.

A staff member comes to you and asks, "I am not sure what a therapeutic milieu really is. We certainly did not have anything like that on the medical unit I just came from. Is it something I am supposed to do or does it just happen? Why have it anyway?"

1. How do you respond?

> A therapeutic milieu is an environment that promotes healing and provides a corrective setting for the client to improve his/her coping skills. It needs to be a safe and comfortable place with qualified staff. There are four general objectives for clients in a therapeutic milieu:
>
> - Correction of the client's perceptions of stressor
> - Changing of the client's coping mechanisms from maladaptive to adaptive
> - Improvement of interpersonal relationship skills
> - Learning effective stress management strategies
>
> A therapeutic milieu can occur in an inpatient unit, partial hospital program, an outpatient setting, or a classroom environment.

Situation: Two staff members have met with the medical director to draft the admission criteria.

2. What would you expect those criteria to include?

- Harm to self or others (critical criterion)
- Unable to provide for basic needs
- Unable to make reasonable decisions regarding health
- In need of hospital treatment

Situation: L.Z. has been on the inpatient psychiatric unit for two days. He is diagnosed with bipolar disorder and has a history of violence. You are his primary nurse. In spite of the prescribed medication therapy, L.Z. remains very active on the unit, often pacing, fidgeting, and restless. He displays aggressive behavior toward others around him. You perceive that he does not trust others. His insurance will only cover 10 days of treatment.

1. Prioritize his problems and describe the most important nursing interventions for L.Z.

- Aggression toward others and history of violence: Monitor his behavior for signs of escalation (agitation, aggressive verbalization or actions) and separate him from the group to help him de-escalate through physical outlets, creative expression, activity, and talking. Provide a safe, quiet place for him to de-escalate. Teach him how to self-monitor his anger and anxiety. Encourage the client to ask for help and to use relaxation and other techniques.

- Pacing and exhaustion: This may lead to L.Z. not sleeping enough and demonstrating poor food and fluid intake and inadequate hygiene. Encourage the client to eat and if he will not sit down, give him finger foods to eat while pacing. Medication may be required for sleep. Take brief rest periods to provide for hygiene needs.

- Administer medication as ordered: This will probably include antipsychotics until a mood stabilizer becomes effective. When he is able, begin mediation education. Also provide education to his family and friends. Ensure that laboratory work is conducted.

- Lack of trust: In developing a one-to-one relationship with him, it is important to establish times to see him. If you cannot make the appointment, he needs to be told the reason and reschedule the appointment. Do not give him false reassurance, or be judgmental. Avoid arguing with the client and respect his views.

- Discharge planning: This is critical, due to the client's short length-of-stay. Involve the client and family in the planning. Identify his aftercare needs and appropriate outpatient treatment setting. Verify that he understands the importance of follow- up care.

Situation: A mother says to the pediatric nurse, "I can't understand why my 3-year-old son throws such a fit whenever we're in the grocery store. He screams and cries for candy at the checkout counter and I always say no. But then he carries on so loudly until everyone nearby is looking at us and I have to give in and buy him candy. I don't understand why he is not learning that he cannot have candy every time he's in the grocery store."

1. What is the target behavior that the mother is trying to change?

    His crying and screaming for candy in the grocery store

2. What has the mother's behavior taught her young son?

    Her giving in to his cries for candy has reinforced his crying and screaming behavior. He has learned that if he cries and screams long and hard enough, he will eventually be given the candy he wants.

Situation: During P.J.'s monthly visit at the Outpatient Clinic, she tells the nurse, "I have started therapy like the doctor recommended and have been going to therapy weekly for about two months. Lately, when I leave the therapist's office, I don't feel good. In fact, I feel kind of upset and stressed about our talking about all the bad things that have happened in my life. I thought therapy was going to help me feel better."

1. What stage of therapy is P.J. currently engaged in?

   The second, or "working stage," of therapy.

2. What occurs in that stage of therapy?

   The client becomes more trusting and discloses significant feelings, thoughts, and experiences that may have led to her current problems. The client may gain insight into problems and behaviors and bring out feelings that she previously could not remember.

Situation: A family, consisting of mother, father, 14-year-old daughter, and 11-year-old son, attends its first family therapy session. The daughter has been withdrawn recently and spends a great deal of time in her room. She is not interested in her friends and prefers to be alone. The son, who has ADHD, continues to struggle in his schoolwork. Last year, he barely passed 5th grade.

1. What is unique about family therapy? How does that apply to this family?

The family is treated as a unit or whole, not as individual members with problems. The symptoms or behavior of the daughter, son, and parents are treated as a sign that the whole family has problems.

The session reveals that the parents disagree and argue about whether or not their son should take medicine for his ADHD. The father says his son "is what's wrong with this family" and should "just buckle down and work harder," but mother says he needs his medication to focus on his work.

2. The father's comments about the son are an example of what communication problem that occurs in troubled families?

Scapegoating

Situation: As an observer to a group therapy meeting, you observe the following: The group is talking about reactions that members have to one another. At times, the group interaction is very emotional. Members seem to feel comfortable with this emotional sharing and confrontation. The group seems close and productive.

---

1. How would you describe the characteristics of this group? State three characteristics that are evident from these data.

    • **The group is cohesive in that its members are working together.**

    • **The group atmosphere is one in which members feel comfortable sharing their feelings about one another.**

    • **The group's interpersonal communication is positive, with members interacting with each other.**

2. What type of group is this? Provide your rationale.

    This is a process-oriented group because it focuses on relationships among members and their communication styles.

Situation: You are the medication nurse for one week on a psychiatric unit. You have a busy week. The following are short client descriptions regarding problems and questions about psychopharmacology that you encountered this week. Respond to the questions for each example given.

1. Your client has been prescribed fluphenazine (Prolixin). The client has never taken this medication. What type of medication is this? Identify four side effects that the client might experience.

   Fluphenazine is an antipsychotic drug.

   Common side effects include orthostatic hypotension, dizziness, and drowsiness during early therapy, and constipation or diarrhea. Skin pigmentation changes and photosensitivity occur infrequently for those on high doses for prolonged periods.

   Extrapyramidal symptoms appear to be dose related, and are divided into three classifications:

   - **Akathisia, which is the inability to remain still, foot tapping, and fidgeting**
   - **Parkinsonian symptoms, which include the mask-like facial expression, shuffling gait, excessive salivation, and tremors**
   - **Acute dystonias, which include muscle rigidity, torticollis, tardive dyskinesia (protrusion of the tongue, lip smacking, and chewing), and other reactions, such as rolling back of eyes and profuse sweating**

2. M.H. is taking procyclidine (Kemadrin). Why would this medication be prescribed?

   M.H. must be taking an antipsychotic medication. Kemadrin is used to prevent or moderate EPS symptoms caused by antipsychotics.

3. A.P. has been prescribed lithium soon after her admission. She is very angry and aggressive. What is wrong with the statement, "The lithium will soon stop that behavior?"

Lithium does not work quickly, and the client may need an antipsychotic medication in addition to the lithium in the initial stages of treatment.

4. A.P. begins to experience hand tremors, polyuria, confusion, and ataxia. What is happening to A.P.? What do you need to do initially?

A.P. is experiencing toxicity to lithium. You need to hold the next dose and call her primary care provider.

5. A.P. will need to be taught about her diet. What will you teach her?

Lithium should be taken with food. The client needs a balanced diet with adequate fluid and sodium intake.

6. B.F. has been taking secobarbital (Seconal) for sleep. He has found that he needs a higher dose to obtain sleep. What has happened to B.F.?

B.F. has developed a tolerance to the drug and may have developed a dependency on the drug.

7. A.K. is taking alprazolam (Xanax). She says, "I have a fear of addiction, but I don't mind taking this medication because I know I can't get addicted to it." How would you respond to this statement?

You can become dependent on antianxiety medications, such as Xanax. These drugs need to be used as prescribed with medical supervision.

8. You are assessing a new client who has schizophrenia. You note that the client has facial grimaces, tongue thrusting, and makes a smacking sound. What is the client's problem? What is a cause of this problem?

The client is experiencing tardive dyskinesia (TD). This is a serious side effect from taking antipsychotic medications.

9. Elderly clients will need higher doses of medications in order to obtain positive results from psychotropic medications. Why is this a false statement?

Elderly clients need lower doses because their kidney and liver function is not usually able to tolerate high doses.

10. A client on the unit has been prescribed isocarboxazid (Marplan). What intervention is critical for this client?

The client requires a special diet and education about it. The diet must be free of tyramine, which is found in beer, red wine, aged cheese, avocados, figs, anchovies, yeast extracts, deli meats, liver, herring, and bananas.

Situation: Unit A provides electroconvulsive therapy (ECT) for clients who need this treatment. V.R. is 60 years old and has been admitted for major depression. She has lost weight, is very withdrawn, and is unable to leave home. V.R. is not able to carry on a conversation for more than a few minutes. She has threatened to kill herself. Her primary care provider has tried her on several antidepressants, but they do not relieve the symptoms. She has been admitted to begin an ECT series. You are assigned to her care.

1. To decrease her risk during the treatment, what interventions are needed? What is the reason for these?

   V.R. will be NPO (nothing by mouth) after midnight the night prior to her treatment. This is important because she will be given general anesthesia for the treatment and there must be no risk of aspiration of vomitus.

2. After the treatment, you are assigned to care for V.R. What should you expect to do?

   Postanesthesia recovery care is required. Vital signs are taken. She will recover quickly, but requires observation until she is recovered. When she is able, she is given food and fluids. She will need assistance walking until stable.

3. Will V.R. experience memory loss? If so, will it be permanent?

   She will likely experience some memory loss, but it is usually not permanent.

Situation: T.C., a 17-year-old girl, comes into the nurse's office at her high school. T.C. says she has been upset, is having trouble sleeping, and has lost her appetite. On further exploration, she reveals that her parents have been arguing quite a bit related to financial difficulties, her college applications are due and she has not started on them, and her grades are suffering. She asks the nurse to help.

1. What symptoms indicate that T.C. is having problem with stress?

She says she is upset, her sleep is interrupted, and her appetite has decreased. Her parents' arguing about their financial problems is upsetting her, she is worried about her college applications, and her grades have dropped.

2. T.C. says she feels worried all the time. What three techniques could help T.C. relax and decrease her stress?

Any of these stress management techniques could help decrease her stress: deep breathing, progressive muscle relaxation, reframing, imagery, and/or positive self-talk.

Situation: G.F. is admitted to the emergency department following a rape. She is 24 years old and lives alone. She was sexually assaulted when returning from work late at night. After she is examined, she begins to shake and cry. She will not let anyone touch her and is unable to decide what to do (e. g., call a friend to take her home, talk with a rape counselor, or agree to follow-up visit). When you try to speak with G.F., she responds rapidly and in a manner that is not clear or understandable.

1. Has G.F. experienced a crisis? And if so, how would you assess her anxiety level?

> **This experience is an adventitious crisis. The assessment reveals G.F. to be in the third phase of crisis, whereby all her internal and external resources are challenged to cope with the situation.**

2. If you had to explain the crisis process and its phases applied to G.F., what would you say?

> **Phase I: G.F. is exposed to an overwhelming event, the rape.**
>
> **Phase II: Her level of anxiety increases. She sees no way of feeling safe at this time.**
>
> **Phase III: Her usual resources for coping, both internal and external, are not leading to relief of her stress, fear, and pain.**
>
> **Phase IV: G.F.'s tension or anxiety increases, she is now experiencing significant disorganization, and deterioration may continue. For example, she is shaking, crying, refusing to let anyone touch her. G.F. is unable to make a decision, her speech is rapid and verbal content is unclear.**

3. What further data about G.F. might be helpful as you plan interventions?

What is her experience with crises in the past?

How does she usually cope? Are these methods effective?

What is her support system?

4. What are some consequences to G.F.'s rape and crisis?

Psychological disequilibrium could continue and cause long-term problems.

After a crisis, the client with impaired coping and overwhelming anxiety is at risk for self-harm.

5. Identify two interventions that you might use with G.F.

Provide a safe, supportive environment for G.F. If she cannot make a decision about calling a friend, get the telephone number from her and call for her. Have a staff member stay with or near G.F. until the friend arrives, consult a rape counselor, and arrange a follow-up evaluation. Give her this information in writing and give it to her friend. Tell her friend that it is important that G.F. come for the appointment.

If she notices G.F.'s anxiety is increasing, or if she appears depressed (crying, withdrawn, not eating or sleeping, etc.), contact G.F.'s primary care provider or counselor. Support groups may be therapeutic when G.F. is ready to attend.

Administer antianxiety medication if ordered. If a prescription is given for home, G.F. and her friend must be educated about its purpose, dosage, frequency, side effects, and dangers (do not use with alcohol, use caution if driving, and potential of medication, etc.).

Situation: G.L., a 44-year-old, comes to the outpatient clinic for her first appointment. She states that she has feelings of restlessness, difficulty concentrating, fatigue related to insomnia, and frequent tearfulness. G.L.'s employment status is in question due to possible downsizing at work. While waiting for the primary care provider, she is pacing and wringing her hands.

1. To fully obtain a complete history, what additional questions would the nurse ask G.L.?

   Is she taking/using any medications (prescription, over the counter, or illegal)?

   Has she been experiencing normal menses/menopausal changes?

   When did the symptoms start?

   Does G.L. drink alcohol? If so, how much?

   What are the stressors in her life?

   How has she coped with stress previously?

   Is there any client/family history of mental illness/anxiety disorders?

   Does she have a support system?

   Is there a history of stress-related physical problems (hypertension, ulcers, ulcerative colitis)?

2. Identify two priority problems that require nursing intervention.

   Overwhelming anxiety

   Impaired decision-making

3. Which medications would you expect the primary care provider to order? What effects of the medication should you expect?

Antianxiety (anxiolytic) medications are important in treating clients with high levels of anxiety. The anxiolytics are the drugs of choice when there are no symptoms of psychosis. These medications are expected to lower anxiety by exerting an inhibitory effect on the neurons in the brain. Antianxiety medications have a high potential for habituation and addiction and withdrawals can be dangerous (e.g., seizures, except for buspirone [BuSpar]), which is not addictive).

The SSRI antidepressants, particularly Paxil, also exert antianxiety effects. Venlafaxine (Effexor) is an SNRI antidepressant that has antianxiety effects. Antidepressants should be ordered to improve the physiologic balance and help G.L. cope more effectively. These medications may take 5-14 days to reach therapeutic levels. The SSRI antidepressants, particularly Paxil, also exert antianxiety effects. Venlafaxine (Effexor) is an SNRI antidepressant that has antianxiety effects.

Situation: J.P. has been having difficulty getting to his job. He tries to leave the house but experiences tremors, shortness of breath, and fear. He is now confined to his home and no longer able to work or maintain social activities. You ask the client what he feels like when he tries to leave, and he responds, "I feel like something awful will happen, I don't know what, but I get this overwhelming feeling of doom." J.P. has agreed to try systematic desensitization.

1. What type of phobia has been described?

   Agoraphobia

2. If you had to describe his specific symptoms that support a diagnosis of phobia, what would you include?

   High level of anxiety (e.g., tremors, shortness of breath, feels overwhelming fear or doom)

   Inability to function (e.g., go to work)

   Withdrawal (e.g., staying at home)

   Dysfunctional social interactions (e.g., he will not leave home for social activities)

3. What is the significance of the fact that J.P. cannot leave his home?

   He no longer can meet his own daily needs and function effectively in the community.

4. What is systematic desensitization?

   This is an intervention in which the client is gradually exposed to the phobic object or situation. The goal is to decrease the fear and increase the client's function in the presence of the phobic stimulus.

Situation: You are assigned a client admitted to a medical unit for colitis. This is the client's first admission for this diagnosis. P.L. is 35 years old and appears to be uncomfortable. She is speaking rapidly throughout the interview. As you speak with her while giving her care, she comments, "This is all just because of stress. Isn't that silly? I should be able to handle my stress better."

1. What responses could you make?

> "Your illness must be very frustrating and being hospitalized is frightening. Colitis is a medical problem, and stress can affect it. We all experience stress, and everyone can learn to cope better with stress. It might make you more comfortable to learn more about stress and coping with it so that you control or manage it, and it does not control you."

2. How can you best help P.L. understand stress?

> Explain that stress is a state of disequilibrium that occurs when a person cannot cope effectively any longer. Learning how to cope with stress and prevent it from overwhelming us will improve our overall health. Support systems can be used to increase coping. When we experience stress, our bodies respond physically, physiologically, and psychologically. This can lead to further problems for us. Improving our problem-solving abilities, recognizing that we need to take time for ourselves, and regularly using stress management techniques such as relaxation and deep breathing, are helpful.

Situation: W.F. is a 75-year-old widow who lives alone. Her daughter lives nearby with her family. Up until this spring, W.F. had experienced few medical problems. In the last three months, she has called her primary care provider weekly with medical complaints and has had numerous appointments. She has insisted on seeing specialists. Her daughter is concerned about her mother's health and also frustrated with the frequent complaints and phone calls about medical concerns. Her mother has now decided that she must have a cardiac problem and is too weak to walk. Her primary care provider cannot diagnosis any cardiac problem.

1. Given the data provided, what is W.F. experiencing?

   She is experiencing a somatoform disorder. This is a disorder in which the client complains of numerous medical problems for which there is no medical basis or cause.

2. Identify five interventions that may be used.

   A complete history and physical that indicates no physical problems is a priority. If there is no physical cause, W.F. is told the facts and supported by saying that you understand that she does feel the symptoms, such as weakness.

   Discuss stress with W.F. and determine how she has dealt with stress. How does she occupy herself living alone? Is it possible and is she willing to live in some type of residential situation? Does she go to day care?

   Teach W.F. new coping methods. Remember at her age, change may be difficult.

   Meet with her daughter and discuss her mother's stress and response to stress. Identify how the daughter will respond to her mother's phone calls and complaints. Consistency is important.

   If antianxiety medications are prescribed, teach the client and daughter about the medication.

Situation: A 40-year-old client is brought to the local emergency room by the police department. The client was observed shouting at customers in a local department store. He frightened many customers by talking to imaginary persons and threatening to harm anyone who attempted to console him. The client was transferred to the psychiatric unit.

On the psychiatric unit, the client keeps to himself and paces and walks away when anyone approaches him. The client talks with a flurry of ideas, laughs to himself and tilts his head to the side, as if listening. When the medical professionals attempt to talk with him, the client shouts, "Get away from me! Stay back! I know that you are one of them!" He picks up a chair, as if for his protection and appears frightened. The client's appearance is unkempt; his clothes are dirty and wrinkled, his hair straggly and uncombed, and he has body odor. The primary care provider's diagnosis is paranoid schizophrenia and the client is prescribed Cogentin and Haldol.

---

1. Identify assessment data from which to formulate a plan of care.

   - **Client picks up a chair and uses it for protection.**
   - **Threatening to staff**
   - **Talks and laughs to himself**
   - **Flurry of ideas**
   - **Tilts his head to the side**
   - **Keeps to himself**
   - **Walks away when approached**
   - **Appearance is unkempt and unclean**

2. Prioritize the appropriate nursing diagnoses for this client.

   Risk for violence directed toward others

   Sensory perceptual alteration (hallucinations)

   Social isolation

   Self-care deficit

3. List the most appropriate nursing interventions that correspond with each nursing diagnosis listed above.

Risk for violence directed toward others: Provide a safe, quiet environment and remove items from the client's environment that could be used to inflict harm to himself or others.

Sensory perceptual alteration (hallucinations): Provide feedback to assist the client in separating reality from fantasy/altered perception.

Social isolation: Establish therapeutic nurse/client relationship.

Self-care deficit: Assess barriers to participation in activities of daily living.

Situation: You are making a home visit to C.K., a client who has a long psychiatric history. She has been on haloperidol (Haldol) for some time. The purpose of your visit is to follow-up about her recent surgery following a broken hip. This is your second visit in four days. On your first visit, she appeared to be pleasant and was responsive to your suggestions. As you enter the home, she seems reluctant to let you in. When you enter, you notice that she is wearing dirty clothes and appears unkempt. She looks tired, and you ask her how much sleep has she been getting. C.K. responds, "How can I possibly sleep? So much has been said about me. I have to be alert for people watching me."

---

1. What data do you have about this client that is important in understanding her current status?

> Her condition has changed in four days. She has a psychiatric history and has been taking an antipsychotic medication, which may indicate that she has had psychotic symptoms in the past. She is experiencing a stressful period, both physiologically and psychologically, due to her surgery. She has a self-care deficit. Although she was responsive on the first visit, C.K. now does not appear to want to have you visit. Her statement is unusual and may indicate that she is delusional, particularly about being persecuted.

2. What further data do you need regarding C.K.'s status?

- What is her psychiatric diagnosis and past psychiatric history?
- What dosage and frequency of Haldol has been ordered?
- Does she have the medication in the home?
- Is she taking the medication?
- If not, how many doses has she missed?
- Does she have support (e.g., family, friends, and neighbors)?
- Assess her physical status and self-care needs.
- Is she safe from harm to self or others?
- Is she capable of caring for her physical and psychiatric problems?

3. You respond with, "C.K., I am sure that no one is watching you." Based on this case description, why might this response not be appropriate?

> This response is not appropriate as it is contrary to what the client believes and could be perceived as arguing with her. However, the nurse should not accept the delusion as true. The nurse should acknowledge how frightening this must be for C.K. to think that people are talking about and watching her.

4. How can you intervene to assist C.K. at this time?

> Ask the client how she is feeling. Express that having surgery is a traumatic experience and having so many different staff to relate to in the hospital and in-home visits can be difficult. You are attempting to assess the feelings associated with the delusion.

> Assess the client's level of anxiety.

> Enlist help of family, friends, and neighbors. Being alone at home and having difficulty leaving home may be increasing her anxiety. Delusions may be her way of coping. If the client does not have Haldol to take, obtain a prescription for her. If she has not taken her medication, ask her why she has not. There may be a problem that can be resolved easily, such as the inability to get to a pharmacy. If she is refusing to take medication, call her primary care provider and report her recent symptoms and probable need for pharmacologic treatment. If C.K.'s condition is deteriorating, and she will not take the Haldol, she may require hospitalization for her own safety.

Situation: C.H. is admitted at 11 p.m. to a secured inpatient unit. The police found him wandering on the street, walking into traffic, and appearing to be talking to someone when there is no one there. He has been on your unit several times, and you know he can be very violent. He calmly enters the unit, thanks the police, and then proceeds to run down the hall screaming, "I will not do it." C.H. hits the wall with his fists. Clients come out of their rooms looking frightened. The shift is changing, and report is just about to begin.

---

1. Based on this description, what do you think C.H. is experiencing?

   The client appears to be experiencing an auditory and/or visual hallucination.

2. What is your priority at this time for C.H.?

   His safety is the top priority.

3. From the perspective of the therapeutic milieu, why is it important for you to act quickly?

   The clients on the unit will become frightened and fear that C.H. might attack them. Since it is nighttime, it is important that the other clients feel that they can go to sleep safely. They will also want to know if the staff can handle someone who is out of control. Some will be fearful that they could become aggressive themselves. The more out of control C.H. becomes, the more difficult it will be to help him. Staff members or other clients may be injured.

4. What interventions are the priority for C.H.?

> Staff members will try to talk with C.H. to help him de-escalate using soft voices and clear, short sentences. Antipsychotic medication will be given to C.H., probably without his cooperation. He will require client protection, a room for seclusion/observation room, and possibly physical restraints. The latter would be required if he were to impose harm to himself in the seclusion/observation room.

5. What are the concerns you should have about client protection interventions?

- Prevent injury to client, other clients, and staff.
- Treat C.H. with respect, and communicate that the staff is there to help him. He must not be abused, verbally or physically.
- Attempt to de-escalate before taking more restrictive measures.
- Establish criteria for terminating more restrictive measures.
- Document interventions, procedure followed, and outcomes of protective interventions.

Psychotic Disorders: Undifferentiated Type Answer Key

Situation: You admit a new client to the Partial Hospitalization Program. E.A. is 55, diagnosed with a psychotic disorder, and was recently hospitalized for three days. When you meet with E.A. for his admission assessment, you discuss his goals for treatment and you assess his needs. E.A. tells you that he is very anxious and cannot seem to think straight. The client is taking risperidone (Risperdal) and benztropine (Cogentin). When you ask the client to tell you when and how much risperidone he takes, he cannot remember. You observe that his clothes are dirty, and he does not appear clean. In the past, E.A. has threatened others with harm and has had difficulty establishing and maintaining relationships.

1. What conclusions can you draw about E.A.'s hospital admission?

   E.A. was hospitalized for only a brief time to begin his medication and other treatment. He also either did not receive any education about his medications, did not have enough time to learn about his medications, or his condition was such that he could not learn about his medications.

2. What outcomes would be appropriate for E.A., who will be in your day treatment program for four weeks?

   - **Experience a reduction in symptoms (e.g., anxiety, hallucinations, aggression).**
   - **Adhere to treatment and participate in treatment planning (e.g., take medications, participate in treatment program).**
   - **Identify medications, their purposes, dosages, frequency, side effects, and when to call a primary care provider.**
   - **Maintain self-care at an appropriate level (e.g., hygiene, ADL).**
   - **Exhibit appropriate behavior with no harm to self or others.**
   - **Demonstrate an interest in and begin skills in interacting with others.**

3. Formulate an education plan for this client.

Medications: Dosage, frequency, purpose, side effects, when to call a primary care provider

Self-care

Coping skills and problem solving

Anger management

Social skills (e.g., communication, appropriate behavior)

Situation: A 54-year-old male is married and is an executive for a large software company. He has no history of mental illness. Lately, the client has been working overtime at the company to meet a deadline. His wife travels out of town during the weekdays. In the past two months, the client has become irritable, isolative, and withdrawn, and has started to drink more than his normal two cocktails after work each day. The client is also less attentive regarding his personal appearance. He is very concerned about the decline in sales over the last year. The client's wife suggests he see a psychiatrist and accompanies him to the appointment.

The psychiatrist's assessment findings include: a SAD affect, insomnia, weight loss, suicidal ideation, and psychomotor retardation. The client is diagnosed with Major Depressive Disorder and is prescribed sertraline (Zoloft) 50 mg. PO every morning. The client is scheduled to return to the mental health clinic in two weeks.

1. Identify the client's priority problems requiring immediate nursing intervention.

    Suicidal ideation

    Feelings of powerlessness and helplessness

    Disturbances in self-esteem

2. Provide the rationale for the priority problems.

    There is a risk for self-directed violence–hopelessness, alcohol abuse, absence of a support network (wife), male gender and high economic status are strong risk factors that increase the potential for suicide.

    Powerlessness decreases the ability to problem-solve and make decisions regarding the self. Feelings of worthlessness and expressions of shame and guilt are common.

    Self-esteem disturbances diminish problem-solving skills. Most clients with suicidal ideation have feelings of lack of hope for the future. Feelings of worthlessness and lack of trust.

3. Identify the appropriate nursing interventions that correspond to each problem.

Instruct the client's spouse regarding the verbal and nonverbal clues that may indicate the client's desire to commit suicide. These clues may be verbal, behavioral, somatic, or emotional.

The nurse should encourage the client to express painful feelings.

The nurse should encourage the client to look at personal strengths and accomplishments, and help the client establish plans for the future.

Situation: D.H., a 22-year-old married female, is diagnosed with bipolar disorder. She lives with her husband and two preschool children. D.H. had numerous mental health problems as a teenager, including anorexia nervosa. She does not take her prescribed lithium on a regular basis, stating, "There's no sense taking it when I'm feeling good! That's for when I'm depressed." Frequently, she leaves her family and travels by herself to other cities to sightsee. She charges the maximum on her credit cards and buys gifts and clothes for friends and neighbors, and buys other items that she then donates to a local charity.

D.H. shows signs of increased manic type behavior. Her primary care provider recommends inpatient admission for assessment and stabilization. She refuses admission and threatens to kill herself if she is admitted. The psychiatrist authorizes an emergency involuntary admission to the hospital for her and she is admitted to the acute psychiatric unit. Admission orders include lithium carbonate 1 gm PO bid.

1. Write the interventions necessary to care for D.H. in the manic phase of the disorder.

   Administer lithium as ordered and antipsychotic medication.

   Reduce environmental stimuli.

   Provide physical activities appropriate to the client's level of functioning.

   Assess behavior, appearance, thought content and self-care.

   Assess learning needs of the client and her husband related to disease process and medication regimen.

   Monitor social interaction.

   Ensure that needs are met (e.g., nutrition, fluids, sleep, exercise, and hygiene).

2. Write the interventions necessary to care for D.H. in the depressive phase of the disorder.

Involve her in one-to-one activities.

Administer lithium and other medications as ordered.

Assist with activities of daily living (ADLs).

Monitor for suicidal plans and place on one-to-one supervision.

Spend short periods of time with her.

Role-play new coping skills.

3. Identify the effects and side effects of lithium therapy.

Lithium therapy is used to reduce the cyclic effects of the disorder, and it is the treatment of choice for bipolar disorders. 600-1800 mg of lithium per day in divided dosages usually produces a serum level of 0.5 to 1.0 eq/L. Therapeutic improvement should be noted in 1-3 weeks.

Side effects include: nausea, vomiting, abdominal pain, fatigue and thirst and polyuria.

Increased fluid intake 2-3 liters per day and slightly increased salt intake are necessary during the initial phase of treatment to avoid dehydration and electrolyte imbalance.

Situation: A roommate found M.B. in her apartment after an overdose of aspirin. She was taken to the emergency department and then admitted to the psychiatric unit. M.B. is 35 years old. She recently lost her job. When her roommate was asked about the overdose, she guessed that M.B. took approximately 30 pills and assumed that her roommate knew that she would be home within the hour. The nurse's physical assessment revealed that she was quiet and responded slowly to questions. She denied wanting to kill herself and stated that she just wanted some peace. She had never tried to harm herself before. M.B. cried through most of the interview. The client said that she had only slept a maximum of four hours per night in the last month or two and had lost 15 pounds. When M.B. was told she would receive one-to-one supervision, she became angry and shouted, "I am not a prisoner."

1. Based on these data, what is the level of risk for M.B.'s suicidal act? Provide your rationale.

    The risk is moderate. M.B. knew her roommate would be home soon, her method could be lethal but she did not take a large number of pills. This method was readily available and did not take much planning.

2. What impact might the job loss have had on M.B.?

    The job loss is a stressor and could have been the precipitating factor; however, it is unknown how long the client has been depressed. She may have been depressed prior to her job loss.

3. What data are provided that indicate M.B. is depressed?

    She talked quietly, responded slowly, cried, has had disturbance in sleep pattern, weight loss, and wanted peace when she made her suicide attempt.

4. How would you respond to M.B.'s outburst about one-to-one supervision?

"All of this is probably frightening to you. We are here to help you and keep you safe. The one-to-one supervision will help us do that. When we feel that you are ready to handle being on your own, we will discontinue it. You will need to help us by talking with us about your feelings."

5. What other intervention is often used with suicidal clients to focus on their responsibility for their own actions? Describe the intervention.

A "no-harm" contract is often used. This is a written contract between the client and staff in which the client agrees not to harm herself, and if she feels the urge to do so, to seek help from staff.

Using the information in the chapters on cognitive disorders and any additional resources necessary, fill in the following table:

Cognitive Disorder	Cognitive Disorder Brief Description	Signs and Symptoms	Nursing Interventions
Delirium	• Usually acute condition characterized by disturbances in consciousness/ changes in cognition following a head trauma or seizure.	• Attention deficits • Disorganized thought • Incoherent speech • Disorientation • Memory loss	• Environmental adjustments (safe environment) • Antipsychotic medications as prescribed • Encourage self care and assure ADLs are met
Dementia	• Can occur concurrently with acute/chronic medical conditions and usually involves impairment in memory, language, emotions, and thought processes.	• Cognitive impairment • Antisocial personality and behavior • Aphasia • Memory loss	• Environmental adjustments (safe environment) • Re-orientation • Family intervention (physical and psychological support) • Antianxiety and antipsychotic medications as prescribed

Cognitive Disorder	Cognitive Disorder Brief Description	Signs and Symptoms	Nursing Interventions
Alzheimer's Disease	• Progressive, pathologic degeneration of biochemical neurotransmitters resulting in remarkable changes in thought and behavioral processes.	• Stage I: Short-term memory loss and mild cognitive deficits • Stage II: Confusion, irritability, agitation, motor involvement, depression • Stage III: Loss of expressive language and reasoning, loss of self-care ADLs • State IV: Disorientation, impaired/absent motor skills, inability to recognize self/ family	• Ensure ADLs are met • Administer prescribed medications • Ensure safety • Latter stages of disease will likely require long-term care provisions
Dissociative Amnesia/Fugue	• A type of retrograde amnesia characterized by a loss of identity (fugue) and can resolve completely and spontaneously	• Amnesias (local, selective, general, continuous, and systematized) • Anxiety • Relocates unexpectedly to new location and forgets own identity (fugue)	• Comprehensive psychological treatment/therapy, including stress management • Family involvement and support if possible • Administer anxiolytic medications as prescribed

---

Situation: E.L. is a client admitted to a medical unit of an acute care facility because of pneumonia. She lives alone and is 80 years old. Due to her illness and limited mobility, she has not taken in an adequate amount of food or fluid. When you enter her room, you notice that E.L. cannot follow your questions. She rambles and speaks incoherently. You ask her today's date and her response is July, when it is December.

When E.L.'s daughter and son come to visit, they express concern about their mother. The daughter says, "Mom is seeing things in the room. We thought she had pneumonia. Our mother has always been a clear thinker. What is wrong with her?"

---

1. What can you tell the family about E.L.'s symptoms?

   E.L.'s symptoms of confusion, disorientation to time, misperceptions, hallucinations, and rambling speech are probably due to delirium caused by her infection and her fluid and electrolyte imbalance. Her perceptual and cognitive alterations may be intensified by the removal from her familiar surroundings.

2. How does delirium differ from dementia?

   Delirium is characterized by a disturbance in consciousness and change in cognition, which develops rapidly when the client experiences a medical condition such as infection, metabolic disorder, fluid and electrolyte imbalance, or hepatic or renal disease. Other causes are drugs (prescribed or non-prescribed) and substance intoxication or withdrawal (e.g., cocaine, hallucinogens, alcohol, etc.). It is also a common postanesthesia event. Delirium resolves once the causative factors are treated; however, dementia is persistent intellectual impairment with disturbances in memory, language, visuospatial ability, emotion, and cognition. Causes may include Alzheimer's, vascular disease, HIV, head trauma, Huntington's disease, Pick's disease, and Parkinson's.

3. Based on the symptoms and probable etiologic factor, what is the prognosis for E.L.'s psychological status?

   E.L.'s psychological status will most likely improve as her pneumonia resolves, and she receives needed fluid and electrolytes.

Situation: B.C. is an elderly male diagnosed with dementia five years ago. He lives with his wife, who is also an elderly person. B.C.'s wife is concerned about his behavior and deteriorating mental status, and is finding it increasingly difficult to care for him at home. He wanders out of the house, is disoriented to time and place, and is unable to dress and groom himself. B.C.'s primary care provider encourages placement in a nursing home, but his wife resists. The primary care provider then arranges for a home health nurse to visit B.C. and his wife.

1. Identify the pertinent client and caregiver information requiring nursing intervention.

   Disoriented to time

   Inability to groom himself

   Wanders

   Angry outbursts

   Pacing

   Caregiver role strain

2. What instructions regarding B.C.'s safety should be given to his wife?

   Keep potentially harmful objects away from B.C.

   Orient him to time and place using clocks, calendars, photographs, and familiar objects.

   Assess his abilities to dress himself and encourage as much self-care as possible.]

   Provide structure to the daily routine.

   Keep environmental stimuli to a minimum.

   B.C.'s wife should also be given information regarding respite care, community services, local support groups, and adult day care programs.

   Lock doors. B.C. should not be left alone.

Alzheimer's Disease Answer Key

Situation: J.L. is a 72-year-old male with Stage II Alzheimer's disease. He lives with his wife. During a routine clinic visit, J.L.'s wife verbalizes concern about her husband's violent, angry behavior and irritability. She tells the primary care provider that her husband often tells her that something is "crawling on the wall" when in reality there is nothing there. He wanders out of the house, is disoriented to time and place, and is unable to dress and groom himself. The client's wife is having difficulty caring for him at home. The primary care provider encourages placement in a nursing home, but J.L.'s wife refuses. The primary care provider then arranges for a home health nurse to visit J.L. and his wife.

1. Identify the pertinent information requiring nursing intervention.

- Disoriented to time
- Inability to groom himself
- Wanders
- Angry outbursts
- Pacing
- Caregiver role strain

2. Identify appropriate nursing diagnoses that pertain to the case study.

- Risk for injury related to confusion and wandering
- Self-care deficit related to impaired cognitive functioning
- Altered thought processes related to confusion
- Sleep pattern disturbance related to wandering and the inability to recognize need for sleep
- Caregiver role strain related to the amount and complexity of home care needs

3. Prioritize the nursing interventions based on the information acquired above:

<u>1</u> Provide safety, keeping harmful objects away from the client.

<u>3</u> Orient client to time and place using posters and signs.

<u>5</u> Assess the client's abilities to dress himself.

<u>6</u> Provide structure to the daily routine.

<u>4</u> Schedule rest periods throughout the day.

<u>7</u> Provide the caregiver with relief by using local support groups and government agencies.

<u>2</u> Keep environmental stimuli to a minimum.

Dissociative Fugue/Dissociative Amnesia Answer Key

Situation: M.L. is admitted to the surgical unit following a fall from a building. He is alert but is unable to remember his name. His wife comes to visit him and he does not recognize her. M.L. becomes agitated and yells out, "I can't remember who I am. What is going on?" At the time of his discharge from the surgical unit three days later, he is still unable to remember anything about himself or his accident. His family takes him home, but he is reluctant to go with them because he perceives them as strangers.

1. What type of amnesia does M.L. have?

   General amnesia

2. What can be done to assist M.L.?

   - **Individual therapy or counseling may be needed to provide support and understanding of the illness process and the effect of the injury on his memory.**
   - **Hypnotherapy may be used at an appropriate time although the success of this treatment is relatively low.**
   - **M.L. will need help in coping with his anxiety and stress about his loss of memory. Teaching him coping mechanisms, such as relaxation techniques, may be helpful.**
   - **Encourage use of antianxiety medications. Provide education about the use, administration, and any side effects of the anxiolytic that should be reported.**
   - **Support from family, if available, without pressure to force him to remember.**

3. Identify three nursing diagnoses that might be applied to M.L.

   Anxiety

   Impaired social interaction

   Ineffective individual coping

Impaired adjustment

Self-esteem disturbance

Personal identity disturbance

Hopelessness

Impaired memory

Altered role performance

Altered family process

Situation: K.T. has been admitted to the inpatient psychiatric unit. She is 16. Her height is 5' 6", and she weighs 75 pounds. This is her first psychiatric hospitalization, but she was admitted last year to the medical unit when she had pneumonia and her weight could not be maintained at home. As you begin the admission assessment, she immediately complains that she is overweight. She asks questions about the calories in the meals and alternate choices. She complains of being tired; however, later you find her exercising in her room with the door shut. You have already told her that the door must remain open. You notice that she has unpacked and neatly arranged all of her clothing and personal items. Her lab work indicates that she has hypokalemia. As you ask about her menstrual cycle, she tells you she has not had her period for one year. Her parents seem over-attentive, but of course, her condition is unstable at this time. You decide to explore more about their relationship later, after K.T. has settled in more on the unit. You do notice that the parents are thin, but not unhealthy in appearance. K.T. has no siblings. She has been unable to attend school in the last two weeks due to her weakness, although she is an excellent student. She expresses concern about getting behind in her schoolwork. You reassure her that a teacher is available who will help her maintain her studies, and this seems to relieve some of her anxiety.

1. What further data do you need to determine if K.T. has anorexia nervosa or bulimia? Describe the difference between the two conditions. What is the similarity?

> **Has K.T. been using self-induced vomiting or misusing laxatives, diuretics, or enemas to control weight?**
>
> **Most persons with bulimia are within a normal weight range. Anorexia is the refusal to maintain a minimally-normal body weight in the absence of a physical cause. Bulimia is an episodic, uncontrollable, compulsive, rapid digestion of large quantities of food over a short period of time (binging), followed by inappropriate compensatory behaviors to rid the body of the excess calories such as self-induced vomiting, laxatives, diuretics, or enemas (purging).**
>
> **Both disorders are exaggerated attempts to control using food intake as the means.**

2. When you conduct further assessment of the family, what factors might have predisposed K.T. to an eating disorder?

> How does the family deal with conflict? Avoidance is typically used in families who have a member with an eating disorder. Power and control issues are also evident. Parents may use criticism that promotes obsessive and perfectionist behavior while the child tries to get love, approval, and recognition. Eventually, the child develops ambivalence toward the parents and eating problems become a way of rebelling.

3. What type of behavior would you expect from K.T. regarding food use on the unit?

> K.T. will want to control all aspects of her meals and snacks. She may hide food, and if she uses self-induced vomiting, she will try to do this without the staff knowing. K.T. will be obsessed with discussing food. At times, she may refuse to eat.

4. Identify three complications that K.T. might experience that require monitoring. Identify one she now has.

> She may experience dehydration, seizures, constipation, and cardiac problems, such as arrhythmias, hypotension, hypothermia, renal problems, and death.
>
> She has hypokalemia, which indicates an electrolyte imbalance, related to gastric losses and laxative or diuretic use.
>
> She also has had amenorrhea for one year.

5. Describe the interventions that might be considered for mealtimes.

> Meals planned with dietitian to ensure that K.T. gets adequate calories.
>
> Allow some choices for K.T., but none that interfere with her health.
>
> Observe her for water loading (prior to meals).
>
> Observe K.T. during mealtime. Staff should be consistent in their responses to inappropriate food consumption during mealtime.
>
> Observe K.T. after meals for specified time to ensure that she does not use self-induced vomiting or exercise to control weight gain.
>
> Plan intervention to use if client does not eat. Tube feeding is a last resort.

6. What is the significance of K.T. wanting to know how many calories are in each of the items on her tray?

This is a way that she can control how much weight she gains. If she knows the calories of each food, she can try to avoid foods that might contribute to a gain in weight.

Situation: You have been told that you must meet with the parents of R.H., who has recently been diagnosed with a personality disorder. You arrange for an appointment with the parents, who tell you they are very concerned and confused about their son's diagnosis and treatment.

---

1. Describe five traits that are frequently found in persons with personality disorders. These traits may be helpful as you talk with the parents about their son's behavior.

    Dysfunctional interpersonal relations

    Suspiciousness

    Social anxiety

    Failure to conform to social norms

    Manipulation and splitting

    Fear of abandonment

2. The parents want to know how long will it take to cure their son. How do you respond to this?

    "There is no cure for a personality disorder. It is a pattern of behavior that develops over time and is a long-term problem. However, your son can be helped to learn new ways of coping and obtain a better understanding of his feelings and how they affect his behavior. Improving the quality of communication with others can positively affect his ability to function in society."

Situation: S.T. has been admitted to the hospital four times within one year. She is 29 years old. Typically, she is admitted after threatening suicide and has been found to burn herself with cigarettes. On the unit, she has complimented one staff member and told that nurse that she is the best nurse and all other staff is awful. This nurse has defended S.T. during team meetings. Other staff members are now angry with this nurse. During group meetings, S.T. has convinced other clients that the staff is incompetent.

1. Describe the data that indicate S.T. may have a borderline personality disorder.

 Multiple hospital admissions in a short period of time

 Suicidal ideation

 Self-mutilation, cigarette burns

 Uses splitting and manipulation

2. What risks are involved in caring for S.T.?

 Serious suicide attempts that may result in medical complications, scarring, or death;

 she may manipulate the staff, undermining care efforts.

3. What is your initial impression for S.T.'s effect on the staff and the unit as a whole?

 S.T. is manipulating the staff by creating triangles and forming conflict among the health care team. The one technique that S.T. uses is to compliment one staff member and complain that the others do not seem to know what they are doing. That staff member may feel an alliance with the client. This technique of splitting is destructive to staff cohesiveness and a team approach to the delivery of care.

Situation: J.E. works in a factory, where he has been employed for three years. His supervisor has noticed over the years that he has certain characteristics. He takes criticism poorly and can become overtly angry and hostile. He tells his peers that he knows the best approach to all problems that they encounter during work and refuses to acknowledge a mistake. His peers do not like working with him. His supervisor has decided to watch J.E. more closely as he is concerned about his behavior. In the last month, the supervisor has overheard J.E. making comments such as, "You don't trust me and are out to get me," and "Get out of my face. I am the only one who knows what to do and who will be successful." The supervisor has been called to the work area because a fight has broken out between J.E. and one of the employees.

1. How can the supervisor best intervene at this time?

   Separate J.E. from the other employee. Ask the other employee to leave the area. Try to discover the reason for the fight but do not get into an argument with J.E.

2. If the supervisor requires that J.E. see a counselor, what data would be important for the counselor to know about? What data might support that he has a paranoid personality disorder?

   Hypersensitivity and poor responsiveness to criticism
   Refuses to acknowledge his mistakes
   Perception that others are out to get him
   Exaggerated self-importance, belief that he is the "only one who knows what to do"
   Hostility and anger
   Suspiciousness of others
   Long-term dysfunctional behavioral pattern

3. Will it be easy to involve J.E. in treatment? Provide your rationale.

   No, it will not. Clients with personality disorders have difficulty adhering to treatment because they do not usually view their behavior as a problem. Many clients who are paranoid will mistrust the intention of the therapist.

Situation: A 20-year-old male, T.J., has no history of mental illness. As a child, he was abandoned by his mother and physically abused by his father. He currently lives with an older sister, but spends most of his time with gang members. He has developed a pattern of altercations with the law, reckless driving, carrying concealed weapons, forging signatures on checks, and theft from neighborhood homes. Recently, he has been involved in more fights. T.J. is presently unemployed and depends on his sister and friends for money. His sister makes excuses for his behavior, stating he had a "rocky start in life."

Recently, T.J. was arrested for theft. During the arrest, he became aggressive and assaulted one of the police officers. Due to his extreme rage, he was taken to the psychiatric hospital for evaluation. He refused to be admitted, and the psychiatrist petitioned for an involuntary admission. The admitting diagnoses are mood disorder and antisocial personality disorder.

---

1. Based on available assessment information, identify the immediate nursing actions.

Aggressive behavior:
- **Observe behavior indicating emotional and cognitive status.**
- **Provide a safe environment for the client and others.**
- **Provide positive reinforcement to the client when tasks are completed according to the guidelines.**

Antidepressant or mood stabilizing medications: observe for desired and side effects and teach about the medications.

Extreme rage:
- **Reduce stimuli in the environment.**
- **Set limits for behavior.**
- **Establish consequences for noncompliance.**
- **It may be necessary to use physical restraints and/or a seclusion/observation room if the safety of the client, other persons, or staff is in question.**

Involuntary admission:
- **Orient the client to the unit rules and acceptable behavior.**
- **Create a therapeutic environment.**
- **Facilitate effective communication.**

2. Write an expected outcome for each of the following nursing diagnoses:

a. Risk for violence to self and others related to aggressive behavior and rage, as evidenced by a history of aggression and association with gang members.

    Expected Outcome:
    The client will not harm himself or others.

b. Ineffective individual coping related to irresponsible behavior as evidenced by illegal actions and sister making excuses for his behavior.

    Expected Outcome:
    The client will conform to expected behavioral norms, display more constructive coping, and assume responsibility for own behavior.

Situation: L.G. is married and has three children. She has always been a very neat and organized person. After the birth of her third child, she wanted to go back to work; however, she could not find adequate childcare, mostly due to her demands of the caretaker. Her husband began to notice that she was more and more concerned about cleaning the house. She developed an elaborate schedule and procedures, which she had to follow. Eventually, the schedule and procedures became so important that if she was interrupted she had to begin all over again. This began to consume more of her time, and she was less able to care for her children. Her husband would come home from work in the evening and find L.G. cleaning while the children were dirty, running wild throughout the house, having not been fed lunch. The husband took L.G. to their family primary care provider.

---

1. What is happening to L.G.?

> **L.G. is experiencing considerable anxiety and is subconsciously dealing with her stress by engaging in compulsive behavior. Her elaborate compulsive motor rituals, which she cannot control, indicate that she has an obsessive-compulsive disorder.**

2. What is the significance of anxiety to L.G.'s problems?

> **Anxiety is a major component of obsessive-compulsive disorder. Although the ritualistic behavior is practiced to decrease anxiety, it is not successful in relieving her perceived stress.**

3. What factors may have predisposed L.G. to a phobic response?

> **L.G. had planned to seek employment outside the home, but has not been able to, mostly due to her need to have everything done her way. Her feelings of anxiety are now intensified because of her compulsivity and lack of ability to cope effectively. She may also have a familial predisposition to OCD.**

4. Describe the impact of biochemical factors on the anxiety L.G. is experiencing.

> An ineffective gamma-aminobutyric acid (GABA) neurotransmitter process may be affecting L.G.'s condition. Fatigue, related to performing her rituals, can also increase her level of distress.

5. How can you best intervene to assist L.G.?

> Her rituals should gradually be limited, but do not prevent them all at once as she may experience panic.

> Work with the husband to allow time for L.G. to have some time for herself. (What does she like to do?) If she will not allow a paid caretaker in the home, maybe he can take time the time or another relative or friend could help out for intermittent periods.

> An antianxiety medication may be prescribed to decrease her symptoms. An SSRI antidepressant will decrease the urge to perform compulsive rituals or engage in repetitive activities.

> Discuss the anxiety process with L.G. Help her to identify the triggers and new methods for coping.

> Include L.G.'s family members in the planning and implementation of her care, as they are likely feeling frustrated with the situation at home.

> Assess L.G.'s sleep pattern and how it can be improved.

> Encourage her involvement with her children.

Child or Adolescent with Attention-Deficit/Hyperactivity Disorder Answer Key

Situation: You are a school nurse in an elementary school. You receive a call from a mother who wants to come in and talk with you about her son who is seven years old. When you meet with the mother, she tells you that her son has been put on Ritalin for attention-deficit hyperactivity disorder. The mother is concerned about her son's behavior in school and at home. Her primary care provider has given her little information about this type of behavioral disorder or the medication that has been prescribed for her son. You tell her that there are other children in the school with this problem and that you will help her gain some understanding.

1. What symptoms would you expect this mother to describe?

   Inattention, hyperactivity, impulsivity, impaired social interactions, risk-taking behavior (without seeming to recognize that his actions are dangerous), difficulty in school, impaired verbal communication, depression, and low self-confidence

2. How would you describe the purpose of Ritalin to the mother?

   Ritalin is a medication that is used to lessen hyperactivity and distractibility and improve attention, focus, and concentration.

3. Why would you suggest that the mother use behavioral contracts with her son?

   A written behavior contract with the son that focuses on specific behavior can be useful in helping the child gain control and use appropriate behavior.

Situation: You are working on the evening shift. The psychiatric unit has been fairly calm, but you do notice that two clients seem to be irritating each other. One of them, E.M., has a history of aggressive behavior and has a diagnosis of paranoid schizophrenia. The other client was admitted for a suicide attempt and will be discharged within two days. E.M. was admitted 12 hours ago. You do not know him. You recognize that both clients are having problems managing their anger. During team meeting, the staff members discuss interventions that need to be taken.

---

1. How might the anger that is felt by these two clients differ?

 E.M. has paranoid schizophrenia. He may be delusional, and this may influence his expression of anger. Due to his illness, he probably has impaired coping and judgment and is likely to respond inappropriately when he feels anger.

 The client with a history of suicide attempts may have anger directed toward self.

2. What will the client who will be discharged in two days need to know about self-monitoring his anger?

 • Identify situations when the client has felt anger.

 • Help him identify triggers for his anger. What sets him off?

 • What are the client's typical coping mechanisms? Are they appropriate? Have they been helpful? How have they affected others?

 • Discuss the difference between appropriate and inappropriate responses to anger.

 • Discuss self-monitoring triggers to anger and coping mechanisms he might use (e.g., seeking out some neutral person to speak to, exercising, removing himself from the situation or stimuli, using relaxation techniques, writing about his feelings in a journal).

 • Encourage him to put together a plan of action to follow when he feels suicidal, or has an urge to harm himself.

 • Help him understand the importance of not turning anger inward.

 • Encourage him to put together a plan of action to follow when he feels suicidal or an urge to harm himself.

3. What needs to be done to assist the new admission, E.M., with his anger?

- Assess his level of anger and aggression.
- Try to determine if delusions are affecting behavior.
- Keep him separate from those who may stimulate his anger.
- Monitor him for need of more restrictive interventions.
- Administer antipsychotics, as ordered.

Situation: You are the nurse admitting a new client to the mental health unit of your facility. Your assessment reveals a client with hand tremors, diaphoresis and agitation. The client reports long-standing relationship problems, depression with thoughts of suicide and mentions concurrent use of alcohol, cocaine, and nicotine.

---

1. Would you classify this as a substance-use disorder, and/or a substance induced disorder? Why?

> As stated in the chapter, the definition of substance abuse is the use of chemicals or materials for non-medical purposes with the intention of producing an altered state of consciousness, sensorium, heightened sensory perception, or change in self-image. In this case, the client appears to exhibit substance use symptoms of alcohol dependency, depression, and relationship difficulties, plus substance-induced symptoms of withdrawal (tremors, diaphoresis and agitation).

2. Provide 3 examples of therapeutic interaction that you could offer this client to build trust and rapport during the initial stages of the admission process.

> Answers will vary depending on type of therapeutic communication used. However, answers could include one of the following types of techniques based on this type of scenario:

- Listening (no statements necessary)
- Broad opening
- Reflection
- Seeking validation
- Summarizing

> Non-verbal actions included in therapeutic communcation include:

- Facial expressions
- Posture
- Gestures
- Proximity to client

3. What discharge needs do you anticipate for this client?

From the information contained in the clinical example, this client will require assistance with abstaining from further use of drugs and alcohol as it has caused problems that are negatively affecting lifestyle. Additional assistance will be needed for developing relationship, coping and problem-solving skills. This client may already have irreversible damage to the liver (cirrhosis), however with abstinence and proper medical care, the symptoms lessen. Additionally, dramatic changes are possible to see enhanced communication and family interdependence, with a greater positive self-image.

Situation: A 45-year-old male was admitted to the hospital at 2 a.m. after vomiting a large amount of blood. In the initial interview, the nurse documents the following data:

The client's father died of complications related to alcoholism two years ago. The client's mother, who is still living, has a past history of substance abuse (Valium). The client relates that he had his first drink as a young teenager when he secretly took it from his parents' stock. He has continuously used alcohol since that time. The client smokes three packs of cigarettes a day, and tells the nurse that he would like to quit smoking, however, does not feel that he can.

The client is married with two teenage children. He has had marital problems but is currently living with his wife. They are having financial problems. His work history is varied and he is unable to hold a job for a long period of time. He has difficulty arriving to work on time and has frequent absences, and asks that his wife call in sick for him. He blames his boss and coworkers for his difficulties at work. Yesterday, he was fired from his job and spent the night at the bars drinking. He was drinking when his hematemesis began.

The client states he was diagnosed with an ulcer three months ago and he has been noncompliant with his medications because he is unable to afford them.

1. Identify the predisposing factors that influence the client's behavior.
   a. Genetic influences:

      1. Mother: history of substance abuse

      2. Father: died of complications related to alcoholism

   b. Past experiences:

      1. Consumed first drink as a teenager

      2. Continued drinking since teenage years

      3. Diagnosed with an ulcer three months ago

      4. Erratic work history

      5. Fired from work yesterday

   c. Existing conditions:

      1. Smokes three packs of cigarettes per day

      2. Severe financial difficulties, unable to afford medications

     3. Marital problems

     4. Fired from work yesterday

2. Identify the expected outcomes for the following nursing diagnoses:

  a. Chronic low self-esteem as evidenced by self-destructive nature of alcohol abuse and inability to take responsibility for self.

    Expected outcome: The client will perform adequate self-care activities. The client will not participate in activities or exhibit behaviors that pose risk for self-injury.

  b. Risk for injury as evidenced by central nervous system agitation and withdrawal.

    Expected outcome: Client will show no sign of self-injury related to alcohol ingestion and/or withdrawal.

Central Nervous System Depressant Abuse and Dependence Answer Key

---

Situation: P.T. is admitted to the substance abuse treatment program from the emergency department. She is 40 years old and has never received treatment for substance abuse. In her admission assessment she reports that she has been taking barbiturates for three years. Her admission was precipitated when she drank alcohol in large quantities and also took barbiturates.

During the assessment, P.T. says she does not know why she had a "bad reaction" to the drugs this time. She has been having more problems holding a job but needs money to buy drugs.

---

1. Describe the effects that central nervous system depressants may have on P.T.'s body.

> **Disruption in REM/NREM sleep states**
>
> **Shallow respiration and bradypnea**
>
> **Renal impairment or renal failure**
>
> **Bradycardia or cardiac arrest**
>
> **Slowed metabolism, leading to longer half-life of the drug**
>
> **Hypothermia**
>
> **Sexual dysfunction**

2. How would you respond to P.T.'s comment about her bad reaction?

> **The combination of barbiturates and alcohol can have a major depressant effect on the body, resulting in slow breathing and heartbeat. It is a very dangerous combination and can lead to death.**

Central Nervous System Stimulant Abuse and Dependence Answer Key

---

Situation: The same day that P.T. is admitted, another client is admitted three hours later. He is experiencing hallucinations and believes that everyone is out to get him. This client, R.G., is 22. His family gave a history of drug abuse over the last five years with no treatment. R. G. arrives wearing dirty clothes and appears to have lost weight, as his clothes are too big on him. Staff members are told he has been abusing amphetamines and cocaine. He has dropped out of college.

---

1. You are told to develop a plan for his initial care. What interventions need to be considered initially for R.G.?

    Safety is important. How are R.G.'s hallucinations and delusions affecting his behavior? Monitoring this to ensure his safety and safety of others.

    Monitor vital signs.

    Assess for withdrawal symptoms of dysphoria, fatigue, sleep disturbances, increased appetite, and increase in heart and respiratory rates.

    Assess his anxiety and provide assistance in decreasing it (e.g., approach calmly, allow him space). Client protection, such as physical restraint and/or seclusion/observation room should be used only after other interventions have been tried.

    Decrease environmental stimuli that could agitate him.

2. Identify two nursing diagnoses that apply at this time and the rationale for them.

    Altered sensory perceptions: He is experiencing hallucinations.

    Altered thought processes: The client is experiencing delusions.

    Risk to self or others: His fear of others may lead to escalating behavior and hurting himself or others.

Situation: The substance abuse unit team meeting is discussing its treatment program for opioid dependent clients. There are a number of new staff members who need to be oriented to the different types of clients and drugs abused, as well as to the treatment program offered. You have been assigned the job of providing this orientation. You make up a list of critical questions that you think new staff might ask. Then, you prepare for your session by answering them.

1. "What are opioids? It sounds exotic but I have no idea what drugs are included."

   Opioids include opioids of natural origin, derivatives, and synthetic opiate-like drugs. Drugs that are frequently abused are morphine, heroin, codeine, and Dilaudid, and synthetic drugs Demerol and Darvon.

2. "How does tolerance develop and what are possible complications?"

   Tolerance for these drugs develops rapidly, requiring larger amounts of the drug to obtain the desired effect. The abuser is at risk for respiratory depression, coma, and death.

3. "Withdrawal is an important topic for us as we are treating clients who are experiencing it. What data are important as the clients are monitored for withdrawal and how long does withdrawal take?"

   Withdrawal symptoms include nausea, vomiting, diarrhea, abdominal cramping, sweating, and fever. These symptoms may begin 6-24 hours after last dose, peak in three days, and are reduced in two weeks.

4. "Are there any medications used to treat opioid dependence?"

   Narcan is used for acute overdose. Methadone hydrochloride (Dolophine) is used for opioid dependency; however, clients must be observed to ensure it is ingested. It can be abused. Clients need to be involved in a support program, such as NA.

Situation: M.H. is admitted to the substance abuse unit from the emergency department, after he was found walking down the street with no clothes on and yelling that he was being chased. He was not being chased. After he became lucid, M.H. admitted to taking PCP at a party. M.H. admits to a long history of PCP use.

1. How can you best intervene at this time?

> **Monitor vital signs.**
>
> **Observe seizure precautions.**
>
> **Protect M.H. from harm to self or others.**
>
> **Decrease stimuli; approach him with a calm voice and simple directions.**
>
> **Ask his friend to stay with him, if both are in agreement.**
>
> **If M.H.'s behavior escalates, may need to use physical restraints or seclusion/ observation room.**

2. What potential medical problems can occur while you are monitoring M.H.?

> **Tachycardia and palpitations, increased blood pressure, seizures, and coma**

3. How might the drug affect him psychologically?

> **The client may experience hallucinations, delusions, depersonalization, derealization, belligerence and escalation, anxiety, and depression. He may experience flashbacks at unpredictable times for years following abstinence from the drug.**

Situation: You have been assigned a clinical rotation with a school nurse in a middle school. During your clinical rotation in a drug rehabilitation unit, you presented an inservice program for new staff. The clinical instructor was very impressed with the information and style of your program. Now he tells you he has a bigger challenge for you. You are to present an educational program to the students on cannabis, which is used by many of the students. You know as much about this topic as you did about opioid abuse, so you approach it in the same way, by asking yourself questions and answering them.

1. What are the typical drugs that are used? What is the active ingredient that causes the physical and mental effects?

   Marijuana and hashish

   THC is the active ingredient in marijuana and hashish.

2. If I wanted to tell the students about the impact that these drugs have on their bodies, what would I tell them?

   Symptoms of use include impaired motor coordination, euphoria, anxiety, a sensation of slowed time, and impaired judgment. All of these affect your driving and decision- making capacity for 8-12 hours. Feelings of paranoia are common. The drugs can have some serious effects on your body, such as increasing your heart rate and decreasing the strength of cardiac contractions. These cardiovascular effects are very serious and can lead to death. THC may cause infertility (low sperm production), an increased rate of spontaneous fetal loss, and birth defects. After you stop taking these drugs, you may experience headaches, fatigue, or restlessness.

Situation: A volunteer at a homeless shelter brought the client, a 35-year-old homeless person, to the psychiatric hospital. The client reportedly had been rocking back and forth on his cot, yelling loudly and hitting himself in the head. The workers at the shelter were afraid for the client's safety.

Upon admission to the psychiatric unit, the client was oriented to time, place, and person and knew identifying information about himself. He told the nurse that he has been homeless for 20 years and stated, "My family thought that there was something wrong with me and sent me away. I wandered from place to place for a while and finally I found a place to stay in a junk yard where the workers would bring me food. The junk yard closed last month. I came to the shelter because I don't have anywhere else to go. I can't stand the noise of the radio. The radio plays in my head all the time and I wish that it would stop."

---

1. Identify the client's immediate needs.

- **Food: Since the junk yard workers have stopped bringing him food, he needs a place to receive food on a regular basis.**
- **Shelter: The client needs a warm, dry place to stay (refer to Maslow's Hierarchy of Needs).**
- **Medical attention: For the client's physical and psychiatric needs, including the hallucinations**

2. Write the most relevant nursing diagnoses.

Impaired thought processes

Self-care deficit

Social isolation

Alteration in family processes

Alteration in nutrition: less than body requirements

3. Identify the realistic outcome criteria for the client.

> **The client will have a safe environment.**
>
> **The client will be provided with, and eat, nutritious meals.**
>
> **The client will be evaluated by mental health professionals.**
>
> **The client will be reconnected with his family, if possible.**

4. List the community resources available for the homeless client.

> **Community outreach programs**
>
> **Transitional care shelters**
>
> **Community-based crisis intervention centers**

Situation: You have taken a new position in an outpatient unit that provides services to children who have experienced abuse or neglect and their families. You know little about child abuse and neglect. On the first day you sit in on a team meeting and hear about abuse and neglect, the family history of abuse, play therapy, and complications from abuse and neglect. When you leave the meeting, you are even more confused about these topics. Now you must get yourself prepared to help the children and their families.

---

1. How would you describe the differences between child abuse and neglect?

   Child abuse is a non-accidental physical or emotional injury usually inflicted by a parent or caregiver. Neglect is not injury, but rather failure to provide for the needs of the child; for example, food, clothing, housing, medical care, or supervision.

2. What does Federal law have to do with child abuse?

   There is a Federal law that requires the reporting of all suspected child abuse or neglect to child protective services.

3. You understand the importance of getting a family history, but you are not sure what important data might be obtained. What would you be looking for?

   Adults who abuse typically were abused themselves.

4. You are going to observe a play therapy session, but what is it?

   Play therapy is used to help the child express internally disturbing feelings. Puppet play is frequently used to help children do this, as well as drawing.

5. As you assess children, you need to be aware of complications that they might experience. Identify what these might be.

- Continued abuse and neglect
- Psychological stress that can lead to major mental illness, such as depression, anxiety, or dissociative identity disorder.
- Feelings of worthlessness
- Physical injuries and disease from prolonged abuse
- Abused child may become an abuser in adulthood

Situation: At midnight, a 39-year-old woman is brought to the emergency department by her husband. Her lip is bleeding and she has a reddened and swollen area around her left eye. She is crying as she tells you that she fell down the stairs at her home. She has 3 children at home, ages 1, 3, and 6 years; she called her mother to stay with them while she came to the hospital. She expresses concern about her children. In the waiting room, her husband is belligerent and repeatedly asks to see his wife.

1. What assessment data do you need to collect about this woman and her injuries?

- Presence of other physical injuries, such as abrasions and bruises
- Likelihood that the physical injuries could have resulted from a fall down stairs and her reason for walking down the stairs at midnight
- Her fears and worries about her children and their safety
- Records of past visits to this or other emergency departments
- Her relationship with her husband
- Eye contact, body language, signs of depression, fear, anxiety, low self-esteem
- The nature of her concerns about her children

2. What concerns do you have about this woman's safety?

- Repeated episodes of battery may be triggered by stress or interventions from persons outside the home.
- Trauma to the eye is serious and can lead to complications, such as retinal detachment or corneal hemorrhage.
- Facial trauma that may result in fracture or neurologic injury
- Concern about the future safety of the children is warranted.
- The husband's level of anxiety is disproportionate to the injury. This may signal suspicion.

3. What nursing interventions are of priority concern?

- Prompt treatment of her physical injuries
- Thorough examination and assessment to search for other injuries that she may try to conceal
- Safety for her and her children; protection of their physical and mental welfare
- Questioning her directly about the nature and cause(s) of her injuries
- Reassurance that she can be protected in a safe environment, such as a women's shelter, if she reveals abuse
- Eliciting a comprehensive history to determine if she has been abused in the past
- Contacting the hospital social worker to assist her in dealing with her husband and social network, and with making plans for her future, including an immediate environment where she and her children can be safe

Human Immunodeficiency Virus Neuropsychological Complications Answer Key

Situation: D.K. is admitted to the medical unit for treatment of Kaposi's sarcoma. He has had AIDS for two years and has been hospitalized twice before for other complications. You know the client well, but notice major physical and psychological changes from his last admission. When you last saw him, he had complaints of chronic diarrhea, fatigue, night sweats, and was experiencing some signs of depression and anxiety. Now, his symptoms include severe weight loss, fever and weakness, and delirium. According to his significant other, D.K. seems more depressed. He talks little and sleeps most of the day. He no longer has interest in what is happening around him and appears to have given up.

1. Based on these data, what stage of illness was D.K. in when he was last admitted and how has that changed?

   On the previous admission, D.K. was exhibiting signs of the middle stage of the disease. Now he shows signs of late stage disease. His depression and perceived hopelessness are likely related to the progression of the disease and the anticipation of the dying process.

2. What interventions need to be considered?

   Provide medical interventions for physical symptoms.

   Use universal precautions.

   Pain management

   Provide supportive care when D.K. is able to talk about his illness and future. This should be an open discussion, as staff should not pretend that death is not a reality. Do not offer false reassurance.

   Administer medications as ordered.

   Those close to D.K. will need support during this time. Support the family and friends' feelings concerning D.K.'s impending death. Include these support persons in the care of D.K.

   Encourage spiritual care.

American Psychiatric Association. (2000). *Diagnostic and statistical manual of mental disorders DSM-IV-TR* (4th ed.). Washington, D.C.: American Psychiatric Association.

Eisen, L. (2003, February). *Health care responses to domestic violence: Module II.* Presentation to Hope House, Independence, MO.

Fontaine, K.L., & Fletcher, S. (2003). *Mental health nursing* (5th ed.). Upper Saddle River, NJ: Prentice Hall.

Folstein MF, Folstein, SE and McHugh PR (1975) Mini-Mental State: A Practical Method for Grading the State of Patients for the Clinician, *Journal of Psychiatric Research*, 12.

Frisch, N.C., & Frisch, L.E. (2001). *Psychiatric mental health nursing* (2nd ed.). Albany, NY: Delmar Publishers.

Hogan, M.A., & Smith, G.B. (2003). *Mental health nursing: Reviews & rationales.* Upper Saddle River, NJ: Prentice Hall.

Johnson, B. S. (2003). *Psychiatric-mental health nursing* (5th ed.). Philadelphia: J. B. Lippincott Company.

Keltner, N.L.,& Folks, D.G. (2001). *Psychotropic drugs* (3rd ed.). St. Louis: Mosby, Inc.

Laraia, M.T., & Stuart, G. W. (2004). *Principles and practice of psychiatric nursing* (8th ed.). St. Louis: Mosby, Inc.

Skidmore-Roth, L. (2002). *2005 Mosby's nursing drug reference.* St. Louis: Mosby, Inc.

Townsend, M. C. (2005). *Essentials of Psychiatric Mental Health Nursing.* Philadelphia: F.A. Davis Co.

Varcarolis, E. M. (2002). *Foundations of psychiatric mental health nursing* (4th ed.). Philadelphia: W. B. Saunders Company.

Videbeck, S.L. (2003). *Psychiatric mental health nursing* (2nd ed.). Philadelphia: Lippincott, Williams & Wilkins.